Mighty Opposites

Zhang Longxi

MIGHTY OPPOSITES

*From Dichotomies to Differences in
the Comparative Study of China*

STANFORD UNIVERSITY PRESS

STANFORD, CALIFORNIA

Stanford University Press
Stanford, California
© 1998 by the Board of Trustees of the
Leland Stanford Junior University
Printed in the United States of America

CIP data appear at the end of the book

To Weilin, Celia, and Caroline

Acknowledgments

In putting the different chapters together in this book, I owe a special note of thanks to Haun Saussy, who carefully read the entire manuscript and offered many insightful comments and helpful suggestions that have contributed tremendously to the coherence of the book's argument as a whole. It gives me great pleasure to acknowledge my indebtedness to a number of friends and colleagues who have helped with the writing of these chapters at various stages. Daniel Aaron, Anthony C. Yu, Kang-i Sun Chang, and Donald Stone have always been generous in their encouragement and moral support. I am grateful to Earl Miner, Hwa Yol Jung, David Stern, and Perry Link for inviting me to contribute to conference or special issues of scholarly journals, for which some of the chapters were originally written. I want to thank Leo Ou-fan Lee, Murray Krieger, Ruth apRoberts, Richard J. Smith, Vincent Pecora, Lothar von Falkenhausen, and Ye Yang for reading earlier versions of some of these chapters and for giving me their much-valued support, suggestions, and criticisms.

In preparing the final version of the manuscript during the summer, I benefited from conversations with David Danow on the Bakhtinian notion of the dialogue, and from Donald Stone's vast knowledge of Western art, especially artistic manifestations of the chinoiserie in the eighteenth century. Reinhold Grimm offered me his insights after reading some of the chapters in an earlier form, and thus gave me more help in the final revision than he was aware of. I am truly grateful to Helen Tartar of Stanford University Press for her enthusiasm in this project from the very start and her efficiency in seeing the production of this book through. I also want to thank my editors, John Feneron and Paul Psoinos, for their remarkable professionalism and meticulous work. For all the defects and flaws that remain in these pages, however, I must bear the responsibility alone.

Earlier versions of chapters 1 and 5 were first published in *Critical Inquiry*, vol. 15 (Autumn 1988) and vol. 19 (Autumn 1992). Chapter 3 appeared in *Poetics Today*, vol. 19 (Summer 1998). I am grateful to the editors for permission to use the materials here in revised form. Chapter 2 originally appeared in *Human Studies*, vol. 16 (April 1993): 51–68, ©1993 Kluwer Academic Publishers, reprinted with kind permission from Kluwer Academic Publishers. Chapter 4 was published in *Modern China*, vol. 19 (January 1993): 71–101, ©1993 Sage Periodical Press, reprinted by permission of Sage Publications, Inc. All these previously published articles have been much revised and expanded in order to highlight the central issue of cross-cultural understanding. I thank the Academic Senate at the University of California, Riverside, for a grant that helps defray the cost of color reproduction of the Boucher painting on the book cover.

To my wife, Weilin, I feel, as always, tremendously grateful for all her care, sacrifice, and unfailing support. I am thankful for the joy and bliss our children, Celia and Caroline, have brought into my life. To all three of them now I dedicate this small volume with gratitude, high hopes, and my tenderest love.

Z.L.

Contents

'Tis dangerous when baser nature comes
Between the pass and fell incensed points
Of mighty opposites.

Shakespeare, Hamlet, V.ii.60

其一也一，其不一也一。
其一，與天爲徒。其不一，與人爲徒。
天與人不相勝也，是之謂眞人。

莊子・大宗師

He is one with what is one; he is also one with what is not one. Being with what is one, he is in company with Heaven; being with what is not one, he is in company with man. The one in whom Heaven and man are not opposed in strife, that is called a True Master.

Zhuangzi, "Following the Great Tao"

Introduction

The present time seems to be a particularly propitious one for American readers, critics, and scholars to understand literatures and cultures other than their own. The predominant influence of critical theories in literary and cultural studies, the challenge to a traditional canon of European writers, the development of multiculturalism—these and many other familiar episodes on the American cultural scene have definitely helped foster a more receptive atmosphere than ever before for the appreciation of non-Western literatures and cultures. At the same time, in post-Mao China, as in many other countries of the Third World and the erstwhile socialist camp, interest in the West and Western culture grows rapidly, and the assimilation of contemporary Western theories forms an interesting parallel to the assimilation of Western technology and consumerism in the Chinese society at large. And yet, given the many important differences in history, cultural perspective, and especially political situation, the growing interest in other cultures does not effortlessly lead to an adequate understanding free from old stereotypes and new distortions. How to read works and texts from a different cultural tradition, and how to interpret things and events in their own social and political contexts, remains a formidable challenge. This book is an attempt at answering that challenge, an attempt to explore the possibilities of understanding cultures other than one's own, of reaching the reality of other cultures through the necessary mediation of one's own language and one's own moment in time. More specifically, it is about the understanding of a non-Western culture, that of China and the Chinese, and thus about East-West comparative studies of literatures and cultures. Since understanding is not easily earned, or, to put it more precisely, since misunderstanding, as Friedrich Schleiermacher tells us, has a far more pervasive presence and provides a far more general background for our effort to know and interpret things, it is perhaps right to say that this book is about misunderstanding as much as it is about understanding.[1] Indeed, understanding as a continuous intellectual endeavor is nothing but the rigorous critique of misunderstanding, misrepresentation, and all sorts of cultural myths and misconceptions.

The very mention of misunderstanding and misconception presupposes, of course, notions of intelligibility, interpretive validity, and verifiability. Indeed, a basic assumption in this book needs to be clearly laid out at the outset, namely, that cultures and histories, no matter how much discursive construction may be involved in their *representations,* are not in themselves entirely and exhaustively discursive; therefore, the understanding of culture and history is not, and not merely, a matter of subjective projection, linguistic coherence, or ideological control. To be sure, cultural representations and historical narratives make use of language and rhetorical devices in much the same way as literary fiction does, but that does not make culture and history reducible to a self-enclosed language game, a rhetorical or fictional discourse, a free play of signifiers. Historians are most likely to disagree. "Against that dissolution of the status of history as a specific knowledge (a stance often taken as a figure of postmodernism)," says Roger Chartier, "one must insist forcefully that history is commanded by an intention and a principle of truth, that the past history has taken as its object is a reality external to discourse, and that knowledge of it can be verified."[2] To insist on the reality of history outside discursive construction is not to go back to a naive, uncritical, positivistic notion of objectivity, but to resist the pervasive influence of the so-called linguistic turn, the much-inflated notion of "textuality" that subsumes everything under a model of linguistic formulation. At the same time, to recognize "reality external to discourse" is also to reaffirm the value of lived experience in shaping our understanding and knowledge. Again as Chartier remarks:

Recognizing that past reality is usually accessible only through texts intent on organizing it, dominating it, or representing it is not the same thing as postulating that the logocentric and hermeneutic logic governing the production of discourse is identical to the practical logic ruling conduct and actions. All historical stances must take it into account that experience is not reducible to discourse, and all need to guard against unconstrained use of the category of the "text"—a term too often inappropriately applied to practice (ordinary or ritualized) whose tactics and procedures bear no resemblance to discursive strategies.[3]

The importance of the differentiation here between the logic governing the production of discourse and the practical logic functioning in conduct and action cannot be emphasized enough, for it sets us free from the proverbial prison-house of language and the self-enclosure of pure subjectivity, both of which have resulted from fashionable critical dogmas—the view of language as an autonomous, impersonal institution of signification, and a totally relativist view of understanding and interpretation.[4] To understand a different culture is, after all, neither an automatic procedure without intention and effort, nor an exercise of solipsism: it is an intense engagement with an alien reality, what Emmanuel Levinas calls "the face-to-face with the Other."[5] To be sure, present understanding is, of necessity, influenced by notions and knowledge formed in the past, for history and tradition always work to shape the present in subtle but significant ways, and interest in the Other is never innocent of motives and motivation embedded in one's own historical moment and cultural condition. Nevertheless, to recognize the tentative nature of understanding, the necessary inclusion of subjective position, and the need of revision and change by no means entails acquiescence to a hermeneutic nihilism that makes relativism the absolute imperative in knowledge, obliterates all criteria of judgment, and makes no distinction between reality and fiction, understanding and misunderstanding.[6] However difficult they may be, understanding and knowledge can be achieved in various degrees, and it is always possible to differentiate a more adequate understanding from ones not so adequate, because no matter how people may construct ideas and images and superimpose them on the reality of things, that which we try to understand will ultimately serve as a constraint or a yardstick: it will challenge our presumptions and disprove our misconstructions. The Other is not, after all, a phantom simply to be called up or exorcised at will, but a presence with a character all its own.

Language itself confronts us as a living presence, a reality to be dealt with in earnest. This is especially evident in the experience of learning a foreign language, which may provide a rather common but telling example of the reality or alterity of things that cannot be reduced to one's own subjective projection, or manipulated by one's whimsies and arbitrary decisions. Without first acknowledging the presence of an alien vocabulary and grammatical rules and accepting them as such, one cannot even begin to understand anything in a foreign language. The very foreignness of the language highlights the otherness of the text we try to read, and in no way can we arbitrarily decide what a foreign word or text means without running into serious problems in understanding. A beginner's knowledge of a foreign language is evidently at a lower level compared with that of someone fluent in that language. From total ignorance to native fluency, there is a whole spectrum of different levels of understanding, and there are many ways of testing the various degrees of proficiency against a set of criteria of correct pronunciation, orthography, standard usage, and so on. Doesn't this already show that something exists outside our mental constructions and can serve as the legitimate ground for judgment and evaluation? Isn't it, indeed, the crucial point of the biblical story of Shibboleth that the presence of language is formidable, beyond control and manipulation, and provides a test to gauge one's adequacy? At the fords of the Jordan, the Ephraimites were found out to be alien and killed because they were brought face to face with a word, but they "could not frame to pronounce it right" (Judg. 12:6). For the Ephraimites, the presence of the word *Shibboleth* was undeniable, indeed inescapable, and they mispronounced it only at their own peril. In *Truth and Method*, experience with a foreign language is one of the examples Gadamer uses to explain the act of understanding as a process of constant revision of our own "fore-meaning" in accordance with the things themselves. "Just as we cannot continually misunderstand the use of a word without its affecting the meaning of the whole," he says, "so we cannot stick blindly to our own fore-meaning about the thing if we want to understand the meaning of another." What that means is not to deny our participating subjectivity, but to "remain open to the meaning of the other person or text," to be "sensitive to the text's alterity."[7] Dialogue—the genuine desire to listen to the voice of the other person or text, and the effort to reach beyond oneself to communicate with that person or text— lies at the core of Gadamer's philosophical hermeneutics.

If for Gadamer Bildung—the process of cultivation in which the self goes out and learns something in the encounter with other people, and then comes back as a new, enriched self with an expanded horizon—describes both the process of knowing and the condition of being, then, in the works of Levinas, the question of being and knowledge takes an intensely ethical form: it puts the Other before the self and becomes an imperative to take responsibility for the life and death of the other person. What Levinas calls *face* indicates the presence and alterity of the Other, not just the expression but also the substance of its vulnerability, its nakedness, its misery, which summon us and command us to take that deeply human responsibility. In a critical reexamination of the Husserlian "pure ego" or "transcendental I," he comes to question the uniqueness and sufficiency of that ego—"the thinking one [*le pensant*]"—and raises the ethical question, "the ethical intrigue prior to knowledge," as the first philosophical question before being, even before the very consciousness to know and understand. "Face to face with the other man that a man can indeed approach as presence," writes Levinas with a strong sense of conviction, the thinking subject is exposed "to the defenseless nakedness of the face, the lot or misery of the human," "to the loneliness of the face and hence to the categorical imperative of assuming responsibility for that misery." For Levinas, it is the "Word of God" that commits us to such a moral responsibility, hence "a responsibility impossible to gainsay."[8] With this religious and absolute moral command, ethics is injected into hermeneutics, and the dialogic relationship with the Other in understanding is recast as the real and practical question of human relationships and responsibilities, that is, relationships with other people in concrete social and political situations. What Levinas has made quite impossible for us is to indulge in the kind of narcissistic subjectivism, the illusion that the Other is what I take it to be. Understanding can no longer be conceived of as a self-enclosed and self-sufficient act of pure subjectivity. "The Other as Other is not only an alter ego," says Levinas; "the Other is what I myself am not."[9] We realize that understanding the Other is an act "outside the subject," an act of always trying to listen to the voice of the other person, to engage that person in a concrete situation, and thus an act with profound moral implications. Then we realize that when we talk about cross-cultural understanding, we are not talking about abstract notions, but dealing with real people in history, in the world of social and political realities.

We may find that it is also rather common in the Chinese philosophical tradition to mix ethical concerns with questions of knowledge and to reason by considering particular cases in making claims to truth of a more general nature. As the Qing scholar and historian Zhang Xuecheng (1738–1801) remarks, "the ancients never spoke of principles detached from particular things."[10] More recently, in a study of the great Confucian thinker Mencius, Huang Junjie observes that much of pre-Qin philosophical discourse depended on thinking in terms of concrete examples drawn from daily experience or historical precedents, and arguing by analogies and associations, of which Mencius was a particularly capable practitioner.[11] This is quite instructive and worth pondering. Given the complexity and multifariousness as well as the ethical import of the many issues in cross-cultural understanding, it seems to me much more helpful to ground our understanding in the particularity of a concrete situation than to draw general conclusions with claims to absolute truth. Discussions in this book are thus very much explorations of the various issues in their concrete circumstances, paying attention to each subject and its specific historical, cultural as well as theoretical, ramifications. Understanding here should be thought of as a process of navigating between the reality of a culture and our ideas, concepts, and preconceived notions about that culture; the emphasis here is not so much on the result as on the process of knowing: an assiduous, open-ended, and self-modifying process, in which we maintain an imaginary dialogue with something new, unfamiliar, even strange, something we try to learn about and comprehend. Dialogue should indeed be the model for understanding between cultures: a dialogue that is forever open to further exchange of answers and questions. Mikhail Bakhtin, for whom dialogue is as essential as it is for Gadamer and Levinas, puts it very well: "To be means to communicate dialogically. When dialogue ends, everything ends. Thus dialogue, by its very essence, cannot and must not come to an end."[12] It is only in and through dialogue with the Other that we may hope to get out of the confinement of self-projection and to arrive at any real understanding. When we say we understand something, we mean of course that we have now grasped something we did not know before, that we feel we are at least capable of making sense, to some degree or other, of that which was heretofore strange and unknown, that we have found some way to bridge over the gaps between the alien and the familiar, between a prior moment of ignorance and the present moment of knowledge. Time, as Levinas argues, "is the very relationship of the subject with the Other."[13]

For any dialogue to happen between at least two voices, for any bridging of gaps and any temporal relationship to occur, there must be a common ground, a shared frame of reference and ways of communication, by means of which new experience and novel concepts can be articulated, appropriated, and transformed from one linguistic and cultural context to another. In understanding different cultures, and especially non-Western ones, however, the main problem today is not so much denying the presence and alterity of those cultures as an excessive emphasis on their difference and alterity, and it is precisely the notion of a common ground, the idea of a shared frame of reference, which is seriously contested in much of contemporary critical theory. Skepticism of commonality is especially strong when we speak of comparison and understanding across the cultural differences between the East and the West. As David Buck observes, the predominant influence in Asian studies at the present time is relativism, namely, the view that cultures are so very different from one another that they become totally incommensurate, that there is no commonality shared by different cultures, societies, and peoples, and that one should be skeptical about "whether any conceptual tools exist to understand and interpret human behavior and meaning in ways that are intersubjectively valid."[14] Such a relativist view is often presented as a critique of old Eurocentric prejudices, a corrective of the imposition of Western views on non-Western cultures in the infamous past of colonialism and imperialism. Insofar as it acknowledges and respects the alterity of non-Western cultures and the validity of their cultural values, relativism seems to be morally superior to Eurocentrism. The problem is, however, that the emphasis on cultural difference is in itself no guarantee of ethical superiority, because Eurocentrism and racism, which exclude groups of people of the non-West from what is considered essentially human and civilized, have always depended on an emphasis on much-exaggerated racial, ethnic, and cultural differences.

Ironically, then, the cultural relativist may find himself making much the same argument as his opponent in the conviction that the non-West is a totally different and alien creature with all its unmitigated alterity. As Patrick Hogan argues with reference to another Eastern culture—that of India, from the colonialist and imperialist days of Rudyard Kipling to our own time—those who celebrate the Eastern difference and those who deplore it "share the most important descriptive presuppositions, differing primarily in terms of evaluation."[15] The danger of such a view of East-West dichotomy lies in its pervasiveness, its diffusion among people on either side of the ideological line; for many who "see themselves as struggling against imperialism, racism, and sexism," he goes on to say, "share with their professed antagonists the bulk of relevant ideological beliefs," as they presuppose, and thus reinforce, the dichotomous view of the East and the West, seeing them as "internally homogenous and mutually contradictory."[16] Inasmuch as relativism has become the predominant influence and, in Buck's words, as many Asianists in the West have frequently advanced "relativist interpretations" of non-Western cultures, the emphasis on East-West difference has put in question the very possibility of cross-cultural understanding.[17] As we shall see in dealing with the various subjects and issues, the skeptic challenge to East-West comparative studies has its philosophical, historical, and political reasons, and the relativist tends to treat the East and the West conceptually as monolithic entities rather than groupings of different individuals. But does difference exist only between cultures? Is there any common ground at all between the East and the West despite their obvious and profound differences? Is China destined to be misunderstood by the West as its imaginary Other, and vice versa?

Perhaps a concrete example may help illustrate the kind of questions and challenges we are likely to face in attempting East-West comparative studies. I want to introduce a specific example of metaphor, with the full conviction that metaphors are not just a figure of speech but are basic to any structure of language, and that they often provide revealing illustrations of how the mind works in articulating sensibilities and experiences. The metaphor I shall discuss is one found in Chinese and English that shows striking similarities across linguistic and cultural boundaries but is formed independently in the two languages, with no actual contact or mutual influence. In chapter 26 of an important philosophical book in ancient China, the *Zhuangzi*, a line that describes the awakening of life in spring comes out in Burton Watson's fine English translation as follows: "In Spring, when the seasonable rains and sunshine come, the grass and trees spring to life."[18] Now Watson's "spring to life" translates the Chinese original *nu sheng*, which literally means "angrily grow." This is probably the earliest instance of the metaphorical use of the Chinese word *nu* or "angry" to describe the irresistible growth of plants and exuberant blossoming of flowers, a metaphorical expression that may strike one as strange and unnecessarily distracting if translated literally. Watson uses an expression that adequately conveys not only the idea but also the action of vigorous growth without mechanically following the original to the letter, for a literal translation of the original phrase in this case would probably sound outlandish and appear to be an instance of "pathetic fallacy." In Chinese, however, *nu sheng* ("angrily grow") or *nu fang* ("angrily blossom") is a familiar collocation with hardly any suggestion of an affected style, and the word *nu* ("angry") is often used in describing flowers. In a poem on Red Plum Flowers, the great poet Su Shi (1037–1101) writes: "The beautiful one with her enraged face looks even more enchanting." This line helps to clarify how this metaphor works, because here, as a commentator explains, the poet is evoking the image of the beautiful face of an enraged woman to portray red flowers, a poetic transference of imagery on the ground that "when a woman is angry [*nu*], her face willturn red."[19] The transference or analogy between a woman's face and a beautiful flower has a long pedigree in Chinese literature, beginning with poem 6 in the canonical *Shi jing* or *Book of Poetry*, where we find peach blossoms compared to so many faces smiling on the branches. The interesting thing about this particular metaphor, however, is the evocation of a woman's angry face rather than a smiling one to portray a full-grown flower, and the commentator, if not the poet himself, made the poetic use of analogy hark back to the phrase in the *Zhuangzi* by way of an implied allusion.[20]

One may marvel at this metaphor as representing a very special and poetic way of making associations, of superimposing one concrete image (an angry face) onto another (a red flower). One may even take this to be exemplary of a uniquely Chinese way of thinking in concrete objects and images, but the sense of uniqueness is quickly undermined when we realize that the specific connection of "angry" with "red" also makes a very respectable appearance in English, in George Herbert's poem *Vertue*, in which we find these famous lines: "Sweet rose, whose hue angrie and brave / Bids the rash gazer wipe his eye." Quoting this and another example from Charles Lamb ("His waistcoat red and angry," *Elia*, Ser. 1.xviii), the *OED*'s definition of this particular meaning of "angry"—"Having the colour of an angry face, red"—sounds remarkably close to that of the twelfth-century Chinese commentator quoted above. Is this a pure coincidence? Probably; but do coincidences like this suggest something ubiquitous in the workings of the human psyche and language, what linguists call "parallel metaphors in different languages"?[21] In a recent study of the articulation of time in several languages, Hoyt Alverson maintains that "the human sciences have greatly exaggerated the ecological, institutional, and ideological differences among cultures of the world and hence the ways in which people experience their daily lives." Against those exaggerated differences, Alverson maintains that "the human experience called 'time' (or alternatively, 'temporality,' 'duration'), like most of human experience in general, is built upon and arises from a panhuman *Bauplan* . . . an underlying universal structure of embodied, enculturated mental experience."[22] Alverson deliberately chooses to examine several languages that cross over the cultural boundaries of the East and the West, and by listing a variety of expressions of time in these languages, including Chinese, he finds that all these expressions are instances of a "universal metaphor" of time based on "universally shared, everyday experience."[23] It is significant that what he calls a "universal metaphor" here refers to a metaphor not of something concrete, but of an abstract concept, and indeed one of the most basic conceptualizations in human experience: the concept of time.

Many scholars in the human sciences—linguists, anthropologists, and certainly literary critics and theoreticians—will probably balk at the very term "universal." Given the predominant influence of a relativist paradigm in these fields at the present, any claim to universality becomes almost automatically suspect. Of course, "universalism" can be a problem and becomes quite meaningless if—and *only if*—it recognizes commonality at the expense of any difference in language, culture, history, political structure, or social institutions. I do not think, however, that Alverson's "universal metaphor" in any way suggests such a reductionist and exclusionary reading of the expressions of time in various languages. In fact, when the word "universal" is used, in most cases it simply means "widely shared" or "common" rather than "totally identical"; it does not require actual agreement of all people on earth without exception, nor does it necessarily lead to a simplistic view of the world as a cemented and monotonous uniformity.

When we recognize the striking similarity in the formation of "parallel metaphors," as in the case of the analogy between an angry face and a red flower in Chinese and English, we of course also notice their significant difference on other levels. The phrase *nu sheng* or "angrily grow" in Chinese is a familiar collocation, but its English equivalent is not equally familiar; hence Watson's paraphrase of the Chinese expression in his translation. More important, the "angrie and brave" rose in Herbert, which constitutes what Helen Vendler calls one of Herbert's "startling conceits" in this poem, serves to highlight the truly enduring "sweet and vertuous soul," whose voice "has been speaking to us all through the poem."[24] If the rose has its roots "ever in its grave" and already indicates the inevitability of death, and if the soul alone, as Herbert puts it, "chiefly lives" when "the whole world turn to coal," the poem and everything in it presuppose an apocalyptic vision of the end of time, which has a specifically Christian connotation of eschatology. The Chinese phrase *nu sheng* or "angrily grow" in the *Zhuangzi*, on the other hand, implies an altogether different philosophical overtone and pro-

ernists, a common strategy they all use to facilitate a program of social and cultural critique. By constantly reversing such crucial concepts and values as "barbarian" and "civilized," however, Montaigne does not try so much to confirm the unyielding alterity of the Other as eventually to overturn the dichotomy between Europe and the New World, thereby greatly mitigating the rigidity of cultural construction in his recognition of a shared, common humanity. The rigidity of dichotomous cultural constructs and their ominous consequences are put under scrutiny in the third chapter in yet another context, where I compare the opposition between Hellenism and Hebraism on the one hand and that between the East and the West on the other. By looking into the Christian typological and allegorical reading of the Bible and the seventeenth-century European debate on "Chinese rites," I try to show that the exclusive claim to spirituality and transcendence in interpretation as opposed to the limitations of a "literal" reading of Scripture or the canon has served to deprive both the Jewish and the Chinese cultural tradition of truth value, and has aggravated cultural rifts and conflicts in history. Indeed, some of the old erroneous views still persist in certain areas of Chinese studies and become serious obstacles to adequate understanding. It is by revisiting cultural constructs of the past and putting contemporary debates in a historical perspective that we may come to realize the limitations and undesirable consequences of an overemphasis on difference, the stubborn tendency to set up a rigid dichotomy between the East and the West.

If the first three chapters move across a wide range of topics, commenting on a variety of works by authors of different time periods and traditions, and mostly dealing with Western understanding of China and the Chinese in the past, the last three chapters in this book are definitely more focused on modern China and Chinese studies today. In these chapters, I am particularly interested in the interactions between Western critical theories and the social and political conditions in China at the present time. Chapter 4 continues to develop the main point

made in the previous chapters about the East-West dichotomy
and argues that such a dichotomy has turned Chinese studies
into a narrow and esoteric field, closed off from the larger intellectual community in Western academic institutions and from
the debates on important theoretical issues. To take the challenge
of Western theory and to engage in theoretical debates in the
study of Chinese literature and culture, as I see it, is a good way
to break the self-imposed ghettoization of Chinese studies, and
to open up the field for deeper and theoretically informed in-
quiries. At the same time, however, a facile and mindless mimicry of Western theoretical discourse without considering the social condition and political reality on the Chinese mainland is not
just useless, but downright harmful, because it not only obscures
our understanding, but brings about consequences that are not at
all ideologically radical or liberating in the specific context of the
Chinese society. The student demonstration and the massacre in
Beijing in June 1989 offer a particularly acute case for testing
theorical discourse and its consequences in practice. Chapter 5
evaluates the rather dismal results of such a testing, and argues
for the importance of paying attention to the reality in China
when discussing issues that have a direct influence on people's
lives. It is morally dubious, I believe, for some self-appointed
leftist intellectuals in the United States to blame the Chinese for
their aspirations for a democratic society simply because these
intellectuals would like to hold China in their imagination as the
sanctuary of revolutionary and utopian dreams, the idealized
Third World country that is everything opposite to the decadent
capitalist West. The ethical question to ask here is whether these
armchair-dreamy revolutionaries have any concern for the quality of life, the suffering, the feelings, desires, and hopes of those
people for whom China is not a place to dream about, but a reality of daily experience with all its petty banalities, tears and
laughters, memories and forgetfulness, as well as its boundless
energy and profound changes. Here again, we find that China in
the theoretical discourse of the West is a myth of the Other, a

symbol of difference, the imaginary foil to whatever the West is supposed to be.

Such an imaginary opposition of China and the West, however, can be found not just in Western discourse, but also in its assimilation and appropriation in mainland China. The last chapter in this book goes to some length to examine Chinese language materials that have recently appeared in Hong Kong and the mainland on the question of postmodernism in China and the debate on its role in cultural and political terms. The use of Said's *Orientalism* and of postcolonial theories by some critics in China to legitimize the cause of a narrow-minded nationalism, the complicated political meanings of the television series *River Elegy* as understood in the cultural and political context of post-Mao China, and the strange convergence in the 1990s of radical Western theories and the conservative forces on the Chinese cultural scene—all these call our attention to the complexity of the issues involved, the persistence of the dichotomous view of East-West cultural difference, and the necessity to adapt Western theories to the new questions and new environment in China. Instead of drawing on the insights of Western theories for a critique aimed at their own culture, society, and political system, certain Chinese "postmodern" critics on the mainland take concepts and notions from Western theories to argue for a "Third World criticism" that has as its main target Western imperialist hegemony, as though the outside pressure of imperialism and colonialism were the immediate danger China faces today. With its edge pointing outward, not inward, such a criticism serves to divert any critique of the status quo from China to its imagined Other, and some of those patriotic "postmodern" critics even ride on the tideway of a xenophobic nationalism in covering up every internal problem with a bogus enemy in the West. It is therefore not a fortuitous conclusion drawn by many that the tendency in the 1990s on the mainland in cultural and political terms is toward conservatism. The debate on Chinese postmodernism and conservatism is still ongoing; it is not a purely academic matter, but has serious implications in social and political life. Given the presence of a rigid dichotomy set up by some in the debate, the serious nature of the debate, and the particularly close relationship with social and political reality, some readers may find that my argument presented in this book often sounds contentious or polemical. I cannot think of a better answer to that charge than to pointing again at the predominance of the relativist paradigm in matters concerning China and the West, and, perhaps, to quote a phrase from the ancient Chinese thinker Mencius, who once said in response to a similar charge, "Not that I am particularly argumentative, but I have no other choice."[25] Whatever the challenge and the answer I can come up with, however, my only goal has always been to promote and enhance cross-cultural understanding between China and the West, to argue for not only the possibility but also the value of such understanding. If anything, this book may have shown that this is a very difficult goal to achieve, but for me that is a goal too important to give up seeking, a goal worthy of all our effort and endeavors.

CHAPTER 1

The Myth of the Other

A book that has been hailed as one of the most important French contributions to philosophy in this century, Michel Foucault's *The Order of Things*, first arose out of a passage in Jorge Luis Borges. As Foucault tells us in the preface, the passage was supposedly taken from a "certain Chinese encyclopedia," in which we find a most curious way of classifying animals:

animals are divided into: (a) belonging to the Emperor, (b) embalmed, (c) tame, (d) sucking pigs, (e) sirens, (f) fabulous, (g) stray dogs, (h) included in the present classification, (i) frenzied, (j) innumerable, (k) drawn with a very fine camelhair brush, (l) *et cetera*, (m) having broken the water pitcher, (n) that from a long way off look like flies.[1]

The strange taxonomy in this passage does not make any sense, and the method of its classification, if there is any method at all in this madness, is totally beyond comprehension. What else, then, can be a normal response to this chaos but an irrepressible laughter, a laughter that points out and at the same time ignores the illogic of the passage?

So Foucault laughed. In this laughter, however, he feels an uneasiness and even distress that the outrageous absurdity has a shattering effect, that the usual categories of thinking and naming in language are being destroyed, and that the monstrous passage threatens to "collapse our age-old distinction between the Same and the Other," casting a spell, an "exotic charm of another system of thought," while showing "the limitation of our own, the stark impossibility of thinking *that*."[2] The juxtaposition of animals in such an unthinkable order or, rather, disorder makes it impossible to find a shared space for them, not even in utopia.

Such a strange taxonomy belongs rather to heterotopia, the inconceivable space that undermines the very possibility of description in language. It belongs, says Foucault, to both atopia and aphasia, the loss of correspondence between place and name. That Borges should designate China as the mythical homeland to this strange taxonomy seems most surprising, since the word *China* should immediately evoke the image of a precise region whose name alone, according to Foucault, constitutes for the West a vast reservoir of utopias:

In our dreamworld, is not China precisely this privileged *site* of *space*? In our traditional imagery, the Chinese culture is the most meticulous, the most rigidly ordered, the one most deaf to temporal events, most attached to the pure delineation of space; we think of it as a civilization of dikes and dams beneath the eternal face of the sky; we see it, spread and frozen, over the entire surface of a continent surrounded by walls. Even its writing does not reproduce the fugitive flight of the voice in horizontal lines; it erects the motionless and still-recognizeable images of things themselves in vertical columns. So much so that the Chinese encyclopaedia quoted by Borges, and the taxonomy it proposes, lead to a kind of thought without space, to words and categories that lack all life and place, but are rooted in a ceremonial space, overburdened with complex figures, with tangled paths, strange places, secret passages, and unexpected communications. There would appear to be, then, at the other extremity of the earth we inhabit, a culture entirely devoted to the ordering of space, but one that does not distribute the multiplicity of existing things into any of the categories that make it possible for us to name, speak, and think.[3]

For the West, then, China as a land in the Far East becomes traditionally the image of the ultimate Other. What Foucault does in his writing is, of course, not so much to endorse this image as to show, in the light of the Other, how knowledge is always conditioned in a certain system, and how difficult it is to get out of the confinement of the historical a priori, the *epistemes* or the fundamental codes of Western culture. And yet he takes the Borges passage seriously and remarks on its apparent incongruity with what is usually conceived about China in the Western tradition. If we are to find any modification of the traditional image of China in Foucault's thought, it is then the association of China not with an ordered space but with a space without any conceivable arrangement or coherence, a space that makes any logical ordering utterly unthinkable. Significantly, Foucault does not give so much as a hint to suggest that the hilarious passage from that "Chinese encyclopedia" may have been made up to represent a Western fantasy of the Other, and that the illogical way of sorting out animals in that passage can be as alien to the Chinese mind as it is to the Western.

How Chinese Is the "Chinese Encyclopedia"?

In fact, the monstrous unreason and its alarming subversion of Western thinking, the unfamiliar and alien space of China as the image of the Other threatening to break up ordered surfaces and logical categories, all turn out to be, in the most literal sense, a Western fiction. Nevertheless, that fiction serves a purpose in Foucault's thought, namely, the necessity of setting up a framework for his archeology of knowledge, enabling him to differentiate the self from what is alien and pertaining to the Other and to map out the contours of Western culture recognizable as a self-contained system. Indeed, what can be a better sign of the Other than a fictionalized space of China? What can furnish the West with a better reservoir for its dreams, fantasies, and utopias?

The passage Foucault quoted appears originally in Borges's essay on John Wilkins, a seventeenth-century English scholar and bishop of Chester, whose mind was full of "happy curiosities," including, among other things, "the possibility and the principles of a world language."[4] As Borges shows, the idea of a precise, artificial language built on a strictly logical system of numbers or symbols ultimately originates with Descartes, that is, from within the Western philosophical tradition and its desire to classify and compartmentalize all phenomena of the world. Such an attempt at universal language, however, has proved to be quite futile, and all kinds of classification of the universe are inevitably arbitrary. It is precisely the "ambiguities, redundancies, and deficiencies" in Wilkins's system that have reminded Borges of similar absurdities "attributed by Dr. Franz Kuhn to a certain Chinese encyclopedia entitled *Celestial Emporium of Benevolent Knowledge*."[5] In Borges's essay, however, the absurdities of the "Chinese encyclopedia" are not recalled to represent an incomprehensibly alien mode of thinking, since he mentions in the same breath "the arbitrariness of Wilkins, of the unknown (or apocryphal) Chinese encyclopedist, and of the Bibliographical Institute of Brussels," all of which tried in vain to sort out things in the universe and exhaustively register "the words, the definitions, the etymologies, the synonymies of God's secret dictionary."[6] Borges greatly admires the courageous, albeit provisional and often thwarted, human effort to penetrate the divine scheme of the universe, and the "Chinese encyclopedia" represents just part of that futile yet heroic attempt to probe God's secret. Though he mentions as his source Dr. Franz Kuhn, a German sinologist and translator of Chinese literature, and even gives the title of that "Chinese encyclopedia," the so-called *Celestial Emporium of Benevolent Knowledge* is nonexistent except in his own invention. As a matter of fact, it is not at all uncommon for Borges in his writings to mix erudition with imagination, blending real names and titles with imaginary ones.

In "The Congress," one of Borges's longest and most diffuse tales, the reader catches another glimpse of the Chinese encyclopedia. This time those fictitious volumes are put among the Britannica, the Larousse, the Brockhaus, and the other "real" encyclopedias in the Congress's reference library. "I recall," says the narrator of the story, "how I reverently fondled the silky volumes of a certain Chinese encyclopedia whose finely brushed characters seemed to me more mysterious than the spots on a leopard's skin."[7] Like the essay on Wilkins, "The Congress" depicts the ambitious intellectual effort to organize everything under the sun and to create order out of chaos. It also dramatizes the failure of this effort by portraying the burning of all the books collected by members of the Congress, including that Chinese encyclopedia. As a matter of fact, the encyclopedia is one of the recurrent images in Borges, with a strong suggestion of the intellect's power to create its own systematic and ideal world in language amidst the labyrinth of the universe. Artificial language systems arise from the desire to impose order on the chaotic universe, and encyclopedias represent the paramount form of such orderly marshaling of things. In "Tlön, Uqbar, Orbis Tertius," one of Borges's best fantastic stories, Uqbar, the strange land of ideal objects, exists nowhere except in the pages of an encyclopedia, quite specifically in volume XLVI of *The Anglo-American Cyclopaedia*, which is, according to the narrator, "a literal but delinquent reprint of the *Encyclopaedia Britannica* of 1902." Yet the article on Uqbar is not to be found there, for it exists only in the copy Bioy Casares acquired "at some sale or other," which miraculously has four extra pages containing that article.[8] In other words, that encyclopedia exists only in Borges's fictional world, to which he has, however, lent some credibility in a playful fashion by mentioning the real *Encyclopaedia Britannica* and Bioy Casares, the name of a real person. In another story, "The Garden of Forking Paths," Dr. Yu Tsun, a Chinese professor who works as a spy for the Germans, finds in the library of an English sinologist "bound in yellow silk several volumes of the Lost Encyclopedia, edited by the Third Emperor of the Luminous Dynasty but never printed."[9] As in Borges's other stories, the encyclopedia here also symbolizes a tremendous but ultimately futile effort to arrange all the irregularities of the universe; its being lost in an obscure little foreign town where a murder is about to occur intensifies the irony of its supposed function as a means to order.

Borges sees the universe as a labyrinth with its innumerable passages, corridors, tortuous paths, and blind alleys, a labyrinth not without its own mysterious order, but an order unintelligible to human beings. Thus the futile attempt at classification in the Chinese encyclopedia, like Wilkins's artificial language, symbolizes the absurd human condition in which the mind, hindered by the limitation of knowledge and the inadequacy of language, tries hopelessly to cope with all vast and labyrinthine Creation. On the other hand, literary creation for Borges is also the making of a labyrinth. By connecting the name of a real sinologist with an invented title, Borges creates a maze that tends to puzzle and mislead his readers. Many critics have noticed Borges's "esoteric erudition," which, besides being genuine erudition, is often esoteric only because he playfully mixes his readings with inventions and blurs the boundaries between the true and the imagined as well as the generic boundaries between essay and story. Borges not only plays jokes with readers who enjoy his fantastic style but plays tricks on critics who try to track down his often obscure references. Thus, we may certainly attribute the Chinese encyclopedia to Borges the mythmaker and writer of fantastic tales, and realize that the incomprehensible passage Foucault quoted is nothing more than a good-natured joke, a fictitious representation of fictitious writing itself.

We have no reason, however, to suspect that Borges invents the Chinese encyclopedia to represent an exotic and alien culture, because Borges is not a cultural relativist and in his dictionary the word *Chinese* is not synonymous with Other. Indeed, in his poem "The Keeper of the Books," as Borges recalls, he even assumes an imaginary Chinese identity: "I was trying to be as Chinese as a good student of Arthur Waley should be."[10] In his effort to transcend the limitations of space and time, and to grasp the essence of different cultures and histories, he always privileges the common nature of all human beings rather than their difference. "We love over-emphasizing our little differences, our hatreds," says Borges, "and that is wrong. If humanity is to be saved, we must focus on our affinities, the points of contact with all other human beings; by all means we must avoid accentuating our differences."[11] Borges is particularly sensitive to the problematic of the Other, and the theme of double identities runs throughout his works. In these works, the Other often turns out to be none other than the self.[12]

Philosophizing the Other

Indeed, we do not have to go very far to seek for the Other. The need to ascertain what makes up our own being, to define our very identity and the features of the world in which we live, that is, the need to have any knowledge of ourselves and our culture, has always to be gratified by an act of differentiation. Spinoza thus formulates one of his propositions: "Every individual thing, or everything which is finite and has a conditioned existence, cannot exist or be conditioned to act, unless it be conditioned for existence and action by a cause other than itself."[13] This is, of course, one of the elementary principles of logic that postulates that the self is invariably correlated with the Other, and that nothing can be determined by and in itself except by being differentiated from what it is not; or, as Spinoza puts it, "determination is negation."[14] Since Ferdinand de Saussure, we are familiar with the structural principle of binary opposition in thinking and in language, the idea that language is a system of terms that define one another in mutual differentiation. When we have one thing among many and can tell the one from the others at all, what we can tell is nothing but their difference. This point is made clearly in the *Parmenides*, that otherwise enigmatic Platonic dialogue: "if we are talking about the others, things that are others must be different; 'other' and 'different' are two names for the same thing."[15]

Philosophical discussions of the Other evidently bear on the problem we have to face when we try to understand different cultures, especially cultures so drastically different as the East and the West. Rudyard Kipling once said, "Oh, East is East, and West is West, and never the twain shall meet."[16] Logically, however, the fact that the poet knows East and West as two separate entities already indicates that not only have the twain met, but each has recognized the otherness of the other. The East or the Orient, which stands for the Other over against which the West has been able to identify itself, is indeed a conceptual given in the process of self-understanding of the West, and an image built up in that formative process as much as the West itself. Thus the philosophical notion of the Other in Plato and Spinoza takes on the quality of a cultural construct in the West when it comes to represent whatever is conceived as different from traditional Western values.

The question of the Other, however, has an inescapably ethical dimension as well, for the Other in cross-cultural understanding is not an abstract notion but the presence of other people in social and historical reality, with whom one forms a relationship and bears the necessary moral responsibility. It is important to remember in this context that "the Other is others," as Levinas puts it; "the departure from the self is the approach to the neighbour."[17] Once the Other is understood as so real and concrete an existence as my neighbor, then differences between the self and the Other are put in perspective, a certain common ground emerges underneath the alterity and particularities, and it becomes impossible for me to deny the humanity of the Other as my neighbor, whose values may also be valuable to me. That should be, as we may infer from the analogy, the relationship that obtains with regard to other cultures, for the concept of culture is meaningless without real people and their values, and the relationship between cultures should be that between neighbors writ large. Just as I cannot displace the reality of my neighbor with an image of my own mental construction, I cannot represent the other culture only as total difference, defined negatively in contrast to my perception of the self. That would not only be epistemologically untenable, but ethically dubious as well. And yet, that is exactly what often happens in the history of cultural conceptions. As a cultural entity conceived in the West, the Orient, as Edward Said argues, is almost a European invention:

We must take seriously Vico's great observation that men make their own history, that what they can know is what they have made, and extend it to geography: as both geographical and cultural entities—to say nothing of historical entities—such locales, regions, geographical sectors as "Orient" and "Occident" are man-made. Therefore as much as the West itself, the Orient is an idea that has a history and a tradition of thought, imagery, and vocabulary that have given it reality and presence in and for the West.[18]

Though by "Orient" Said means the Middle East, what he says here also make sense in the context of the Far East, especially of

China as the paradigm and locale of the Other with its own history and tradition of thought, imagery, and vocabulary. Vico's famous principle of *verum factum* is of special import for Said. It defines the criterion of truth in terms of the convertibility of the true and the made, thus elevating the humanities to a higher level than the natural sciences because, says Vico, while the secret of nature is known only to God the Creator, "the world of civil society has certainly been made by men, and . . . its principles are therefore to be found within the modifications of our own human mind."[19] In the Greek sense of the word, men are poets, that is, makers, who not only have created the world they inhabit and myths that account for their experience of the world, but have "created themselves."[20] According to Vico, nothing can be known unless it is experienced; and nothing makes sense unless it is accommodated to the shape of the human mind, which imposes its own shape on the world and our experience of it. Studies of the modifications of the human mind from prelogical thinking in concrete images to logical conceptualization constitute the bulk of Vico's theory of knowledge, which fully recognizes the epistemological value of myth and mythic thinking in primitive societies while refusing to accept Cartesian rationalism as the sole criterion universally applicable to all times and cultures.

This seems to anticipate a benign kind of cultural and historical relativism that acknowledges the value of each culture or historical period and judges it solely by its own standard and criterion, a relativism that seems to open a new historical vision, to which Erich Auerbach enthusiastically attributes the widening of the aesthetic horizon in the West since the beginning of the nineteenth century. Owing to Vico, Auerbach declares with perfect assurance, we are now able to acknowledge the independent values of early and foreign civilizations and to cultivate the true catholicity of aesthetic taste and judgment. Under the impact of Vico's *New Science*, which for Auerbach is nothing less than a great " 'Copernican discovery' " in historical studies, no one would condemn a Gothic cathedral or a Chinese temple as ugly because they are not in conformity with classical models of beauty or consider the *Chanson de Roland* as a barbaric and ugly monster, unworthy of being compared to the civilized perfection accomplished in Voltaire's *Henriade*. Our historic way of feeling and judging is so deeply rooted in us that we have ceased to be aware of it. We enjoy the art, the poetry and the music of many different peoples and periods with equal preparedness for understanding.[21]

Vis-à-vis Foucault's remark on the Other, it is no wonder that Auerbach should have singled out a Chinese temple to represent an alien concept of beauty. In the eighteenth century, however, those who grew tired of the vogue of chinoiserie often mentioned the Gothic and the Chinese in tandem as equally grotesque and extravagant, as these satirical lines from Robert Lloyd's *Cit's Country Box* (1757) clearly show:

> Now bricklay'rs, carpenters and joiners,
> With Chinese artists and designers,
> Produce their schemes of alteration,
> To work this wondrous reformation.
> The trav'ler with amazement sees
> A temple, Gothic or Chinese,
> With many a bell, and tawdry rag on,
> And crested with a sprawling dragon.[22]

Since China has been for so long a myth and symbol of cultural difference, the appreciation of the elegance of a Chinese temple would indeed be a real proof of the true spirit of cosmopolitanism, an undeniable testimony to the triumph of aesthetic historicism.

The surmounting of dogmatic precepts and provincialism, the cultivation of historical sympathy with a genuine interest in the totality of human experience of creation, and the preparedness to accept and enjoy the artistic achievements of ancient and foreign cultures may all be logical outgrowths of Vico's theory, but the recognition of the aesthetic values of Chinese architecture and Chinese art in general owes more to Auerbach's view than to Vico's. For in the *New Science*, Vico characterizes China and the

Chinese in an unmistakably traditional scenario, in which China appears to be a site of space stubbornly inaccessible to the revolution of time. The Chinese, Vico observes, "are found writing in hieroglyphs just as the ancient Egyptians did"; they "boast a monstrous antiquity because in the darkness of their isolation, having no dealings with other nations, they had no true idea of time."[23] The Confucian philosophy, like "the priestly books of the Egyptians," is "rude and clumsy," almost entirely devoted to "a vulgar morality."[24] Chinese painting seems to Vico "most crude," for the Chinese "do not yet know how to make shadows in painting, against which highlights can stand out." Even Chinese porcelain fails to impress him, as he thinks the Chinese "just as unskilled as the Egyptians were in casting."[25] The comparison between the Chinese and the Egyptians Vico constantly emphasizes indicates how they both represent, as traditionally understood in the West, totally alien civilizations that are oblivious to any progress in history and lifelessly frozen in their vast, timeless immobility. The irony, however, is that this traditional image of China has itself proved to be quite frozen and timeless, as we find it almost intact in the writings of Foucault and some other contemporary thinkers who, notwithstanding the better knowledge now made available to Western scholars by the progress in sinology, still think of China in very much the same terms as Vico did some two hundred years ago: "as a civilization of dikes and dams beneath the eternal face of the sky; . . . a culture entirely devoted to the ordering of space, but one that does not distribute the multiplicity of existing things into any of the categories that make it possible for us to name, speak, and think."[26]

China Idealized

Vico's view, however, does not represent the whole picture of China in the Western mind of his time. The eighteenth century, as Adolf Reichwein argues, saw the first "metaphysical contact" between China and Europe, and the Western view was then largely favorable. Reichwein maintains that the age of the rococo was imbued with a spirit akin to that of Chinese culture, a spirit manifested in those graceful products imported from China: "Sublimated in the delicate tints of fragile porcelain, in the va- porous hues of shimmering Chinese silks, there revealed itself to the minds of that gracious eighteenth-century society in Europe a vision of happy living such as their own optimism had already dreamed of."[27] Indeed, in Alexander Pope's *Rape of the Lock*, that famous mock-heroic drawing-room drama, one can see how im- portant porcelain becomes as a symbol of the feminine compo- nent of the rococo, the daintiness of eighteenth-century high so- ciety: for the cutting of the curl from fair Belinda, which forms the fatal climax and the central action of the poem, is always foreboded by the breaking of a "fragile China jar" or some por- celain vessels.[28] Indeed, porcelain, silk, lacquer, wallpaper, Chi- nese gardening, and *ombres chinoises* all became fuels that fed the craze in Europe for things Chinese, the curious eighteenth- century vogue of chinoiserie. But chinoiserie, as Hugh Honour argues, has little to do with China or Chinese objects as such, but "may be defined as the expression of the European vision of Cathay."[29]

Largely based on favorable reports from Jesuit missionaries and their translation of some of the Chinese classics, on the influ- ential pioneer works by Juan González de Mendoza, Louis Dan- iel Le Comte, and especially Jean Baptiste Du Halde's *Description géographique, historique, chronologique, politique, et physique de l'em- pire de la Chine et de la Tartarie chinoise*, many eighteenth-century philosophers found in China and the Chinese the model of a na- tion well organized on the basis of lofty reason and good con- duct. After Montesquieu's *Lettres persanes*, dozens of imitations commented on contemporary European life through the mouth- piece of a foreigner, including some collections of "Chinese let- ters." An example of this particular genre in English is Oliver Goldsmith's *Citizen of the World*, which fully exploits the oppor- tunity for satire on the unsatisfactory conditions in contemporary England. In France, Michel de Montaigne already spoke about China in the sixteenth century as a great nation, whose history made him realize "how much ampler and more varied the world is than either the ancients or we ourselves understand."[30] Donald Lach rightly points out that Montaigne "uses the East to support his beliefs about the uncertainty of knowledge, the infinite variety in the world, and the universality of moral precepts"; and that he saw in China "an example for Europe that he never discerned elsewhere in the overseas world."[31] In Montaigne as well as in Goldsmith, the use of China serves a purpose that is obviously not concerned with China per se but with learning about the self in the West.

In the late seventeenth century and the early eighteenth, Gottfried Wilhelm Leibniz ardently promoted the mutual understanding of the East and the West, and he saw China as opening up the possibilities of a great civilization beyond the confines of his own and offering a good remedy for many of the moral and social problems in the Europe of his time. "Certainly the condition of our affairs, slipping as we are into ever greater corruption," says Leibniz, "seems to be such that we need missionaries from the Chinese who might teach us the use and practice of natural religion, just as we have sent them teachers of revealed theology."[32] For Leibniz, it was almost a deliberate divine plan that China and Europe should develop such different but equally great civilizations at the opposite ends of the earth, "so that as the most cultivated and distant peoples stretch out their arms to each other, those in between may gradually be brought to a better way of life."[33] China, in other words, held out great hopes for Leibniz's vision of the world as a family of nations in harmonious relationships.

In the eighteenth century, chinoiserie became more than just a vogue in daily social life. Great French painters like Antoine Watteau and François Boucher all contributed to French rococo chinoiserie not only by creating their own works, but also by providing models for others to follow. Boucher's output in this vein was rather extraordinary, "ranging from paintings through tapestry designs and stage sets to engravings, and would on its own have been enough to sustain the career of a lesser artist."[34] He depicted his Chinese figures in some fanciful settings, with such standard items of exotic fauna and flora as elephants, camels, palm trees, as well as gorgeous canopies and delicate pavilions, but by and large, they are recognizable as sophisticated, urbane Parisians as they might imagine themselves in exotic costumes. This "Chinese never-never land," as Alastair Laing observes, is "in no sense an imitation of actual Chinese pictures," but "an invention of Boucher's own."[35] What appears in Boucher's paintings, drawings, and tapestries is the life of the Chinese as he imagined it: joyful, peaceful, harmonious, and strange at the same time, a happy land of bright colors and fascinating details depicted with a typical gaiety and suavity that are the signature of Boucher's art. But that is not all. "Behind all the bright elegancies of French rococo chinoiserie," as Honour remarks, "there is a serious philosophical strain."[36] For Voltaire, China was "le plus sage empire de l'univers."[37] He admitted that the Chinese, like the French two hundred years earlier or the ancient Greeks or Romans, were not good mechanics or physicists, "but they have perfected morality, which is the first of the sciences."[38] He greatly admired Confucius for counseling virtue, preaching no mysteries, and teaching in "pure maxims in which you find nothing trivial and no ridiculous allegory [rien de bas, et rien d'une allégorie ridicule]."[39] Philosophers of the Enlightenment came to know Confucius at a time when they were extremely critical of all existing European institutions, trying to differentiate Christian morality from dogmas of the churches. They suddenly discovered, to their astonishment, that in great antiquity in China—a country whose material products had won the admiration of city dwellers in the market—Confucius had taught the philosophy of a state built on the basis of ethical and political *bon sens*, and that the Chinese civilization had developed for centuries on principles different from, yet in many respects superior to, those of the West. "Thus," says Reichwein, "Confucius became the patron saint of eighteenth-century Enlightenment. Only through him could it find a connection link with China."[40]

Reichwein declares that in the year 1760, with Voltaire's *Essai sur les moeurs,* Europe's admiration of China reached its zenith. In a substantial study of China in English literature of the seventeenth and eighteenth centuries, however, Qian Zhongshu shows that Reichwein's book has unduly left out English literature and that the situation was quite different in England, where sinophilism was at its height in the seventeenth century, but suffered an eclipse in the eighteenth, particularly as seen in its literature.[41] Qian's study provides many examples of how fact and fiction about China were commingled in the minds of the English, as China was yet more legendary than real, and English men of letters could still reflect on China in a leisurely manner, with an interest more humanistic than pragmatic. For all the false information they may have had and all the strange ideas and popular misconceptions they may have helped to propagate, those writers are extremely interesting precisely because they spoke of China as the Other, as a country whose unfamiliar outline could be filled in with all sorts of fantasies, philosophical speculations, and utopian idealizations.

Of great interest is their discussion of language and writing in China. Probably reflecting Mendoza, Francis Bacon remarks that the Chinese "write in characters real, which express neither letters nor words in gross, but things or notions."[42] Here Bacon is talking about language as the "organ of tradition," defining, after Aristotle, words as "images of cogitations" and letters as "images of words." But words, Bacon continues, are not the only medium capable of expressing cogitations, for "we see in the commerce of barbarous people, that understand not one another's language, and in the practice of divers that are dumb and deaf, that men's minds are expressed in gestures, though not exactly, yet to serve the turn."[43] It is in this context that he mentions how the Chinese use characters to communicate among themselves without understanding one another's spoken language. If that is a sign of the "barbarous," if Chinese characters express neither words nor letters—namely, images of cogitations and their transmission in alphabetic writing—the obvious inference must be that Chinese is a primitive language. And that, as we shall see, is precisely the point some writers of that age tried to prove in their vigorous quest for the "primitive language"—"primitive" in the sense of belonging to the times of the beginning or origin: the first language God created and the antediluvian people used, a language pure and simple, yet unaffected by the confusion of tongues at Babel.

Many Jesuits had propagated the view that the Chinese were descendants of Noah and had received from him the principles of natural religion, which had prepared them well for accepting the revealing light of Christianity. Under the influence of such a truly mythical view, Walter Ralegh asserts in his *History of the World* (1614) that Noah's ark finally landed in the East, somewhere between India and China; and Thomas Browne declares that "the Chineses who live at the borders of the earth . . . may probably give an account of a very ancient languadge" because by using common written characters the Chinese are yet able, in spite of their confusion in spoken language, to "make use of the workes of their magnified Confutius many hundred yeares before Christ, and in an historicall series ascend as high as Poncuus, who is conceaved to bee Noah."[44] However, it is John Webb who has presented, in a small octavo volume, the most intriguing argument on the Chinese language, and probably the first extensive treatment of this subject in the West. The thesis of his book is clearly stated in its title: *An Historical Essay Endeavoring a Probability That the Language of the Empire of China Is the Primitive Language*. In his dedicatory epistle to Charles II, dated 29 May 1668, Webb professes to "advance the DISCOVERY of that GOLDEN-MINE of Learning, which from all ANTIQUITY hath lain concealed in the PRIMITIVE TONGUE."[45] He explains that his intention is "not to dispute what in Possibility cannot, but what in Probability may be the First Speech."[46] Given the authority of the Bible and the "credible History" in the seventeenth century, Webb's argument must have impressed his contemporaries as logically simple and forceful. With his syllogistic argument firmly grounded on Scripture and history, Webb says:

Scripture teacheth, that the whole Earth was of one Language until the Conspiracy at BABEL; History informs that CHINA was peopled, whilst the Earth was so of one Language, and before that Conspiracy. Scripture teacheth that the Judgment of Confusion of Tongues, fell upon those only that were at BABEL; History informs, that the CHINOIS being fully setled before, were not there; And moreover that the same LANGUAGE and CHARACTERS which long preceding that Confusion they used, are in use with them at this very DAY; whether the Hebrew, or Greek Chronology be consulted.[47]

Webb did not know Chinese himself, but drawing on all the important works then available, he was able to argue with assurance that "*China* was after the Flood first planted either by *Noah* himself, or some of the sons of *Sem*, before they remove to *Shinaar*," and that "it may with much probability be asserted, *That the Language of the Empire of CHINA, is, the PRIMITIVE Tongue, which was common to the whole World before the Flood.*"[48] In no small feat to trace the changes of sound and spelling, he even proved to his own satisfaction that the Chinese emperor Yaus or Jaus (obviously the legendary Yao) was the same as Janus, whom many distinguished authors had identified as Noah himself! Finally he proposes "six principal guides" for discovering the primitive language: antiquity, simplicity, generality, modesty of expression, utility, and brevity, to which may be added consent of authors.[49] As he finds in Chinese plenty of these features, he has no doubt that Chinese is the primitive or first language.

Webb's enthusiasm for Chinese civilization is obvious; so are the Western values that underlie his appreciation of China. For him, as for many others in the seventeenth century who sought to see an ideal country where their dreamed values became true, China was that dreamland. He finds no difficulty in seeing China as realizing both Christian and Platonic ideals, for the Chinese are "*de civitate Dei*, of the City of God," and "their Kings may be said to be Philosophers, and their Philosophers, Kings."[50] Chinese poets win his acclaim for not stuffing their works with "Fables, Fictions, and Allegorical conceits, such as when the Authors Poetical rapture is over, himself understands not."[51] He observes that in Chinese poetry there are "*Heroick* verse[s]" for didactic purposes, poems of nature, and also poems "which treat of Love, not with so much levity nevertheless, as ours, but in such chaste Language, as not an undecent and offensive word to the most chaste ear is to be found in them." And most amusingly, he informs his readers that the Chinese "have no Letters whereby to express the *Privy parts*, nor are they to be found written in any part of all their Books." This remarkable phenomenon, he claims, is due to "the detestation of that shame, which *Noah* received by the discovery of his nakedness."[52]

For Webb as for Voltaire a century later, the perfection of morality in China, the outcome of a pure and uncorrupted state of natural religion, deserves the greatest admiration. Webb's book, as Qian comments, represents the best knowledge then available about China; it is full of inspiration and insight, putting its emphasis on "the cultural aspect of China instead of being interested in a *mélange adultère de chinoiseries*."[53] It is therefore no exaggeration to say that in England, as the works of Webb and some other writers can testify, the enthusiasm for China and Chinese culture reached its zenith in the seventeenth century.

China Scandalized

After a period of infatuation, there is bound to be disenchantment and a change of heart. And indeed we find a quite different picture of China in eighteenth-century English literature. This, of course, corresponds with the social changes in England of the time on a much larger scale. The seventeenth-century idealization of China can be partly traced to religious interests that prompted the Jesuit missionaries to go to China and study its culture. Such evangelistic zeal, however, seems less characteristic of the so-called Age of Reason: in English literature, the fictional character who goes to China is significantly not a missionary but a practical-minded fellow like Robinson Crusoe, the famous character created by Daniel Defoe, whom Honour calls "a violent and unreasonable China-phobe."[54] In the second part of Defoe's novel *Robinson Crusoe*, the protagonist gives running comments as he travels through Chinese cities; and his extremely negative impressions amount to a total rejection of the more favorable view we find in the literature of an earlier period. This famous earthy traveler constantly compares the "reality" he sees in China with that of Europe, predictably always to the disadvantage of the Asian country, striking a note of colonial militarism that is so typical of the time of the British Empire:

What are their buildings to the palaces and royal buildings of Europe? What is their trade to the universal commerce of England, Holland, France, and Spain? What are their cities to ours for wealth, strength, gaiety of apparel, rich furniture, and an infinite variety? What are their ports, supplied with a few junks and barks, to our navigation, our merchant fleets, our large and powerful navies? Our city of London has more trade than all their mighty empire. Our English, or Dutch, or French man-of-war of eighty guns would fight and destroy all the shipping of China.[55]

If Webb saw the Chinese as being "of the City of God," Crusoe, on the contrary, finds them "a barbarous nation of pagans, little better than savages." He cannot understand why the English "say such fine things of the power, riches, glory, magnificence, and trade of the Chinese, because I saw and knew that they were a contemptible herd or crowd of ignorant, sordid slaves, subjected to a government qualified only to rule such a people."[56] If the Chinese enjoy a reputation for wisdom, says Crusoe, they are wise only "among the foolish ones"; their religion, being "all summed up in Confucius's maxims," is "really not so much as a refined paganism"; and their government is nothing but "absolute tyranny."[57]

Such a pungently critical view indeed contrasts sharply with the seventeenth-century enthusiasm for China, but Defoe's is not the only voice of depreciation. Dr. Johnson, for example, despite his "particular enthusiasm with respect to visiting the wall of China," calls the Chinese "barbarians," for he sees it as a sign of "rudeness" that "they have not an alphabet. They have not been able to form what all other nations have formed."[58] The word "rudeness" with which Johnson justifies his view reminds us of

Vico, but in this case, as in many others in his conversation, the Doctor may be arguing for the sake of argument, behind which he would rather stand firm simply because Boswell is proposing a different view. Yet there is another example in his introductory note to Sir William Chambers's *Chinese Architecture*, a book with which he was much pleased. In that introduction, Johnson declares that he does not want "to be numbered among the exaggerators of Chinese excellence." He believes, in fact with very good reasons, that much of that exaggeration is due to "novelty"; and he tries to counterbalance the "boundless panegyricks which have been lavished upon the Chinese learning, policy, and arts."[59] Evidently, when French philosophers were paying very high tribute to Confucius and Chinese civilization, their English contemporaries were having many serious doubts and reservations.

To be sure, the picture Reichwein paints of China in the perception of eighteenth-century Europe is not all that rosy. He mentions the reaction against Voltaire's excessive praise: the marked indifference of Frederick the Great; the profound skepticism, disparagement, and critique as expressed by Rousseau, Montesquieu, Frédéric-Melchior Grimm, François de Fénelon, and many others; but Reichwein dismisses all these detractors of China as "hemmed in by the limitations of an arbitrary system" and presents Goethe's enthusiastic remarks on the Chinese as a kind of grand finale to his book. He regards the *Chinesisch-deutsche Jahres- und Tageszeiten* as a work indicating Goethe's warm reception of the Chinese world during the last years of his life. "Everything belonging to that world," says Reichwein, "seemed to him light, delicate, almost ethereal, the relations of things cleanly and clearly defined, the inner and the outer life serene and free from convulsions, something like battledore and shuttlecock perfectly played, without a single clumsy movement."[60] But after Goethe, the concept of China underwent a radical change in nineteenth-century Europe as the influence of the Jesuits began to wane and a more practical, commercial view gained the upper hand. As a result, China lost its spiritual significance for the West, and "the idea of China as, above all, a first-rate world-market is beginning to be the sole concern of public opinion."[61] Many misconceptions were cultivated by philosophers and historians, particularly the one that China was in a state of eternal immobility and standstill, an idea elaborately developed and explained in the works of Hegel, Leopold von Ranke, and others—an idea that has become an integral part of the traditional image of China in Western eyes.

In America, whose cultural roots are firmly planted across the ocean in Europe, we find the change of attitudes and concepts often following patterns similar to European ones. Having interviewed many people who all play an important role in shaping the public opinion about China and India, Harold Isaacs is convinced that there are in fact "all sorts of scratches on American minds about Asia," that is, all sorts of images and concepts that are more or less distorted, but all "have in common a quality of remoteness, of the exotic, the bizarre, the strange and unfamiliar, and—until the day before yesterday—a lack of connection with the more visibly important affairs of life."[62] In 1942, four months after Pearl Harbor, a national poll found that 60 percent of Americans could not locate China or India on a world map, but by the end of the war, because the Chinese were allies who fought the Japanese, knowledge about China increased slightly among Americans. Evidently, Americans have two sets of images, of which the modulation, with one advancing and the other receding alternately, is tuned in to the social and political atmosphere of the time. China is seen as both static and restlessly chaotic; the Chinese are both wise and benighted, strong and weak, honest and devious, and so on, and so forth. In popular Hollywood movies, there is on the one hand the famous villain Fu Manchu; on the other there is the clever pseudo-Confucian sleuth Charlie Chan. Of course, the actors who played Fu Manchu and Charlie Chan were not Chinese, and this fact speaks for itself. As Isaacs observes, "by examining the images we hold, say, of the Chinese and Indians, we can learn a great deal about Chinese and Indians, but mostly we learn about ourselves."[63]

It is indeed the image of the self that appears through the mirror that we call the Other, and this is no less true of the Chinese than of the Europeans or Americans. But there is perhaps this essential difference: while the Westerners tend to see the Chinese as fundamentally Other, sometimes the Chinese would think the Westerners eager to become like the Chinese themselves, that is, if they want to become civilized at all. In chapter 52 of the *Dream of the Red Chamber*, also known as *The Story of the Stone*, the best-known novel in classical Chinese literature, we find a Western girl "from the country of Ebenash" who not only "had a perfect understanding" of Chinese literature but "could expound the *Five Classics* and write poems in Chinese."[64] In fact, the poem she composed is so good that it wins high praise from the poetically talented protagonists of that famous novel. For the Chinese of classical education, literary art was the hallmark of the cultured, and here the writing of poetry would become a symbolic act of the ritual of initiation by which a foreigner was admitted into the society of culture, for which the only culture worth having was Chinese, and the Other as a cultural issue did not seem to arise.

Such an egocentric attitude may prove to be disastrous in actually dealing with the Other in reality. In the first few centuries of East-West contact, the Chinese emperor and his ministers could hardly bring themselves to understand the relation between China and other countries except in terms of an outmoded tributary framework, in which the Chinese emperor as the Son of Heaven and sovereign of the Middle Kingdom graciously accepted the respect and tribute foreign kings had to pay if they wished to contact or trade with the Celestial Dynasty. In as early a record as the *Rites of Zhou* (*Zhou li*), we already find that "nine different kinds of tribute" were being collected from the king's vassals in smaller states by officials of the central Zhou government.[65] In the *Doctrine of the Mean* chapter of the *Record of Rites* (*Li ji*), Confucius is recorded as teaching the nine principles (*jiu jing*) in the political art of rulership, of which the last two are "to pacify people of remote places [*rou yuanren*], and to appease the lords and vassals [*huai zhuhou*]." The anticipated results in implementing these principles are surely the consolidation of the king's power at the center: "when people of remote places are pacified, all from the four directions will come over to pledge allegiance; and when the lords and vassals are appeased, all under heaven will be struck with awe."[66] Numerous commentaries and elucidations made these early concepts articulated in Confucian classics into deeply ingrained ideas of rulership in China, and the tributary system was later used in handling relations between China and its neighboring countries. In the minds of Chinese rulers and officials, China was the sole center of civilization whereas all foreigners were barbarians. What we find in this inadequate picture of the Other is of course nothing but the incredible ignorance and arrogance of the Chinese ruling elites. Such an attitude is shown clearly in Emperor Qianlong's letter to King George III in 1793. Here the emperor told the king of Britain that "the virtue and prestige of the Celestial Dynasty having spread far and wide, the kings of the myriad nations come by land and sea with all sorts of precious things. Consequently there is nothing we lack, as your principal envoy and others have themselves observed. We have never set much store on strange or ingenious objects, nor do we need any more of your country's manufactures."[67]

The "principal envoy" mentioned here is George Macartney, whose refusal to perform the ritual of kowtow to Emperor Qianlong was one of the major reasons why his mission to establish trade relations with China and to install a permanent British embassy in Beijing failed, because that ritually required gesture of humility and submission was, in the mind of Qianlong, crucial in defining the tributary relationship between the emperor of China and foreign barbarians.[68] In two recent articles comparing the historical documents involved in the Macartney embassy, especially the letters and memoranda written by the British and the Chinese translation at the time presented to Emperor Qianlong, the Chinese scholar Ge Jianxiong found that the Chinese version of those documents had been rendered in such a way that its language "turned all the [British] documents originally meant to be communication between equals into reports submitted by subordinates to their superiors."[69] Comparing the two versions of those documents, Ge maintains, a Chinese reader today would feel amused, exasperated, and sad at the same time, but more important for such a reader is the lesson to be drawn from these historical events that may prove useful for the present, because "this is a page in the history of Chinese diplomacy that we would do well always to remember and take notice of."[70] Not surprisingly, the emperor's foreign policies based on such ignorance, arrogance, and self-deception later proved to be disastrous for China. In the painful experience of modern history, the Chinese—and Chinese intellectuals in particular—have recognized the significance of the presence of a powerful West. Perhaps it is no exaggeration to say that the whole history of modern China has been a long record of the clashes between cultures of the East and the West, tradition and modernity, and that the future of China depends on a successful reconciliation of the two. To achieve that success, however, a better knowledge of the Other is absolutely vital, and that explains why the desire for knowledge of the West may be said to characterize the Chinese intelligentsia during the entire modern period. From the point of view of Chinese intellectuals, however, the effort to learn about—and from—the West is not a purely epistemological issue, stemming out of mere curiosity; it is rather the necessary means to the aim of the survival and self-strengthening of the nation, and thus a historical mission and a social responsibility.

In the West, however, knowledge of China and Chinese civilization seems to be still a specialty limited to a small number of sinologists. In 1963, when Raymond Dawson edited a collection of essays on China as one of the companion volumes to the highly acclaimed *Legacy of Greece*, he felt that "a generation ago it would not have been possible to produce anything fit to occupy a place on the same shelf as the illustrious first volume of the series."[71] Even then, he still thought it necessary to entertain "a healthy scepticism" in reading anything about China. "Old misconceptions of her civilization live long and die hard," says

Dawson, "for there is a certain inertia in our historical beliefs, so that they tend to be retained until they are ruthlessly questioned by original minds perhaps centuries after they have ceased to be true."[72]

Indeed, an old misconception tends to remain alive despite all improvement in knowledge and judgment, that is, the misleading idea that Chinese is a pictographic language. We have seen this idea in Bacon and Vico, and we find it again in Foucault when he talks about the difference between cultures of the East and the West in terms of different conceptions of writing. Foucault claims that in Western culture writing "refers not to a thing but to speech"; therefore, the "presence of repeated speech in writing undeniably gives to what we call a work of language an ontological status unknown in those cultures where the act of writing designates the thing itself, in its proper and visible body, stubbornly inaccessible to time."[73] The reference is obviously to nonphonetic writings in Egyptian hieroglyphs or Chinese characters, which are allegedly transparent signs of things: writings that exist not in and for themselves, not ontologically. But when Foucault describes the ontological status of writing in the sixteenth century, the "absolute privilege" and "fundamental place accorded in the West to Writing," he recalls, with Blaise de Vigenère and Claude Duret, a time when the written word was primary and the spoken word was "stripped of all its powers," when the possibility was emphasized that "before Babel, before the Flood, there had already existed a form of writing composed of the marks of nature itself."[74] This naturally reminds us of Webb's view that Chinese is the primitive language before the Flood, but it reminds us even more of the sensible and accurate observation of a sixteenth-century missionary in China, Father Matteo Ricci, who noted in his diary that "from time immemorial, [the Chinese] have devoted most of their attention to the development of the written language and did not concern themselves overmuch with the spoken tongue. Even up to the present all their eloquence is to be found in their writings rather than in the spoken word."[75] If ontological status implies "privilege" and "fundamental place" accorded to writing as Foucault suggests, then Chinese may certainly be called a language that has achieved such an ontological status in its own cultural context. As Chinese scripts are much less directly phonetic as compared with Western alphabetic writing, they may give the appearance of being truly ontological in the sense of being detached from the spoken word.

Contrary to popular misconceptions, however, Chinese writing is not pictographic or ideographic, because the characters are linguistic signs of concepts and represent the sound and meaning of words rather than pictographic representations of things themselves. Many Chinese scripts do contain a phonetic element, showing how they should be pronounced, and it is simply wrong to believe that Chinese writing refers not to speech but to things directly, that it is a kind of pictographic writing unrelated to the spoken word. When the French sinologist Henri Cordier (1849–1925) tried to define the Chinese writing system, he remarked with good reason that "as the graphic system is not hieroglyphic, or symbolic, or syllabic, or alphabetic, or lexigraphic, but ideophonographic, we shall, in order to avoid misconception and for the sake of brevity, call its characters *sinograms*."[76] This coinage evidently tries to differentiate Chinese written characters from both alphabetic and hieroglyphic writing; the key word used here to describe Chinese scripts is "ideophonographic." More recently, George Steiner astutely uses the word "logographic" in talking about the Chinese language.[77] But long before Steiner and even Cordier, as William Boltz points out in a recent study of Chinese writing, Peter Du Ponceau (1760–1844) already argues in his *Dissertation on the Nature and Character of the Chinese System of Writing*, published in 1838 by the American Philosophical Society in Philadelphia, that Chinese characters represent ideas as words in language, that they are connected with sound in the same way as a group of letters in the English alphabet is, and that Chinese characters form "a *logographic* system of writing."[78] A writing system can represent speech on a number of different levels: a given graph may stand for a single sound, as is the case with most letters in an alphabetic system, or it can stand for a syllable or a whole word. "A graph that stands for a syllable is called a *syllabograph,* and one that stands for a word is," says Boltz, "a *logograph,* or, less commonly, a *lexigraph.*" The last is the case with Chinese characters, which differ from Western alphabetic writing only because they "render sounds visible a whole word at a time, whereas alphabets (the stereotypical phonetic script) do it, *grosso modo,* sound by individual sound."[79]

To see Chinese characters as minipictures of a myriad of things with no relation with the sound of speech, however, is a perennial Western misconception that simply refuses to die. Its life is made even stronger in modern times with an injection of poetic vigor by Ernest Fenollosa and Ezra Pound, who formulated one of the most powerful modern theories of "ideogrammic" poetry based on a creative misreading of the Chinese written characters. Based on Fenollosa and Pound, Jacques Derrida sees in the "nonphonetic" Chinese language "the testimony of a powerful movement of civilization developing outside of all logocentrism."[80] Again the Chinese language becomes a sign of a totally different culture, which sets off, for better or for worse, whatever is conceived as Western culture. But is China, its language, or its culture, only to be understood in terms of the West's Other, defined negatively as whatever the West is not? Is cross-cultural understanding possible when the Other is seen as the opposite to a Western self-image? It is about time such misconceptions and their underlying dichotomous assumptions were questioned and rejected: China as the Other should not be required to serve as the antithesis to the West, as a mere foil or contrast to a Western self-conception.

Fusion of Horizons

The question is, then, can we ever know the Other as the truly Other? When we have argued with Foucault and others who entertain a variety of distorted images of China as the Other, it seems that we have argued, ironically, not against Foucault but for him completely. All we have shown is precisely the validity of his proposition that it is hardly possible to get out of the confinement of the historical a priori, the *epistemes* or fundamental codes of cultural systems. Apparently, the misconceptions of China we find today form part of the traditional repertory of cultural concepts in the West; they are deeply rooted in its history and ideology. The image of China in the Western eye, as our discussion shows, has always been historically shaped to represent values that are considered different from Western ones. China, India, Africa, and the Islamic Orient have all served as foils to the West at one time or another, either as idealized utopias, alluring and exotic dreamlands, or lands of eternal stagnation, spiritual purblindness, and ignorance. Whatever change and progress we may make in understanding the Other, that understanding has to be mediated through language, which is itself a product of history and therefore not outside of it. As Dawson observes, the "polarity between Europe and Asia and between West and East is one of the important categories by means of which we think of the world and arrange our knowledge of it, so there can be no doubt that it colours the thoughts even of those who have a special interest in Oriental studies."[81] As there is no other language or other way of thinking available to us except our own, and no understanding of the Other except in relation to the self, a purely "objective" or "correct" understanding unaffected by historical and ideological givens is indeed hard to find. But does that mean that our thinking and language are a kind of prison-house, from which there is no escape? When Dawson speaks about the pervasive influence of popular misconceptions, he is speaking not only as a sinologist who understands China better than those who are yet to be initiated into the range of his knowledge, but also as a scholar and editor whose book will provide knowledge to disperse hazy fantasies and help readers understand the rich cultural legacy of China. He is, in other words, suggesting that it is not just necessary but also possible to expose and rectify cultural misconceptions.

It is true to a certain extent that our thinking and knowledge are determined by the historical givens of the culture in which we are born, that we can name, speak, and think only within the boundaries of our language. Understanding begins with a set of historical givens—what Martin Heidegger describes as the fore-structure of understanding—and the process of knowing seems to move only within limits of a hermeneutic circle. Anything understood, says Heidegger, is conceptualizable through interpretation that is already "grounded in *something we have in advance*— in a *fore-having*."[82] The forestructure of understanding is not, however, a fixation of presuppositions never to be challenged or modified, but a necessary yet provisional beginning, whose further development will depend on the things and events that we come to encounter in the hermeneutic process. "Our first, last, and constant task," says Heidegger, "is never to allow our fore-having, fore-sight, and fore-conception to be presented to us by fancies and popular conceptions, but rather to make the scientific theme secure by working out these fore-structures in terms of the things themselves."[83] In Heidegger's hermeneutic theory, therefore, while presuppositions are fully recognized, the fore-structure of understanding does not preclude, but rather invites, challenges and modifications based on the claims of "the things themselves." And that, as Gadamer points out in a lucid gloss to this important passage, is precisely what Heidegger works out here. "The point of Heidegger's hermeneutical reflection," Gadamer observes, "is not so much to prove that there is a circle as to show that this circle possesses an ontologically positive significance."[84] To know the Other certainly begins with interpretive givens, the *epistemes* or fundamental codes of a cultural system, but as the hermeneutic process evolves, those givens will be challenged and revised. As Gadamer remarks, in the Heideggerian hermeneutic process "interpretation begins with fore-conceptions that are replaced by more suitable ones," and "methodologically conscious understanding will be concerned not merely to form anticipatory ideas, but to make them conscious, so as to check them and thus acquire right understanding from the things themselves."[85] If it is right to remember how our language largely determines the way we can talk about the Other, it would

be wrong to forget that the Other has its own voice and can assert its own truth against various misconceptions. It is by forgetting and indeed silencing the voice of the Other that many of the
misconceptions rise to the status of dubious cultural representation, and those who come to study the other culture and society
in order only to find alternative visions to their own can afford to
fantasize about the Other. What gets lost in such self-projection
and fantasizing is the true concern about the Other, the moral responsibility for the other person, which Levinas holds to be prior
to knowledge and crucial for our own being. But when the voice
of the Other is forgotten or silenced, as we shall see more con-
cretely in discussing some of the real events in recent history, the
talk about the Other becomes little more than empty chatter, and
worse still, a distortion of the social and political reality of the
other people, in place of which a Western theoretical discourse
prates on, hardly aware of its ominous implications in the other
people's home. What is important then is to remain open to the
claims of the Other and to listen to its voice, which will make us
aware of our own preconceptions and limitations as well as the
fact that Orient and Occident as polarized cultural entities are
cultural constructs widely different from the physical entities
they are supposed to represent.

Images of national characters, those popular, caricaturelike
generalizations, are often generated by representational systems.
In 1889, Oscar Wilde put it in clear and witty language that the
discrepancy between reality and representation can be enormous. Take Japan for example, says Wilde. "The actual people
who live in Japan are not unlike the general run of English people; that is to say, they are extremely commonplace, and have
nothing curious or extraordinary about them. In fact the whole of
Japan is a pure invention."[86] In proclaiming that Japan as represented in art and literature is a myth and fiction, Wilde, as
Eugenio Donato argues, has dismantled the illusion of realism
and revealed "what we know only too well after Derrida,"
namely, "the play of representation."[87] As a typical aesthete
Wilde certainly prefers artistic myth to reality, but his insight

into the play of representation emphasizes precisely the false nature of cultural myths. Perhaps that is why Wilde, though admittedly making deliberate overstatements, appears more sober-minded than many scholars of our own time, who, for all the knowledge now made available about the language and culture of China and Japan, seem either to take myth for reality or simply to refuse to acknowledge their difference.

An interesting modern reflection on Japan as "a fictive nation" and a consciously "invented name" is Roland Barthes's *Empire of Signs*. Like Wilde, Barthes is fully aware that the Japan that emerges in his writing is not a real country: "I am not lovingly gazing toward an Oriental essence—to me the Orient is a matter of indifference, merely providing a reserve of features whose manipulation—whose invented interplay—allows me to 'entertain' the idea of an unheard-of symbolic system, one altogether detached from our own." He knows very well that the desire to use the language of the Other to reveal "the impossibilities of our own," a desire Foucault shares, is merely a "dream."[88] Having warned his readers that his writing is pure mythmaking, however, Barthes indulged in the dream of a totally different Other and produced a number of charming myths about Japan: when he asserted, for example, that "chopsticks are the converse of our knife (and of its predatory substitute, the fork)," thus setting West and East again in the frame of a fundamental polarity.[89] It would be interesting to see what symbolic meaning our modern dreamers will attribute to, say, fortune cookies, which are so popular in every Chinese restaurant in the United States but unheard of in China; and what reflections they may have on the mixture of fantasy and reality, the colorful Chinatown mythologies.

Barthes has indeed a short piece on China, and his China is anything but colorful. That was the China of the Cultural Revolution, the painful, disastrous period of political upheavals and self-destruction in recent Chinese history. As a semiotician and politically leftist intellectual, Barthes fails completely to read China as a text, to understand the Chinese society, its people, and its politics. In fact, the very point Barthes tries to make in his short piece is precisely the nonunderstanding of China, or the lack of meaning and significance of his experience in China. Having visited Red China, the group of French intellectuals went home "with: *nothing.*" The words Barthes used to describe that vast land are "bland," "flat," "not colorful," and "nothing picturesque."[90] "In China," he says, "meaning is annulled, exempted from being in all those places where we Westerners track it down, but it remains standing, armed, articulated, and on the offensive where we are loath to put it: its politics."[91] But putting China in the East-West dichotomy as the opposite of whatever the West represents, Barthes could not even begin to decipher the meaning he located in Chinese politics. What he found in the "current campaign against Confucius and Lin Piao," for example, was "a certain playfulness." Even the name of the campaign in Chinese (*Pilin-Pikong*), he asserts, "rings like a joyful sleigh-bell, and the campaign is divided up into invented games."[92] Given the numerous instances of senseless cruelty in which many Chinese men and women were tormented and physically abused, beaten, maimed, or even murdered in those political campaigns during the Cultural Revolution, Barthes's characterization of such campaigns as "playful," "joyful," and "invented games" sounds like an outrageously sadistic joke. He of course did not "mean" it, nor did he have any way of knowing how to read Chinese politics in terms of "the things themselves." What he says, as Simon Leys puts it mildly, is nothing but the typical elegant Parisian chatter: Barthes is bestowing "an entirely new dignity on the old and unjustly disparaged activity of small talk," by keeping up "the exquisite drip-drip-drip of a tiny little tap of lukewarm water."[93] More recently, Lisa Lowe gives an excellent discussion of this short piece by Barthes along with Julia Kristeva's bizarrely psycholinguistic fantasizing of a "pre-oedipal matriarchal" Chinese culture and the *Tel quel* group's political fetishizing of Maoism. In all these cases, says Lowe, "the subversive China is invoked according to a logic of opposition; it is described in terms of how it thwarts the will to decipher, and is described for the purpose of more thoroughly elaborating the western observer's hermeneutic desire."[94] Here the French intellectual's leftist political persuasion does not guarantee a benign attitude toward the people in the East. Indeed, as Barthes acknowledges openly, to him "the Orient is a matter of indifference," an excuse for writing. Lowe calls it Barthes' "poetics of escape," which shows a surprising affinity with the Orientalist exoticization of the East:

Ironically, Barthes's attempt to resolve the dilemma of criticizing western ideology while escaping the tyranny of binary logic takes a form not unlike that of traditional orientalism: through an invocation of the Orient as a utopian space, Barthes constitutes an imaginary third position. The imagined Orient—as critique of the Occident—becomes an emblem of his "poetics of escape," a desire to transcend semiology and the ideology of signifier and signified, to invent a place that exceeds binary structure itself.[95]

And yet the binary structure is precisely what gets consolidated in Barthes's reflections on China and Japan. The desire to "transcend semiology and the ideology of signifier and signified" projects itself on an imaginary Orient of complete emptiness, a flat and bland surface "exempt from meaning." For Barthes, China is "the end of hermeneutics."[96] Japan is indeed called an Empire of Signs, but a name that needs immediate qualification: "Empire of Signs? Yes, if it is understood that these signs are empty and that the ritual is without a god."[97] That is to say, these Oriental signs are not for reading or deciphering, as "there is nothing to *grasp*."[98] This Orientalist semiology of emptiness is just that—emptiness, whose only meaning is the exemption from meaning or the reversal of Western hermeneutics of meaning and depth.

Needless to say, insofar as the Orient is conceived and defined in Western terms of differentiation as its Other, what is seen in the Western eye as the Orient is only a cultural myth. But once China or Japan is recognized as truly different, that is, not as the imaginary Other with its history of imagery in the Western tradition but as a country with its own history, and once the desire to know the Other is genuine enough, being part of the desire to expand the horizon of knowledge in the West, it becomes necessary to demythologize the myth of the Other. The traditional imagery of the Other has, of course, an aura of mystery, exotic beauty, and what Victor Segalen calls "the aesthetic of the Diverse." As poet and sinophile, Segalen develops a highly personal theory of the Other, celebrating the faraway in space or time, which he terms *l'Exotisme*. For him China is not so much a real country as a myth that inspires his *Stèles*, *Equipée*, and other works; demythologization of the Other would seem to him a threat to poetic charms, because exoticism, according to Segalen, is nothing but "the power to *conceive the Other*."[99] In the increasing contact of East and West, he sees a depressing loss of exoticism. "The exotic tension of the world is diminishing. Exoticism, the source of mental, aesthetic, or physical energy (though I do not like to confuse the levels), is diminishing," laments our poet. "Where is mystery? Where are the distances?"[100]

Mystery, however, may contribute to fear as well as to charm, and distances may blur the view of true beauty. To demythologize the Other is surely not to deny its distance, its alien nature, or the possibility of its poetic charms, but to recuperate real rather than imaginary differences. The beauty of real difference or the aesthetic of the Other cannot be truly appreciated unless various misconceptions are exposed and the false polarity between East and West totally dismantled. The question of the beautiful or the aesthetic judgment of taste is of course not to be solved by logical reasoning or a scientific method. As Gadamer notes, "the validity of an aesthetic judgment cannot be derived and proved from a universal principle. No one supposes that questions of taste can be decided by argument and proof."[101] At the same time, he also observes that "*the concept of taste* was originally more a *moral* than an aesthetic idea," and that taste can be improved or trained through Bildung or "cultivation."[102] The dialectic in questions of beauty and aesthetic taste lies in its irreducible particularity on the one hand, and the possibility of a social norm and common standard on the other. Therefore, in arguing for the necessity of demythologization, I do not venture to propose any magical way of knowing the true beauty of the Other, only to discourage any illusory and irresponsible construct of cultural difference. What I want to emphasize here is the moral rather than the aesthetic idea, the cultivation of taste in the appreciation of the Other's alterity. By "moral idea" I mean first of all to acknowledge the presence of the Other as real human beings, to have a sense of their desire and interest, and to guard against the danger of subjective projection that may render the Other voiceless and irrelevant. To demythologize the Other for adequate understanding is not to become self-alienated in adopting alien values, but eventually to come back to the self with rewarding experiences. Here another important concept Gadamer develops in his work may prove to be helpful, namely, the concept of Bildung.

In Hegel's concept of theoretical Bildung, there is first this move to self-alienation: "Theoretical Bildung leads beyond what man knows and experiences immediately. It consists in learning to affirm what is different from oneself and to find universal viewpoints from which one can grasp the thing, 'the objective thing in its freedom,' without selfish interest." Yet the basic movement of the spirit is a tendency of returning to the self from the Other; thus "what constitutes the essence of Bildung is clearly not alienation as such, but the return to oneself."[103] Bildung is not, however, just attaining to the universal, the perfection of the absolute knowledge of philosophy, as Hegel insists. Instead Gadamer emphasizes the openness of the process: the importance of "keeping oneself open to what is other—to other, more universal points of view"; for him the universal viewpoints are not absolute, "not a fixed applicable yardstick, but . . . the viewpoints of possible others."[104] That is to say, to know the Other is a process of Bildung, of learning and self-cultivation, which is neither projecting the self onto the Other nor erasing the self with the Other's alterity. It is rather a moment when self and Other meet and join together, in which both are changed and enriched in what Gadamer calls "the fusion of horizons."[105] That moment of fusion would eliminate the isolated horizon of either the self or the Other, the East or the West, and bring their positive dynamic relationship into prominence. In the fusion of horizons, we are able to transcend the boundaries of language and culture so that there is no longer the isolation of East or West, no longer the exotic, mystifying, inexplicable Other, but something to be learned and assimilated until it becomes part of our knowledge and experience of the world. Thus, in demythologizing China as the myth of the Other, the myth disappears but not the beauty, for the real differences between China and the West will be fully recognized, and China's true otherness will be appreciated as contributing to the variety of our world and the totality of what we may still proudly call the heritage of human culture.

CHAPTER 2

Montaigne, Postmodernism, and Cultural Critique

The previous chapter tries to delineate a certain historical continuity in the Western imagination of China or the Orient, and one of the things that one sees in such a historical survey, which is especially relevant to the current cultural scene, is precisely the complexity of historical continuity, the constant search for self-understanding, the ironic relationships and unexpected affinities between the old and the new, the Orientalist discourse and contemporary views that are sharply critical of Orientalism. History is, of course, both continuity and change, but in the polemical gesture of radical breaks and transformations, which may be seen as a major characteristic of the contemporary and postmodern discourse, affinities and continuities based on similar principles and modes of thought are often neglected, even deliberately overlooked, by advocates of new theories and new historical movements. In talking about China and the West, what seems to have persisted and thus made the continuity possible, as we have seen, is a dichotomous opposition between the self and the Other, the West and the East. How the Other is viewed, whether it is regarded with admiration or looked down upon with contempt, does change from one form of the dichotomy to another, and from one historical period to the next as well as within the same period, but the perennial dichotomy itself seems seldom to relax its grip on people's minds in the perpetuation of cultural myths. This is not to say that binary opposition is in itself necessarily reductionist and untenable, for we do need to understand things in mutual differentiation, but a rigid opposition that makes self and Other mutually exclusive and puts the East and the West in an *absolute dichotomy* does indeed reduce the one to the other's negative mirror image, and thus completely fails to recognize the reality of cultures and their interrelations. Different formulations of this dichotomy tend to look like radical breaks in thinking about other cultures, but the way in which other cultures are conceived and thought often turns out to be the same. How to recognize cultural differences without putting them in an absolute dichotomy—that is, without falling into the fixation of cultural myths—remains a difficult challenge. It is one of the most important challenges we must face if we are serious about acquiring adequate understanding of other cultures and other peoples, and if we want to make the world a happier place for all cultures and traditions to coexist in peaceful harmony rather than conflict and violent clash.

According to many theorists and critics, cultural breaks are characteristic of postmodernism.[1] Here again, the tension and relationship between the modern and the postmodern may be worth exploring: we may ask the question whether there is historical continuity despite the claim to radical breaks, if that is indeed how postmodernism understands itself, and whether the use of the Other, especially with regard to the construction of cultural differences, the construction of a non-European, non-Western Other, plays a similar role in the self-knowledge or self-critique of the West at different historical times.

Postmodernism and Postmodernity

In spite of much argument and discussion, the concept of postmodernism seems to remain hopelessly ambiguous, and it seems still difficult to specify just what constitutes postmodernity and distinguishes it from the merely modern. The postmodern condition, as Jean-François Lyotard describes it in a rather dry narrative of the decline of classical metanarratives of legitimation, is the condition of knowledge in postindustrial societies where scientific research and knowledge, funded and controlled by the state and multinational corporations, engage in a lan-

guage game of which the goal is "no longer truth, but performativity—that is, the best possible input/output equation."[2] Research and knowledge seem to have nothing to do with discovery, invention, and what Francis Bacon called, in the early days
of modernity, the advancement of learning. In contemporary societies of "perfect information," where data is in principle made
accessible to any expert by advanced computer and telecommunication technologies, postmodern knowledge is characterized
not by acquiring new facts, additional information, or truth, but
by generating new paradigms, new and imaginative ways of arranging the data for better performance and efficiency. So the
question for today's "professionalist student, the State, or institutions of higher education," says Lyotard, is "no longer 'Is it
true?' but 'What use is it?'" Or more directly and honestly, "Is it
salable?" "Is it efficient?"[3]

For anyone who still believes in pursuing truth and loves
knowledge for its truth value, Lyotard's report on the postmodern condition of knowledge may be rather disconcerting. But it
would be interesting to reflect whether such a disconcerting
statement about the postmodern condition applies to Lyotard's
own text as well, since his text, as the author acknowledges, is
commissioned by a government agency, "the Conseil des Universitiés of the government of Quebec."[4] Indeed, considering
Lyotard's report on the mercantilization and self-legitimation of
knowledge in today's postmodern societies, one may wonder
whether it is still possible at all for Lyotard to write *A Report on
Knowledge* that can be valued for its information of facts rather
than discursive performance, for its reliability rather than salability. Of course, questions like these hardly ever come up in the
debate on postmodernism, but the irony is, though unintended,
that Lyotard's report on the postmodern condition cannot but
implicate itself as knowledge disseminated under the same condition as he describes. At any rate, whether contemporary Western societies have reached the condition of "perfect information"—and there is some doubt about this[5]—the postmodern
condition as Lyotard describes is clearly a Western phenomenon,

and postmodernism, as Linda Hutcheon puts it, is "primarily European and American (North and South)."[6]

If postmodernity refers to the situation of postindustrial societies in the West, postmodernism as a cultural concept designates, on the other hand, radical changes in ways of perception and representation, conceptual and stylistic transformations and fractures that have occurred in Western art and literature in the last fifty years. As Fredric Jameson argues in his at once supportive and contesting foreword to Lyotard's book, concurrent with the decline of metanarratives that legitimate science by way of evidence and proof located in an objective reality outside the language of science, is the so-called "crisis of representation, in which an essentially realistic epistemology, which conceives of representation as the reproduction, for subjectivity, of an objectivity that lies outside it—projects a mirror theory of knowledge and art, whose fundamental evaluative categories are those of adequacy, accuracy, and Truth itself."[7] This linkage of postmodernity conceived exclusively in terms of science and technology with a concept of postmodern culture and aesthetics, which Jameson finds regrettably lacking in Lyotard's book, serves to reformulate the question of the postmodern both historically and politically, since for Jameson the "problem of postmodernism is at one and the same time an aesthetic and a political one."[8] The turn to the aesthetic is politically significant because, according to Jameson, the experimental art of the avant-garde, the self-conscious new forms of high modernism, embody a politicized aesthetics, "the conception of the revolutionary nature of high modernism that Habermas faithfully inherited from the Frankfurt School."[9] In opposition to the popular taste and accepted values of a philistine society, the avant-garde art of high modernism has an almost inherently revolutionary potential, while postmodernism, understood as a reaction against modernism and producing, however ironically and paralogically, a "new conflation of the forms of high and mass culture," is "no longer at all 'oppositional' in that sense; indeed it constitutes the pervasive hegemonic aesthetic of consumer society and significantly serves the latter's commodity production."[10] Postmodernism, in other words, is "a kind of aesthetic populism."[11] But by linking up postmodernism with modernism, though not in a strictly chronological order, Jameson is able to historicize postmodernism and to conceive of postmodernity as a late stage of capitalism rather than a totally new social order, and therefore a social structure that can still be analyzed in classical Marxist terms, as an index "of a new and powerful, original, global expansion of capitalism, which now specifically penetrates the hitherto precapitalist enclaves of Third World agriculture and of First World culture, in which, in other words, capital more definitively secures the colonization of Nature and the Unconscious."[12] In view of this global expansion of capitalism, then, postmodernism would not be just European and American but also implicates the Third World and its non-Western cultural manifestations.

Jameson's argument is richly suggestive for the three aspects just mentioned above, namely, the historicization of postmodernism, the turn to the aesthetic, and the cultural interplay between the Western world and the Third World. Putting the three aspects together, one may raise some interesting questions about postmodernism as a cultural concept. If postmodernism can be historicized and related with the past, what can then be identified as its historical antecedents? What relationship obtains between the postmodern moment as a Western phenomenon and the non-Western (Third World) Other? By calling attention to Lyotard's own reflection on postmodernist culture, which is included in the English version of Lyotard's book as an appendix, Jameson notes that Lyotard himself is "quite unwilling to posit a postmodernist stage radically different from the period of high modernism and involving a fundamental historical and cultural break with this last."[13] What is *post*modern indicates a paradox in social and cultural changes, for the displacement of what goes before, the kind of Oedipal relationship between successive generations of poets and artists, which Harold Bloom calls the anxiety of influence, is especially visible in the transformation of art from the modern to the postmodern. Such a relationship, as

Lyotard recapitulates it, runs through the history of art from the Impressionists to Cézanne, from Cézanne to Picasso and Braque, from Picasso and Braque to Marcel Duchamp, and from Duchamp to Daniel Buren: "In an amazing acceleration, the generations precipitate themselves. A work can become modern only if it is first postmodern. Postmodernism thus understood is not modernism at its end but in the nascent state, and this state is constant."[14] Postmodernism thus becomes synonymous with a constant search for the ever new, the breaking of existent boundaries of the known, the same, the self, and at the same time a strong desire to reach out to the unknown, the different, the unrepresentable Other. In this respect, then, postmodernism, or at least that part of it which is, in Lyotard's words, "not modernism at its end but in the nascent state," may preserve much of the radical, if not revolutionary, nature of high modernism. Indeed, the attitude postmodernism maintains toward the past, especially in its various theoretical formulations, is a fundamentally critical one. To the extent that everything modern is already superseded by something that comes after it, postmodernity appears to be symptomatic of an extreme impatience in the psychosocial condition of contemporary Western culture, in which the notion of the traditional, timeless classic is threatened to be supplanted by Andy Warhol's proverbial fifteen-minute fame, and the need to make something new and militantly avant-garde becomes in itself the aim of artistic creation. Postmodernism seems impatient of what was or has been in the past, and yet, insofar as the search for ways of representing the new and the unrepresentable characterizes the creative impulse and desire, postmodernism does not belong exclusively to the present; that is to say, it is not without historical precedents.

Montaigne in Postmodern Perspective

Like any other cultural movement or tendency, postmodernism is situated in its own historicity and should be understood, again as Lyotard remarks, "according to the paradox of the future (*post*) anterior (*modo*)."[15] This temporal paradox projects postmodernity as a concept from the immediate present onto a much larger conceptual space and relates it to those moments in the past that were also in search of what was once new. Lyotard exemplifies this paradox by making the surprising remark that "the essay (Montaigne) is postmodern, while the fragment (*The Athaeneum*) is modern."[16] Seeing postmodernism as an ironic revisit of the past and ironic use of the already used language to represent what cannot otherwise be represented, Umberto Eco also defines postmodernism as an ahistorical "ideal category—or, better still, a *Kunstwollen*, a way of operating" not limited to a particular period of time. If postmodernism can be so defined, Eco continues, "it is clear why Sterne and Rabelais were postmodern, why Borges surely is, and why in the same artist the modern moment and the postmodern moment can coexist, or alternate, or follow each other closely."[17] But in what sense can we say Montaigne is postmodern? How does his essay partake of the desire and strategies we call postmodernist? What are the shared concerns in Montaigne and in the writings of postmodernism? Taking Lyotard's remark as a starting point, I shall explore the implications of the temporal paradox of the "future (*post*) anterior (*modo*)" and understand postmodernism not as uniquely of the present moment but as rooted in other moments of cultural critique, namely, the critique of the self and of subjectivity, which constitutes the driving force that lies at the heart of both modernist and postmodernist transformations. I shall argue that the use of a non-Western Other as an alternative cultural vision in questioning the Western self forms an important aspect of the common ground on which Montaigne's essay seems to meet with postmodernist writings.

It is a critical commonplace that Montaigne in his *Essays* is concerned with the problem of knowing the self, but he is concerned not so much with his own self as the self of a more general nature, for the subject of his study is not himself as such but is "man."[18] Needless to say, the self or the concept of man in his writings is culturally specific, that is, conceived within the range of Western culture that Montaigne inherits most consciously by copiously citing classical writers whose works constitute the Western tradition. In his quest of the essence of man, however, Montaigne starts and proceeds by putting that essence in question. The pervasive and healthy skepticism, clearly demonstrated in his *Essays* and his famous motto—*Que sais-je?*—reveals a profound sense of change and transformation, a sense of the limit and uncertainty of the knowledge of man. The uncertainty or "crisis" of identity is of course a typical postmodern question. As Lyotard observes, the question raised by much of contemporary art, the challenge of works like Duchamp's "ready-made" art objects to aesthetic theory, is not "What is beautiful?" but "What can be said to be art (and literature)?"[19] In the postmodernist aesthetics, the very identity of a work of art becomes a question the work raises about itself, a question that does not seem to arise in the traditional aesthetics of the beautiful. But when art raises the question of identity and self-knowledge, as Arthur Danto argues eloquently, art comes to its end in precisely the way Hegel has described, that is, it raises a theoretical question to which only philosophy can provide the answer. "Without theory, who could see a blank canvas, a square lead plate, a tilted beam, some dropped rope, as works of art?" But when such questions were raised in works of art themselves, says Danto, "the history of art attained that point where it had to turn into its own philosophy. It had gone, as art, as far as it could go. In turning into philosophy, art had come to an end. From now on progress could only be enacted on a level of abstract self-consciousness of the kind which philosophy alone must consist in."[20] Art loses its identity in turning into philosophy, but art in the postmodern mode is not just moving into the realm of philosophy, but crossing into a lot of other areas as well. The blurring of boundaries between art and nonart, fiction and reality, and the deliberate breach of traditional norms of the beautiful and the artistic have pushed the postmodernist work into an identity crisis in which, as Hans Robert Jauss argues, the *poiesis* and *aesthesis*, or the creative and the receptive sides of the aesthetic experience, are increasingly mixed up, and consequently the viewer or the reader "is called upon to decide whether this can *still* or *also* claim to be art."[21] No longer grounded in the authorial subjectivity but shaped by individual viewers or readers from their changing perspectives, the identity of the work of art becomes as a result indeterminate. This indeterminacy of art thus shows an affinity to Montaigne's philosophical reflections.

Uncertainty or indeterminacy, we may recall, is the first of eleven "definiens" on Ihab Hassan's "paratactic list" of postmodern features.[22] Such uncertainties and indeterminacies are very much at the center of Montaigne's *Essays* and their general theme—the problematic of knowing the self—and his pre-Cartesian skepticism seems to reveal an attitude extremely congenial to the contemporary critique of Cartesian subjectivity and rationalism. Norman Holland maintains that the identity problem also marks the advent of postmodern psychoanalysis, the crucial moment when "Freud's *intra*psychic picture of the mind" has given way to an "*inter*psychic model," in which the self is understood not as an autonomous entity like a high modernist text but intersubjectively, in an intricate nexus of relationships with the Other. "The most personal, central thing I have, my identity," says Holland, "is not in me but in your interaction with me or in a divided me. We are always in relation. We are among. Whereas psychoanalysis began as a science of human individuality within each human skin, Postmodern psychoanalysis is the study of human individuality as it exists *between* human skins."[23] For a postmodern analyst, as for Montaigne four centuries ago, the identity of the self is understood only through its interactions with others; it is defined, in much the same way as a linguistic sign, with regard to other identities in mutual differentiation. This interpsychic identity, however, is nothing unique in postmodernism or Montaigne, because we find in Dostoevsky, via Bakhtin, a similar emphasis on the interpsychic: "Not that which takes place within, but that which takes place on the *boundary* between one's own and someone else's consciousness, on the *threshold*. And everything internal gravitates not toward itself but is turned to the outside and dialogized, every internal experience ends up on the boundary, encounters another, and in this tension-filled encounter lies its entire essence."[24] That is to say, in examining interactions between the self and the Other, what seems to be uniquely postmodern becomes an indication of historical continuity. Therefore, to see Montaigne as a precursor of postmodernism is not as absurd as may appear at first blush, and it is perfectly justifiable to situate postmodernity in other times and other locales if only because the postmodern desire for the new and the unprecedented is at the same time a desire for the Other, a desire revealed in Montaigne's *Essays* or Dostoevsky's novels.

Let us recall that the word *essai*, as Montaigne used it, did not signify an established literary genre but an experiment, a new way of writing in which he tested the concept, the language, and the components of the self. His was the time when some of the most important experiments in history were being carried out, when old beliefs were shaken by the Copernican revolution and the discovery of the New World, and when the horizon of the Western man was expanding rapidly, whereas the limitation of his knowledge and capacity was inevitably brought to his critical consciousness. "Why do we not remember how much contradiction we sense even in our own judgment? How many things were articles of faith to us yesterday, which are fables to us today?" Thus Montaigne describes the fast pace of dynamic changes in his time.[25] Like Socrates, he lays emphasis on the importance of the "consciousness of our ignorance and weakness," and argues that it is as wise as it is necessary to give up one's established opinions, to abandon accepted "limits of truth and falsehood."[26] Like the postmodern rejection of a realistic epistemology, Montaigne's willingness to abandon established notions of truth and falsehood is based on his realization that any grasp or comprehension of reality is mediated through the apparatus of thinking and language, which operate, mostly and for most of the time, by applying to each situation what can only be described as norms, formulas, and conventions. "We are nothing but ceremony," says Montaigne; "ceremony carries us away, and we leave the substance of things."[27] The contrast between convention (Montaigne's "ceremony") and reality here evinces his sober recognition of human knowledge as structured information, determined by what is conventionally held as true or false, right or wrong, and so forth. But once the conventional nature and limitation of knowledge are exposed, self-complacency is no longer possible. "I am as doubtful of myself as of anything else," he says, and his relentless quest for the truth of the self leads him into the wilderness of doubt, the agonizing yet exhilarating experience of self-questioning. At the same time, it also leads to a fascination with "far-off governments, customs, and languages," a fascination with whatever is unknown and unfamiliar.[28] All that is known to us "would be less than nothing compared with what is unknown," Montaigne argues. "If we saw as much of the world as we do not see, we would perceive, it is likely, a perpetual multiplication and vicissitude of forms."[29] With such awareness of the limitation of one's own knowledge and values, Montaigne seeks to go beyond the boundaries of European culture and to understand sympathetically what seems to be the strange and alien, the non-European Other.

In one of his earlier essays on Montaigne with special reference to the relationship between the self and the Other, Tzvetan Todorov argues that Montaigne's "radical relativism" leads him to "the two great politico-ethical opinions," that is, "conservatism at home, toleration for others."[30] Todorov's argument, however, aims to expose Montaigne as a universalist, who imposes his own values and value judgment on others rather than taking the position of a real relativist, who accepts the Other on its own ground. "Confronted with the other, Montaigne is undeniably moved by a generous impulse: rather than despise him, he admires him, and he never tires of criticizing his own society." But, asks Todorov, "does the other receive his due from this little game? It is doubtful. The positive value judgment is founded on a misunderstanding and on the projection upon the other of an image of the self—or more precisely—of an ideal Ego (*idéal du moi*), incarnated for Montaigne by Greek civilization. The other is never apprehended, never known."[31] Much of this is fair enough, for in reading Montaigne's many comments on the non-European Other, the reader may constantly sense that Montaigne is projecting upon the Other what he sees, or, rather, does not see, in the tradition of European culture. According to Todorov, Montaigne uses Greek civilization as his universal yardstick to measure everything that belongs to the Other; what appear to be his open-minded magnanimity and acceptance of the Other thus turn out to be "a detailed plea for the autonomy of the subject," a plea for the self conceived totally within the limits of Western culture and leading "directly to individualism and egoism."[32] Montaigne's self defines and manipulates the Other rather than being defined with regard to the Other, and what seems a self-critique is in fact a disguised self-assertion, a deceptive kind of paranoia. In Todorov's portraiture, therefore, Montaigne eventually comes out as a bad "unconscious universalist," one who "pretends to be a relativist," whose tolerance of different social and cultural values is in fact "an indifference to values, a refusal to enter the world of others."[33]

Todorov's debunking of Montaigne as one of the early thinkers who anticipated the postmodern desire for the Other raises a significant question. It is not so much a question about Montaigne's intention or consciousness as one about the way in which a relationship can be established between the self and the Other, and about the function of Montaigne's sympathetic view of the Other. To be sure, when Montaigne argues for the acceptance of alien customs and values, he often does so by referring to historical precedents in the Western tradition, especially examples recorded in Greek and Roman antiquity. This can be seen clearly in "Of Cannibals," an essay Todorov also discusses at length, in which Montaigne reflects on the character and customs of the natives in the "newly discovered" Brazil. By choosing the New World aborigine cannibals as his topic, Montaigne puts into question the quintessential idea in all discussions of culture, namely, the very definition of the civilized and its necessary opposite, the barbarous (*barbare*) or the savage (*sauvage*). All these words are used and examined in Montaigne's essay, and each of them is given an unconventional meaning, or, rather, the conventional meaning of each is seriously questioned and invalidated.

'Des cannibales'

The essay begins with an anecdote that bears on the relationship between the civilized and the barbarian not with direct reference to the Brazilians but indirectly, by reflecting on the meaning of "barbarism" as used by the Greeks with regard to the Romans. The real Other—in this case the native Brazilians—is yet undefined and therefore unrepresentable; the only way to speak of that Other, as Montaigne demonstrates, is by means of analogy and historicization, in terms of what has been appropriated in the tradition of Western culture. The only language available is the language of the self, which for Montaigne is historically meaningful, originating from classical antiquity. Thus, instead of speaking of the New World cannibals, Montaigne first examines the original meaning of the word "barbarian" as used by King Pyrrhus, who exclaimed, when deeply impressed by the well-disciplined troops of the Roman army, "'I do not know what barbarians these are' (for so the Greeks called all foreign nations), 'but the formation of this army that I see is not at all barbarous.'" This anecdote immediately brings the word "barbarian" to its Greek origin, its etymological sense, which does not, Montaigne suggests, carry the derogatory meaning usually attached to it in popular usage. From this, Montaigne remarks, "we should beware of clinging to vulgar opinions, and judge things by reason's way, not by popular say."[34] It is thus by a critique of language that Montaigne prepares the reader for a new way of speaking of the yet undefined Other, a new language in which words like "barbarian" and "barbarity" may turn out to be something very different from what they signify in conventional usage.

Throughout the essay, Montaigne tries to undo the conventional way of speaking of the Other by further developing the discrepancy between the etymological sense of "barbarian" as simply "foreign" and the cultural notion of "barbarian" or "barbarous" as "uncivilized." Both meanings exist in Montaigne's essay as he writes:

I think there is nothing barbarous and savage in that nation, from what I have been told, except that each man calls barbarism whatever is not his own practice; for indeed it seems we have no other test of truth and reason than the example and pattern of the opinions and customs of the country we live in.[35]

For Montaigne, the anecdote clearly shows that we all live in an enclosure of accepted opinions, customs, conventions, or, to put it in a modern idiom, a prison-house of language. By bringing to consciousness this imprisonment, however, he aims precisely to break out of it by challenging conventional meaning and usage, by expanding his horizon of knowledge to embrace the New World not just geographically, but conceptually as well. He suggests that the discrepancy between "barbarian" as simply "foreign" and "barbarian" as "uncivilized," which already exists in King Pyrrhus's comment on the Romans, has grown increasingly aggravated in the history of Western civilization, which is at the same time a history of the corruption of nature by culture, reflected in the corruption of language itself. The semantic shift of the word "barbarian" from a more "natural" and descriptive term into a culturally loaded one is a manifestation of the corruption of language. That is to say, Montaigne uses a sort of counternarrative of the degeneration of language and civilization to facilitate his critique of the familiar metanarrative of Western cultural progress, and in that critique the Brazilian cannibals function as a shock force to subvert and shatter accepted cultural values and conventional use of language. Todorov is quite right to observe that Montaigne has "a unique scheme at his disposal" in outlining this history of degeneration: "Originally, man was natural; during his history, he has become more and more artificial."[36] This implied narrative of degeneration makes it possible for Montaigne to unite the Greeks, who represent the very origin of Western civilization, and the New World cannibals, who stand in opposition to that civilization. Since the ancient Greeks lived in a time more natural than the present, they could have understood the natural condition of the native Brazilians better than the modern Europeans. It is a pity that "Lycurgus and Plato did not know of them," says Montaigne; "for it seems to me that what we actually see in these nations surpasses not only the pictures in which poets have idealized the golden age and all their inventions in imagining a happy state of man, but also the conceptions and the very desire of philosophy."[37]

When nature is privileged over culture, the Brazilians are found superior not only to modern Europeans but also to the ancient Greeks, and the Greeks, being closer to the natural condition, are in turn superior to the moderns. In their propinquity to pure naturalness, the Greeks and the native Brazilians have more in common with each other than with the modern Europeans. Even the horror of cannibalism, the ultimate sign of the barbarous Other, so Montaigne argues, is not unknown to the Greeks and the ancient French, since "Chrysippus and Zeno, heads of the Stoic sect, thought there was nothing wrong in using our carcasses for any purpose in case of need, and getting nourishment from them; just as our ancestors, when besieged by Caesar in the city of Alésia, resolved to relieve their famine by eating old men, women, and other people useless for fighting."[38] In their courage and unconquerable spirit the cannibals are compared to King Leonidas at the pass of Thermopylae; their polygamy is justified by citing biblical and classical parallels, and their love song is found to be "altogether Anacreontic."[39] One may object to such an argument, as Todorov does, that Montaigne uses Greek precedents to absorb the Other, but it is not very persuasive to say that Montaigne is neither interested in the Other nor cognizant of its integrity. On the contrary, it makes more sense to argue that for Montaigne the Greeks and the Brazilians, the imaginary self and the Other, are not positioned at the two poles of an absolute and mutually exclusive opposition, that there is no either/or dichotomy between the two. For Montaigne and his contemporaries, the cultural value of the legacy of Greek and Roman antiquity was a historical given not much in doubt, and certainly not rejected; therefore, the effective way for Montaigne to persuade his readers of the "natural superiority" of the New World cannibals is to put the Brazilians and the Greeks together, rather than position them in an either/or dichotomy. Montaigne is not, after all, confined in what Todorov calls an "all-or-nothing alternative."[40] In putting the ancient Greeks and contemporary New World cannibals together under the rubric of naturalness, he is using an old rhetorical strategy, namely, the topos that connects, as Victor Segalen puts it, "the remote in the past (historicism) and the far-off in space (exoticism)."[41] In Montaigne's essay, the Greeks and the cannibals come to share the same side of superior nature, whereas the modern Europeans are left on the other side, alienated from naturalness by the very culture that claims to lord over the "barbarians" not as "foreign," but as the "uncivilized."

It is obvious even in a casual reading that the meaning of "barbarian" constantly changes throughout Montaigne's essay, and that its conventional usage is always put in question. Edwin Duval identifies five different and contradictory perspectives from which "barbarism" in Montaigne's essay undergoes a shift of meaning.[42] Michel de Certeau also notes that Montaigne highlights the inadequacy of the conventional usage of "barbarian" in three ways: "an ambivalence (cannibals are 'barbarian' because of their 'original naturalness'; Occidentals are barbarian because of their cruelty); a comparison (our ways are more barbarian than theirs); and an alternative (one of us has to be barbarian, us or them, and it's not them)," which finally designate "us" as the real barbarians. Montaigne's performance, Certeau concludes, is thus "a critique of language, carried out in the name of language and nothing else."[43] But if the semantic shift of the word "barbarian" is tied to an attitude always favorable toward the Brazilians, then we must admit that Montaigne's essay offers more than a mere critique of language, or rather, his critique of language must indicate at the same time a cultural critique, a critique of the Western self and the cultural values that constitute it. J. M. Blanchard considers the essay on cannibals part of Montaigne's meditation on the problem of autobiography, "a problem which arises when and where the consciousness of a difference between what constitutes the self and what constitutes the other remains unclear."[44] Again, it is necessary to emphasize that what is at stake in Montaigne's essay is not just writing of the self but self-critique in examining one's own cultural values vis-à-vis those of the Other.

Indeed, it is this cultural critique that underlies and determines the change of perspectives in Montaigne's essay. As Duval comments, "despite this disconcerting flux in value and point of view, no reader of the essay has ever failed to notice that Montaigne's judgment of the Brazilian natives themselves remains steadfastly favorable from beginning to end."[45] Once we realize the purported social and cultural critique in Montaigne's essay, the vagaries of its changing argumentation become rather understandable as they fall into a simple pattern that assigns positive values to the ancient Greeks and contemporary New World cannibals, while depriving the modern Europeans of their pride and self-complacency. When the word "barbarian" or "savage" is shown to be positive rather than negative, it is always used to refer to the Brazilians, but when the word is used in its pejorative sense, it designates the condition of modern Europeans. Thus, Montaigne argues that the cannibals can be called wild only in the sense that they are purely natural, that "the laws of nature still rule them, very little corrupted by ours." Their practice of cannibalism is indeed barbarous, but they at least eat men when they are dead, while in Europe there is "more barbarity in eating a man alive."[46] Toward the end of the essay, conventional meanings and values are completely overturned as "cannibals" prove to be less barbarous than the "civilized," and the Europeans, Montaigne insists, surpass the cannibals "in every kind of barbarity."[47] The entire essay, as Todorov concludes correctly, "is in fact a praise of the 'cannibals' and a condemnation of our society."[48] That is of course what often happens in cultural self-critiques.

In Montaigne's essay, the Brazilian cannibals evidently serve a polemical purpose: the Other is evoked not so much for its own sake as for the critique of the self by the self. In presenting the cannibals as superior in their naturalness to cultured Europeans, Montaigne, as Todorov remarks, is indeed creating a myth, "the myth of the noble savage."[49] Eventually, therefore, it is the Western self that resides at the polemical center of the essay, around which the whole argument is methodically organized, while the Other, Todorov complains, is "never apprehended, never known."[50] In denying Montaigne any genuine interest in, or knowledge of, the New World cannibals, however, Todorov presumes that Montaigne's discussion of the non-European Other is completely predicated on an either/or dichotomy, or what he calls an "all-or-nothing alternative." That presumption, however, may not be adequate in discussing the modus operandi in Montaigne's essay, and in Renaissance humanism in general, because Montaigne, as I mentioned earlier, did not reject the cultural value of the Greeks when he approved the virtues of the Brazilians; instead he put the Brazilians and the Greeks together in contrast to the modern Europeans. In other words, Montaigne did not set up an absolute cultural dichotomy between the self and the Other, and his subversion of conventional usage and meanings of such words as "barbarian" and "civilized" worked precisely to overturn such a dichotomy. In this, I would argue, Montaigne is indeed very different from a postmodern relativist with his view of the Other as the opposite of whatever is thought to be the West. But if Montaigne used the Other as an instrument for self-knowledge or self-critique, does that make his essay essentially different from decentered postmodernist writings and theories? The answer, I venture to say, is emphatically negative. Instead of seeing Montaigne as a universalist whose philosophy differs from a postmodern relativist, I would argue that the use of a non-Western Other for a Western self-critique is precisely what makes Montaigne a precursor of postmodernism, and that Todorov's relativist who "does not judge others" does not yet exist.[51]

In a more developed study of universalism and relativism,

Todorov presents a somewhat different argument. He differentiates "good" universalism from ethnocentrism, which imposes one's own particular values on others as falsely "universal" and thus becomes a caricature of universalism. "'Good' universalism is based," Todorov now argues, "on familiarity with at least *two* particulars," while ethnocentrism arises from "the deduction of the universal on the basis of a *single* particular. The universal is the horizon of understanding between *two* particulars; we shall perhaps never attain it, but we need to postulate it nevertheless in order to make existing particulars intelligible."[52] In this study, Todorov presents Montaigne as not a universalist but a relativist or an "unconscious universalist," who tolerates and even admires the Brazilian cannibals only because he finds in them virtues that are also found "among the Greeks, who embody Montaigne's personal ideal."[53] And yet, familiarity with at least two different cultures and value systems, though highly desirable in itself, seems to me not the necessary prerequisite for "good" universalism. To avoid the pitfall of ethnocentrism, it would be more basic to cultivate the sense of common humanity shared by different peoples and cultures, even if one does not yet possess sufficient knowledge of, and much less familiarity with, alien peoples and alien cultures. Understanding other cultures necessarily begins by way of mediation through one's own linguistic and cultural perspective, but the important thing is always to revise and change one's own perspective to include what was the alien and the different. It is only at that point that one may claim to have attained a certain degree of familiarity with another culture.

    Perhaps it is necessary here to note that Todorov himself later came to realize the limitations of relativism in a courageous self-examination and sober-minded reflection on contemporary criticism. He was prompted to make such self-examination through his study of history and ideas, and especially his brief encounter and conversations with Arthur Koestler and Isaiah Berlin, two intellectuals who were, like Todorov himself, born in Eastern Europe and knew cultures and political realities quite different

from that of Western Europe, who "knew what it was to be up-
rooted, had experienced cultural otherness," and, most important, had held to their principles and moral integrity, their com-
mitment to truth and freedom, living their "personal otherness,
that state in which one acknowledges the other while keeping
one's distance."[54] This last clause is particularly noteworthy as it
describes a state of mind and a condition of being in which all
three of them, Koestler, Berlin, and Todorov, find themselves as
intellectuals in the West with a background and experience very
different from that of the average Western academic. "After I became a French citizen," says Todorov, "I began to feel more
acutely than ever the fact that I would never be a Frenchman like
any other, because of my simultaneous participation in two cultures. A double belonging . . . sensitizes one to the problems of
cultural alterity and the perception of the 'other.'"[55] It is surely
the other culture, especially the social and political reality in
Eastern Europe, deeply ingrained in his memory not as some
imaginary Other, but as lived experience, that has made it impossible for Todorov to become "a Frenchman like any other."
Todorov is not alone in feeling this cultural and personal otherness, however, for it is a feeling shared by many Chinese in the
West as well. "By virtue of my self-chosen marginality," as Leo
Ou-fan Lee puts it, "I can never fully identify myself with any
center." But this feeling of marginality or personal otherness
does not have to be an anxiety-ridden crisis of cultural identity.
"The feeling of self-torment, perhaps representing the negative
side of a bicultural marginal person," says Lee, "can be turned
into a positive character strength."[56] As I shall argue in some of
the later chapters, experience of a different cultural and political
reality, and our personal and collective memory of such experience, ought to provide us with a rich source of insight and moral
strength, and above all an independent mind that will not follow
any trend blindly, not even the influential trends in Western literary and cultural theories.

Knowledge of a different culture and political reality as well as
a consciously kept distance from the center enabled Todorov to

question the paradigm of relativism he had embraced earlier, which had relinquished the moral responsibility of making choices and judgments in cultural criticism. If in his essay challenging Montaigne, Todorov argued for the position of a relativist who "does not judge others," he now realizes that tolerance and respect of other cultures do not mean that we must "refrain from making any judgment about societies other than our own."[57] Judgment is necessary as a moral and political responsibility, but it is not a simple pronouncement of one's own values and beliefs; rather, it is the result of learning and dialogues. Instead of seeing universalism and relativism as hermetically sealed and isolated from one another, he now argues that "without turning one's back definitively upon universal values, one may posit them as a possible area of agreement with the other rather than as an a priori certainty." Cross-cultural understanding is possible, he declares with optimism and confidence, because "we can go beyond mere 'points of view,' and it is in human nature to be able to transcend one's own partiality and one's parochialism."[58] Like Montaigne, Todorov finally acknowledges shared humanity as the basis for maintaining dialogues and making connections, and for establishing a more sensible relationship among different peoples and cultures. Here, as in Montaigne's essay on the Brazilian cannibals, humanity should not be understood as a purely abstract and a priori notion; it is an idea grounded in some basic human values manifested in specific actions and concrete situations.

The discourse on human nature in ancient China, notably in the philosopher Mencius, is also characterized by specific examples and practical reasoning. In trying to prove his thesis that all human nature is essentially good, Mencius uses a particular example that not only concretizes his argument but also breaks up what he meant by good human nature into distinct good qualities or virtues that make up the general category. "People all have a heart that cannot bear to see other people being hurt," says Mencius, and he goes on to prove his point by describing potential human reaction in a hypothetical situation: "Now upon seeing, all of a sudden, a child about to fall into a well, everyone would feel horrified and compassionate not because one would want to make friends with the child's parents, not because one would want to make a reputation among neighbors and friends, nor because one hates to hear the child crying. From this we may conclude that he who does not have a heart of compassion is not human."[59] That all human beings will react in the same way to the situation of a young child in danger is simply presumed here as an axiomatic statement, which means that for Mencius a morally good nature is so unquestionably shared by all human beings that he could safely rely on it to draw a general conclusion without having to articulate it explicitly. Instead of positing human nature as an abstract idea whose various attributes are to be expounded in a systematic argument, he simply starts his argument by assuming that general idea, whose manifestation is what we find in that particular example of human interactions. Therefore, it would be wrongly hasty to infer that human nature as Mencius understood it never attains to the status of a general notion meant to be universally shared and applicable. In another passage, his rival Gaozi makes an analogy between human nature and water, contending that human nature is neither good nor bad, just as water is not predisposed to flow eastward or westward: it all depends on external conditions rather than an innate nature. Mencius replies by exploring the same analogy further, saying, "It is true that water is not predisposed to go east or west, but is it also not predisposed to go up or down? Human nature is inherently good just as water necessarily goes downward. No man is not inherently good, just as no water will not flow downward."[60] In this case, again, a general conclusion is drawn from particular analogies, but it is understood as a notion invariably true and beyond question. The particular and the general, the concrete and the abstract, the practical and the theoretical are thus not mutually exclusive, but dialectically related, in Mencius's argument on human nature. This is quite significant for comparative philosophy, and thus also for cross-cultural understanding. Despite the way his argument proceeds by concrete examples, there is no question that Mencius, as Irene Bloom observes, is proposing a concept of "common humanity," an essentially good human nature that *"all* human beings *share."*[61] Mencius's concept of human nature, then, should be general and capacious enough to encompass a notion of humanity similar to what made it possible for Montaigne to connect the New World cannibals with the ancient Greeks in his essay.

Beyond Heterotopia

But the idea of a shared, common humanity is anything but postmodern. The postmodern condition as Lyotard describes it is a condition of difference and heterogeneity, which manifests itself in the dissolution of every kind of totalizing narrative, the waning of the cultural authority of the West, and the celebration of all sorts of cultural and ethnic differences. For such a condition, for "such a situation of 'pure difference, '" as Steven Conner argues, Foucault's *heterotopia* provides "the most famous image," "a name for the whole centreless universe of the postmodern."[62] We may recall that heterotopia is the name Foucault adopts to designate the inconceivable space inscribed in a certain "Chinese encyclopedia" found in one of Borges's postmodern "essays," where strange and strangely categorized animals are put together in one locale despite their radical incommensurability and according to an absurdly illogical method of classification. Such an inconceivable heterotopia thus reveals, so Foucault claims, a totally different way of thinking and speaking, "another system of thought."[63] As I have argued in the previous chapter, the hilarious passage from the so-called Chinese encyclopedia" is in fact a Western fiction, and in citing that fictitious Chinese encyclopedia as a metaphor of an exotic, non-Western Other whose conceptual monstrosity threatens to destroy the usual categories of thinking and naming in language, Foucault is also creating a myth, a cultural myth of the Other whose function in postmodernist theories, very much like that of the cannibals in Montaigne's essay, is already predetermined by a critical view of the Western self and traditional Western values.

Even Lyotard's report on knowledge in the highly developed Western societies at the postmodern moment would be incomplete without evoking an image of the Other at a clearly premodern moment—a Cashinahua storyteller, whose ritualistic narrative formulas provide a model of the pragmatics and self-legitimation of narrative knowledge, which is said to be incommensurate with the classical Western conception of scientific knowledge, but to which the entire postmodern scientific and cultural discourse returns.[64] But, one may ask, what is that Cashinahua storyteller doing in a report on the postmodern condition of contemporary Western societies? What function does he perform in Lyotard's text except that of an instrument of contrast and illustration? It may be useful here to compare Lyotard's evocation of the Cashinahua storyteller with *The Storyteller* by the Peruvian writer Mario Vargas Llosa, in which a modern novelist seeks in vain to write about the Machiguenga Indians and their storyteller or *hablador*, whose narrative performs a communal function of uniting his people together, in contrast to the modern novelist's fragmented individualism. Vargas Llosa is fully aware, however, that to evoke a Machiguenga storyteller is but to repeat a romantic myth and nostalgia of a paradise of innocence. "All my attempts led each time to the impasse of a style that struck me as glaringly false," says the novelist in *The Storyteller*, acknowledging his incapacity to represent the Other, "as implausible as the various ways in which philosophers and novelists of the Enlightenment had put words into the mouths of their exotic characters in the eighteenth century, when the theme of the 'noble savage' was fashionable in Europe."[65] This recognition of the failure of representing the Machiguenga storyteller in Vargas Llosa's text contrasts sharply with Lyotard's appropriation of the Cashinahua storyteller in his. As Keith Booker argues, "Lyotard's turn to the Cashinahuas as an alternative to the totalizing and impoverishing metanarrative structures of the Enlightenment reveals a strand of Utopian thinking," whereas Vargas Llosa's book effectively undermines such thinking and romantic nostalgia, "suggesting that the solutions to the problems of contemporary society are to be found not in Utopian fantasies but in direct, hard-nosed confrontation with reality."[66] Obviously, the image of the Other in postmodernist theories—whether Lyotard's Cashinahua storyteller or Foucault's heterotopia—often harks back to the myth of the "noble savage," a myth Montaigne also employs in his essay on the Brazilian cannibals. As a Latin American writer, however, Vargas Llosa is more sensitive to the complexity of the problems of representation, especially the problem of representing a non-Western Other as an idealized, utopian alternative to Western ideas, values, and systems.

As Conner remarks in commenting on this Western myth of the Other with special reference to Foucault: "Once such a heterotopia has been named, and, more especially, once it has been cited and re-cited, it is no longer the conceptual monstrosity which it once was, for its incommensurability has been in some sense bound, controlled and predictively interpreted, given a centre and illustrative function."[67] In point of fact, the heterotopia has never been really the conceptual monstrosity Foucault claims it to be; the inconceivable heterotopia or the incommensurate Other is conceived, after all, by and for the Western self, and therefore it is contained at the very moment when it is created. However positively presented or represented, the Other in postmodernist discourse performs a predictable role, an assigned function of an oppositional system of thought, language, or value, and its containment makes the discourse of postmodernism a totalizing force, which it purports to deconstruct. Conner argues:

Something similar can be said to happen repeatedly in postmodernist theory, or theory of postmodernism, which names and correspondingly closes off the very world of cultural difference and plurality which it allegedly brings to visibility. What is striking is precisely the degree of consensus in postmodernist discourse that there is no longer any possibility of consensus, the authoritative announcements of the disappearance of final authority and the promotion and recirculation of a total and comprehensive narrative of a cultural condition in which totality is no longer thinkable.[68]

By positing a number of concepts and ideas and claiming their absolute validity, the "total and comprehensive narrative" of postmodernist theory becomes itself a totalizing discourse, a new master narrative of the West, which defines and produces the terms in which critical discourse is conducted, and which determines what is centrality and what is marginality, and what relationship persists between the two. Insofar as the Other is not allowed to speak for itself but is defined and spoken of only in the interest of the Western self, as its foil—even though for the express purpose of a self-critique—all the emphasis on cultural difference and heterogeneity tends to lose its efficacy despite good intentions and genuine concerns. Quite contrary to its intended or hoped-for effect of openness and liberation, the discourse on difference may actually prove to be repressive once it precludes any possibility of commonality. A case in point is the discourse on racial difference. Henry Louis Gates, Jr., certainly one of the most eloquent voices speaking for a distinct tradition of African American literature, calls "race" a dangerous metaphor, "the ultimate trope of difference" that does not correspond to reality or an ontological essence. To use language carelessly as though racial difference is a "natural" given, says Gates, "is to engage in a pernicious act of language, one which exacerbates the complex problem of cultural or ethnic difference, rather than to assuage or redress it."[69] In quite the same spirit as Martin Luther King's famous "I Have a Dream" speech, Gates emphasizes "the basis of a shared humanity" as the cultural value too precious to be yielded by *inscribing* "race" as an essence.[70] Racial discrimination, the vice and violence that infect almost all modern nations, thrives precisely on the pernicious act of language that internalizes and naturalizes racial difference while denying any shared humanity. In our effort to fight racism, therefore, we need to rethink the postmodern discourse on difference and the consequences of a rigid dichotomous thinking and cultural relativism. As Gates puts it succinctly: "To attempt to appropriate our own discourses by using Western critical theory uncritically is to substitute one mode of neocolonialism for another."[71] If this is true of the discourse of African-American criticism, it is certainly true of the discourse of cross-cultural understanding, particularly that between China and the West.

In this connection, then, we may recognize a virtue in Montaigne's essay on the cannibals that is rarely found in postmodernist discourse on the Other, namely, the virtue of *reconstituting* humanity as shared by the cannibals and the Greeks, the self and the Other. As Blanchard observes, in reading this essay, one is struck by Montaigne's repeated assertion that "far from being strange, [the cannibals], more than we perhaps, are plain ordinary folk."[72] That is to say, in evoking the cannibals as Other, Montaigne did not *prescribe* and *fix* the Other as pure difference, as strange and grotesque animals roaming about an unthinkable heterotopia, which is the image of the Other we find in much of postmodernist as well as traditional Western discourse. Instead, he reaffirmed a shared, common humanity between the self and the Other, thereby going beyond the trap of a rigid cultural dichotomy, the danger of constructing an arbitrary opposition between different cultures and races. As for the use of a non-Western Other in cultural critique, that is a strategy we find repeatedly adopted by thinkers of many different centuries. The perennial emergence of such a strategy, the reappearance of the Other in Western discourse, helps put the issue in a historical perspective. To borrow the words of Ernst Robert Curtius on the recurring mannerism in European literature, we may say that to call the question of the Other a uniquely postmodern concern "is possible only as a result of ignorance and of the demands of pseudo-historical [or ideological] systems."[73] Montaigne, as Lyotard claims, is indeed postmodern, but he is of course also a humanist with his firm belief in a common humanity.

The example of Montaigne's essay, especially the idea of a shared humanity with which he connects the Brazilian cannibals and the ancient Greeks, suggests a way out of the deadlock of a rigid dichotomy between self and Other, universalism and relativism. To understand the Other means, as I have argued at the end of the last chapter, to go beyond the self and the Other in a "fusion of horizons," that is, to move to a new horizon, a new beginning open to other questions and dialogues. This Gada-merian concept of "fusion of horizons" implies the coming to-gether of the self and the Other and at the same time the tran-scending of both in their self-enclosure. This does not entail a simple negation of subjectivity on the part of the self, for Other-ness is reciprocal: the self is also other to the Other. However, it is from the vantage point of the self that the ethical import of the Other becomes significant, and Levinas's emphasis on moral re-sponsibility makes perfect sense. Therefore, to understand the Other does not mean to eliminate one's own forestructure of un-derstanding, but to be sensitive to a different kind of structure, to be attentive to the voice and claim of the Other, and to be willing to engage in dialogues and change one's own views with regard to those of others. In that moment of fusion, that is, in the tran-scending of self and Other, we may finally realize that self and Other are all psychological and social constructs, albeit useful and perhaps necessary constructs, and that the voice of the Other is not a single, unitary voice, but a multiplicity of voices, a diver-sity of actual utterances. Perhaps Bakhtin's description of the en-vironment of utterance is most relevant here. "The authentic en-vironment of an utterance," he says, "the environment in which it lives and takes shape, is dialogized heteroglossia, anonymous and social as language, but simultaneously concrete, filled with specific content and accented as an individual utterance."[74] Of course, Bakhtin is concerned with language as dialogic in nature, and "dialogized heteroglossia" describes the environment he conceived of for all utterances, within the same language and culture as much as between languages and cultures. Bakhtin's insight is even more significant, however, in situations of cross-cultural understanding, in which the Other must not be thought of as a monolithic, unified entity. From Bakhtin's remarks we may conclude that there is no single utterance or voice that can speak, or can claim to speak, for the Other, but there are many different voices of others as individual utterances. The conceptu-alization of the Other as one unified entity speaking in one voice—for example, the claim that all Chinese think and speak in a certain way—often serves as a prelude to the construction of an East-West dichotomy. But it is a false dichotomy, based on a false conceptualization, because there is no such thing as *the* Other, only a multiplicity of others, and there is no one unified voice but a diversity of voices, all engaged in a "dialogized heteroglossia." The fact that a text is written by a foreign author in a foreign language, responding to specific concerns of a foreign culture and history, does mark it out for special attention as articulation of a different perspective, but we should engage it in a dialogue just as we engage many others, and regard it as an individual utterance rather than some representative specimen of an entire culture. This is not to deny the importance of cultural representation; but representations are diversified, and no single one can claim to speak for all others. Once we recognize the diversity and heterogeneity of the Other, as we do of the self, cross-cultural understanding can be seen as part of our effort at understanding in general, of our endless dialogue with others, with ourselves, and with the world at large.

CHAPTER 3

Jewish and Chinese Literalism

The conceptualization of cultural difference as an opposition between real or imagined entities, systems, or values, as we have seen, is by no means new: it is neither modern nor postmodern. As Aeschylus's play *The Persians* and Herodotus's *Histories* made very clear, the ancient Greeks had a strong sense of their own civilization defined against that of the Persians. When Dionysius of Halicarnassus wanted to assert the primacy of Greek or Attic style in rhetoric and oratory in the first century B.C.E., he contrasted the Attic with "her antagonist, an upstart that had arrived only yesterday or the day before from some Asiatic death-hole."[1] Greece and Asia, Occident and Orient, the West and the East, these are fundamental categories or conceptual building blocks by means of which people in different times and places have thought about the world and constructed their self-identities. Various differences provide powerful metaphors and conceptual paradigms for understanding both the character of one's own tradition and that of other people, and when differences assume the foreground, each culture as a form of life takes on the characteristics of a unique, self-contained entity, and difference between cultures tends to be polarized as an opposition of cultural forms, concepts, and values that are said to be incommensurate with one another.

What Dionysius called Asia we of course call Asia Minor, but the contrastive principle underlying his reference has a general applicability that goes far beyond the specific location of a Mysia, Phrygia, or Caria. As John Steadman remarked in a sobering argument many years ago, such antitheses are abstract categories of formal logic that the exponents of "metahistory" or

Kulturgeschichte often employ to fulfill the tasks of "rationalizing cultural geography and idealizing cultural history." When those philosophical historians apply the logical principle of opposition to the study of civilizations, they drastically simplify complex cultural phenomena and reduce them to neatly differentiated groups. "To define the Orient, they contrast it with the West. To elucidate European civilization, they emphasize its opposition to Asia. In their hands, the terms become mutually exclusive—what is true of the one cannot be true of the other."[2] The contrastive principle imposes a logically necessary exclusion on both sides of the dichotomy—Europe and Asia, the Occident and the Orient—without taking into consideration internal differences that may inhabit each of the two sides or overlapping similarities that may undermine a clear-cut opposition. Thus the advocates of the contrastive principle often ignore or deemphasize differences *within* one culture so that they may highlight differences *between* cultures. All concepts, values, and human activities lose distinction on the level of individual subjectivity and utterance, only to be reassembled into collective categories, general characteristics, even entire cultural systems, which are said to be mutually exclusive. It is only by reducing cultures to such totalizing collective identities that cultural differences are constructed as absolute and rigidly antithetical.[3]

In a highly suggestive passage of his book, Steadman maintains that the Western tradition seems to have a deeply embedded propensity toward thinking in binary opposition and dichotomies. "As the spiritual heir of two of the most self-conscious of cultures—the Hellenic and the Hebraic—Western civilization has, almost from the beginning, retained much of their inherent spiritual exclusiveness. The one thought in terms of the difference between Hellene and barbarian, the other in terms of Jew and Gentile."[4] Martin Hengel makes much the same point when he comments on the tension between the Greeks and the Jews in the Hellenistic period and remarks that "the Greek feeling of superiority with its contrast between 'Hellenes' and 'barbarians' was matched on the Jewish side by a sense of elec-

tion, unique in antiquity, which was expressed in the contrast between 'Israel' and the 'nations of the world.'"⁵ I may add that this
divisive propensity is the symptom of ethnocentrism that can be
found anywhere, not just in the West. The traditional, sinocentric
Chinese also thought in terms of the difference between the civilized Chinese (*hua*) and foreign barbarians (*yi*). The Chinese
ruler's great desire has always been, as Mencius tells us, "to
reign over the Middle Kingdom [*Zhongguo*] and to appease the
barbarians from all four corners [*si yi*]."⁶ The distinction may
well refer originally to tribal, ethnic, or racial difference as a
simple fact and does not necessarily imply a cultural value
judgment, but the quick semantic shift of the word *barbarian* from
the etymological sense of "foreign" to the culturally charged
meaning of "uncivilized," as Montaigne reminds us in his essay
on New World cannibals, indicates how small a step it needs to
take to move from a purely ethnic distinction to an ethnocentric
notion of cultural difference.

Steadman is concerned with the dichotomy between the West
and the East, and thus he speaks of the Western tradition as the
coming together of two highly self-conscious cultures to form a
unified civilization that tends to see itself as distinct from the
various non-Western cultures. Of course the two cultures he
mentions—the Hellenic and the Hebraic—have themselves often
been set up in a dichotomous relation with one another, a dichotomy within the Western tradition itself, which does not appear so very different from the one between the Occident and the
Orient. Indeed, the same set of terms is often employed in the
traditional discourse on Hellenism and Hebraism, the latter of
which is often considered to be "Oriental." The inherent spiritual
exclusiveness of the contrastive principle seems to operate everywhere and to feed, as it were, on the Western civilization itself.
Before the non-West—a construction that depends on and con-
tributes to the construction of the West itself, and vice versa—
comes directly within purview, a persistent opposition is already
established between the Hebraic and the Hellenic, representing
virtually all sorts of opposition that one finds in the later con-

struction of the East-West dichotomy. If the opposition between Hellenism and Hebraism is not the only manifestation of the contrastive principle in the West, it is certainly one of the most important and persistent ones, an opposition invoked by almost all major Western thinkers as the source or basis of two opposite sets of concepts, categories, and values. It is therefore worthwhile to examine how the contrastive principle is played out in two different situations: how the opposition is set up inside the Western tradition between the Hellenic and the Hebraic, and how it is established "outside it," between the West and the East. In the two cases, we may find surprising similarities in the construction of cultural difference in a binary opposition. Indeed, the will to differentiation, or the desire for difference, bears a far more complicated and ambiguous relationship with tradition and traditional ideology than those who celebrate cultural difference—like some proponents of multiculturalism—may have realized. There is, as I shall argue in this chapter, another side or dimension of cultural difference that may not promise a liberation at all, but rather the danger of exclusion and repression. Putting the two kinds of dichotomy together, we may recognize that they are both cultural myths whose construction may have serious, even undesirable consequences in the interaction of cultures.

Origen and Rabbinic Interpretation

The interaction of the Hellenic and the Hebraic cultures has a long history that goes as far back as the time before Alexander the Great. The many Greek loanwords used in Hebrew, including the word for the Jewish supreme council, Sanhedrin, which is derived from the Greek word *sunhedrion* (a " sit-together"), give a good indication of such interaction or "the existence of a continuous Hellenistic pressure in the very heart of Judaism."[7] Martin Hengel observes that by the third century B.C.E., the Greek language was widely used in Palestine and became the effective bond of the Hellenistic world, that Hebrew assimilated many Greek loanwords, that many Jews adopted Greek names, and that Greek education had its influence on Palestinian and Diaspora Judaism.[8] The rabbis in Palestine might not have read Plato or the pre-Socratic philosophers, nor did they employ any Greek philosophical terminology, but they did acquire firsthand knowledge of Gentile laws and made use of Greek and Latin legal terms.[9] On the other hand, the Greek translation of the Hebrew Bible, the Septuagint, had its own influence on the Hellenistic culture and "may be said to have created a new form of Greek, which contributed to the formation of the idiom in which the gospel was preached, and the New Testament written, and the oldest Christian liturgy and theology worked out."[10] These three words—Greek, Hebrew, and Christian—already suggest that the coming together of the Hellenic and the Hebraic cultures, as well as the tension between the two, became nowhere more apparent than in the formation of Christianity as a new religion in late antiquity. To be sure, in a polemical gesture to differentiate their own religious belief from all other religions and cultures, many Christians may think of the nascent Christianity in terms of a new faith that supersedes the old belief in Judaism on the one hand, and renders all the gods of paganism obsolete on the other. The moment Christ is born in Bethlehem, as Milton envisions it in a famous ode,

> The Oracles are dumb,
> No voice or hideous hum
>   Runs through the arched roof in words deceiving.
> *Apollo* from his shrine
> Can no more divine,
>   With hollow shriek the steep of *Delphos* leaving.[11]

Here the advent of Christ manifests itself, among other things, as a transformation of language, for Apollo is deprived of his "voice," and the Greek speeches (*logoi*) Apollo used to utter were hushed by the true Logos of the Christian God. In the minds of many devout Christians, the numerous Greek gods may have been supplanted by the one God. "All Olympus now became an aerial hell," as Heine puts it ironically, and the Christian knight

Tannhäuser could tell Venus right to her face: "O Venus, lovely lady mine,/You're nothing but a devil!"[12] What had been divine in ancient Greece was then demonized and became a mere superstition, "and in this transformation of an earlier national religion," says Heine, "the idea of Christianity manifests itself most profoundly."[13] And yet, the spirit of Greek culture has a pervasive influence on Christianity. Hengel's classic study, *Judaism and Hellenism*, concludes in presenting early Christianity as growing out of Judaism after the failure of a Hellenistic reform, as a response to the conflict between the syncretic tendency of Hellenistic universalism and the Judaic nationalistic legalism.[14] In late antiquity, Hellenism in its various forms provides a vast background for considering many of the historical events and cultural phenomena, and whatever theories one may propose to explain the rise of Christianity as a religious movement, one must take into account the Hellenistic background.[15] That the New Testament was written in Greek and that many of the earliest Christians were Greek-speaking Jews have profound implications for understanding the relationship between Christianity and the language and culture of the Hellenistic world.

The relation of Christianity with Judaism runs even deeper in terms of Scriptural, liturgical, and theological traditions. The first Christians formed a messianic sect within Judaism; they considered themselves as faithful Jews and their faith in Jesus as the fulfillment of the prophetic message in Judaism. It is not until the time when the Fourth Gospel was written, as Morna Hooker shows, that the followers of Jesus became largely Gentiles rather than Jews and Christianity was turned into a new religion that "cut across racial boundaries."[16] The fact that the Christian Bible retains the Hebrew Scripture along with the New Testament demonstrates not only the close ties Christianity had with Judaism in its formative period, but also its inheritance of both the Hellenic and the Hebraic traditions. A careful look at the historical process of the coming together of the Hellenic and the Hebraic in early Christianity reveals so much dynamic interaction and syncretic blending that no rigid opposition would seem capable of sustaining its claims or credibility. The importance of the Jewish background to the teaching of Jesus has been emphasized in a number of works in New Testament scholarship. E. P. Sanders argues that the contexts within which the Gospels present Jesus—the theological context of a "Jewish salvation history" and the eschatological context of a sense of living in the end of time—are both Jewish, "both are orientated towards the future, and both assume that God will do something in *history* that agrees with other things he has done."[17] Hooker challenges the so-called criterion of dissimilarity in New Testament scholarship that accepts as authentic only those of Jesus's teachings that are differentiated from the beliefs of Judaism on the one hand and those of the early Church on the other, thus constructing an isolated Jesus with "no roots in Judaism, and no influence on the Christian community."[18] More recently, Averil Cameron puts in question the "separability" of the early Christian discourse from either Hellenism or Judaism. She considers it misleading to present the "rise" of Christianity against a background of the "decline" of the Greco-Roman tradition, and she argues that the connection here is not even a matter of Greek or Jewish "influence" on early Christian writing, but "their integral relationship."[19] Unfortunately, however, in their attempt to establish the ideological supremacy of the Christian doctrine, theologians of the early Church often ignored the "integral relationship" recognized by modern historians. Of course, the Pauline letters in the New Testament already established the basis for a polemical reading of the Torah, and Paul's language is filled with the typological contrasts of the old and the new, the letter and the spirit, death and life (2 Cor. 3:6 ff.). He made use of exegetical strategies of traditional Jewish interpretation, notably that of the *pešer*, but radically changed them to suit his Christocentric hermeneutics. "The mixed language of allegorical typology which reads God's plan of salvation from the accounts of Israel's history, and of typological allegory which locates this salvation in the realm of truth beyond history," as Karlfried Froehlich remarks, "became characteristic of Christian exegesis in the second century."[20] In setting up a rigid opposition between Christianity and the other forms of ancient culture, especially Judaism, early Christian theologians constructed differences with inherent spiritual exclusiveness that had unfortunate influence and consequences in history.

In the early Christian interpretations of the Bible, the opposition between Hebraism and Hellenism manifests itself in a most egregious form, in the often evoked opposition between the letter and the spirit, between a supposedly Jewish bondage to an exaggerated anthropomorphism or purblind literalism and the transcendental voice of the divine Logos heard through Christian allegorical interpretation. Athens and Jerusalem, or, more precisely for the cultural geography of late antiquity, the Hellenistic Alexandria and the Syrian Antioch, name the prominent sites of that tendentiously constructed opposition. The usual picture presents the Alexandrian school as eminently Hellenic and essentially Platonic in its pursuit of a higher and spiritual meaning of the biblical text over its bodily sense, while it depicts the Antiochene school as largely Hebraic, laying emphasis on the historical and literal sense of the Holy Scripture. The two schools certainly engaged in methodological rivalries, and it is likely, as Robert Grant says of Antioch, "that wherever the influence of the synagogue was felt by the church the interpretation of scripture had a tendency toward literalism."[21] In late antiquity, there was evidently a thriving Jewish community in Antioch, whose Haggadic and other interpretive traditions may have had some impact on Christian interpretation of the Bible. Wayne Meeks and Robert Wilken note that "exegesis depending ultimately on Jewish models becomes a hallmark of the Antioch school."[22] Nevertheless, Alexandria and Antioch are not diametrically opposed to one another to form a simple dichotomy between Hellenism and Hebraism. Under a closer examination, the historical context of those rivalries reveals a much more complicated situation of interaction than the picture of a rigid dichotomy would lead us to believe.

Although Alexandria was indeed the most important center of

Hellenistic culture, it was a Jewish writer, the prolific Philo, who first exemplified Alexandrian allegorism in the exegesis of the Pentateuch and exerted a profound influence on Christian patristic hermeneutics. In Philo's reinterpretation, the rabbinic understanding of the Law as God's revelation to Moses on Mount Sinai was combined with the Greek notion of divine inspiration, which gave the biblical text a deeper truth or spiritual meaning that could be recuperated only through allegorical interpretation. The deeper truth, Philo insists, "loves to hide itself." Whenever the biblical text makes "the inspired words of God" seem "base or unworthy of their dignity," the literal sense must be rejected in order to understand the spiritual truth allegorically.[23] Philo's allegoresis is often said to represent a Jewish apologetics that tendentiously presents the Hebrew Bible vis-à-vis a rich and highly developed pagan culture, but this apologetics finally leads to nothing less than the bold claim that all Greek philosophy, law, and wisdom were ultimately derived from ancient Hebrew sources, that Heraclitus might be "snatching" ideas from Moses "like a thief," and that Plato also "borrowed from the Prophets or from Moses."[24] Philo's allegorical reading of Scripture, as David Dawson remarks in a recent study, can be seen as an effort "to make Greek culture Jewish rather than to dissolve Jewish identity into Greek culture," an interpretive strategy to "reshape, redefine, or 'rewrite' formerly nonscriptural, cultural meanings."[25] Philo combined the Greek philosophical approach to ancient texts, especially the allegorical reading of Homer, with the legacy of Jewish Halakic and Haggadic traditions, with which he was apparently familiar. His allegoresis, as Jean Daniélou observes, was not "a case of Hellenistic gnosis dressed up in biblical imagery," but had its inspiration "truly biblical, for he was a devout and believing Jew."[26] On the other hand, while reacting against the excess of Alexandrian spiritualism, the Antiochene exegetes also drew on the Greek tradition of classical rhetoric and textual criticism, and they also aimed at a higher sense of Scriptures, what they called *theoria*, a Platonic term they adopted to counter the overly spiritualist Alexandrian allegorism. Thus both the Alexandrian and the Antiochene schools attempted to interpret the biblical text for a higher sense, and despite the rivalries that did exist between them, "the sharp antithesis," as Froehlich maintains, "is a construct. . . . The difference between Alexandria and Antioch seems to reflect more the methodological emphases and priorities of the schools than soteriological principles."[27]

Given these shared concerns about the higher sense of the Bible, how was the "sharp antithesis" between the Hellenism and the Hebraism of the early Church constructed? For one model, we can turn to the exegetical works of Origen. Representative of the exegetical method of Alexandria, Origen is the most allegorical of all early Christian interpreters of the Bible and the first to formulate patristic hermeneutic theory in a systematic treatise, *On First Principles*. He sees the divine writings as inspired and containing deeper meanings that are deliberately obscured by the historical and literal sense of the biblical text. The Word of God, says Origen, "used actual historical events wherever they could be accommodated to these mystical [meanings], hiding the deeper sense from the multitude." He argues that Scripture has a threefold meaning, which he compares to the body, soul, and spirit, and in his biblical exegesis, he always aims to bring out the spiritual sense. "For with regard to divine Scripture as a whole," he claims, "all of it has a spiritual sense, but not all of it has a bodily sense. In fact, in many cases the bodily sense proves to be impossible."[28] In all these aspects, Origen is deeply indebted to Philo.[29] Daniélou provides a list of five elements or principles that Origen took from Philo and that, he argues, generally lead to untenable overinterpretations. Especially suspicious is the idea borrowed from Philo "that *everything* in Scripture has a figurative meaning." Such an overstatement, says Daniélou, becomes "the starting-point of all the exaggerations of the medieval allegorizers."[30] But Origen's indebtedness to Jewish interpretation does not end with Philo, for he learned Hebrew from his Jewish contacts, possibly some rabbis, and often mentions some Hebrew source for the reading of a particular phrase or passage. Daniélou briefly discusses the influence of Jewish rabbis on Origen;[31] Nicholas de Lange devotes an entire book to that subject and goes so far as to declare that "much of what Origen says cannot be understood without a knowledge of the Rabbis, and some of the arguments which have been produced by modern scholars crumble to dust when the evidence of the rabbinic writings is adduced."[32]

His dependence on Hebrew source or indebtedness to Philo notwithstanding, however, Origen relentlessly excludes the Jews summarily from the possibility of understanding the Bible correctly. In his writings, the subtle difference between the word "Hebrew" (*Hebraioi*) and "Jewish" (*Ioudaioi*), as de Lange notes, reveals a conscious effort to separate the Old Testament from the Jews: "If the connotations of *Hebraioi* are philological, those of *Ioudaioi* are polemical. *Ioudaioi* is used in the context of the confrontation of the Church and the Synagogue: in recalling debates or disputations, in condemning the Jews for rejecting and killing Jesus, in criticising Jewish literalism in the interpretation of the biblical law."[33] That is to say, though the Old Testament is Hebrew, its true meaning is not, according to Origen, accessible to Jewish understanding. Origen's hermeneutics is resolutely Christocentric and firmly based on the interpretive strategies of Christian typology, which appropriates the Hebrew Scripture while making it devoid of historical substance and denying Jews true understanding. He maintains that descriptions of an anthropomorphic God or the records of historical events in the Old Testament "point figuratively to some mysteries by means of a historical narrative which seems to have happened but did not happen in a bodily sense."[34] This polemical move not only robs the Hebrew Bible of historical reality but also makes it meaningful only as prefiguration of the coming of Christ. "It must be admitted," says Origen, "that the divine quality of the prophetic statements and the spiritual character of the law of Moses came to light only with the coming of Jesus. Before Christ's advent it was hardly possible to present clear evidence that the old writings were inspired."[35] In other words, only Christianity can reveal the holiness of the Hebrew Bible; the Jews may have Scripture in their language, but they do not know how to read it because they read only the letter of the biblical text and understand the Holy Scripture literally.

Literalism in the polemical sense is not just reading the canonical text according to its literal or historical sense, but it also means—and this is what Origen repeatedly emphasized—the impossibility of spiritual understanding, the blindness that blocks the Jews from getting the spiritual truth hidden behind the literal sense or the historical narrative of the Holy Scripture. The Jews are bound to the letter, says Origen, and their view is still blocked by the veil that covered the face of Moses and dimmed the light of the spirit. It is only the Christian allegorists who are able to see the spiritual light beyond the letter. "The veil has been removed," he declares, "and the good things whose shadow the letter displayed have gradually been raised to the status of knowledge [cf. 2 Cor. 3:13–16, Heb. 10:1]."[36] The Pauline dichotomy of the letter and the spirit legitimizes Origen's polemical reading, but the tendentiousness of that reading is also clearly discernible in that dichotomy. Origen's emphasis on the spiritual meaning of the Bible at the expense of the literal and historical sense was later criticized as excessive and excessively Platonic, even heretically Gnostic. Against what he perceived to be "the danger of a mechanical literalism," as Gerard Caspary observes, Origen may have lapsed into the opposite danger of a "overweening intellectualism. . . . the disembodied spiritualism of Platonists and Gnostics."[37] We can see that in Origen's exegesis a sharp antithesis was set up that combines and reinforces all those dichotomies: the opposition between Alexandria and Antioch, the Hellenic and the Hebraic, Christian allegorization and Jewish literalism.

But what is Jewish literalism, anyway? To be sure, rabbinic interpretations, and midrash in particular, generally work with specific words and phrases in the biblical text. "What the midrashist addressed himself to was not first and foremost the book as a whole, i.e. not the allegory itself," says James Kugel, "but single verses, isolated in suspended animation."[38] This is not to say, however, that Jewish interpretation of the Bible is unconcerned with spiritual meanings or that there is absolutely no possibility of allegorism. The very term *midrash*, as Wolfson points out, denotes the "non-literal method of the rabbis." In discussing the background of Paul's allegorical method in the New Testament, Wolfson argues that the various nonliteral interpretations Paul used are all "of the rabbinic midrashic kind."[39] In one of the oldest works of midrash, the *Mekilta de-Rabbi Ishmael*, Rabbi Joshua and Rabbi Eleazar Hisma maintained that the verse *Then came Amalek* (Ex. 17.8) "is to be taken in an allegorical sense" to indicate the vital importance of the words of the Torah, "because [the Israelites] separated themselves from the Torah the enemy came upon them." To *Tomorrow I will stand upon the top of the hill* (Ex. 17.9), Rabbi Joshua gave a literal reading, but Rabbi Eleazar of Modi`im went far beyond the literal, saying, "Let us declare tomorrow a fast day and be ready, relying upon the deeds of the forefathers. For the 'top' [*rosh*], refers to the deeds of the fathers; 'the hill' refers to the deeds of the mothers."[40] What is known as the Oral Torah in Judaism is a tradition of free interpretation in which the letter of the Scriptural text is not followed closely, and that tradition, as Wolfson remarks, is the basis on which Philo established his allegorical method of interpretation. "The principle that Scripture is not always to be taken literally and that it has to be interpreted allegorically," says Wolfson, "came to him as a heritage of Judaism; his acquaintance with Greek philosophic literature led him to give to the native Jewish allegorical method of interpretation a philosophic turn."[41] If it makes sense at all to speak of Jewish "literalism," it does so only because these midrashic spiritual readings tend to be based on some "literal" feature, that is, relating to the particular words and letters of Scripture. The function of midrash, however, is precisely to go beyond the obvious meaning of the text, to make some ingenious and sometimes far-fetched interpretations, and ultimately to make connections between the world of the Bible and the midrashist's own world. "For in midrash the Bible becomes," as

James Kugel argues, "a world unto itself. Midrashic exegesis is the way into that world . . . the Bible's time is important, while the present is not; and so it invites the reader to cross over into the enterable world of Scripture."[42] For the midrashist, the precise entry into the biblical world is through the actual words and phrases in the biblical text, the small details of every verse. This is markedly different from Christian allegorism, which often posits a spiritual meaning of the text as a whole that bears only a tangential relation to its literal sense. In rabbinic interpretation, the literal and the spiritual meanings are thus not as mutually exclusive as they tend to be in Origen's exaggerated spiritualism, and one may add that Christian allegorism was further facilitated by the fact that the Christians were using the Greek Bible, not the Hebrew, and that they knew they were working with a translation, however inspired they might believe it to be, and thus less bound to the letter of the biblical text than the midrashist.

If allegory does exist in rabbinic interpretation, the literal sense, on the other hand, is not completely abandoned by Christian exegetes, either. Origen's excessive spiritualism does not, after all, have universal acceptance in the Christian tradition of biblical hermeneutics. Augustine argues that the Bible contains both plain and obscure passages and that "hardly anything may be found in these obscure places which is not found plainly said elsewhere."[43] Thomas Aquinas also remarks that "nothing necessary to faith is contained under the spiritual sense which is not elsewhere put forward clearly by the Scripture in its literal sense"[44] Following this line of argument, Martin Luther claims that the words of the Holy Spirit "can have no more than the one simplest meaning which we call the written one, or the literal meaning of the tongue."[45] For Luther, as for Augustine and Aquinas, Scripture is its own interpreter (*scriptura sui ipsius interpres*), and in that Christian hermeneutic tradition, as Karlfried Froehlich argues, no either/or was intended: "The literal sense did not exclude the spiritual, or vice versa. Rather, the two were related in a dialectical movement from one to the other."[46] Seen in this perspective, then, Origen's talk of Jewish literalism appears all the more polemical and is clearly intended to distinguish Christian exegesis from the tradition of Jewish interpretation. The constructed myth of Jewish literalism does not come from any particularly Jewish essence of rabbinic interpretation, but from the will to differentiation, the desire to make cultural difference absolute across racial and religious boundaries. Underlying this notion of literalism is the work of the contrastive principle, the inherent spiritual exclusiveness of the either/or thinking, according to which Origen simply must argue that if spiritual truth is revealed to the Christians, it cannot be also understood by the Jews in spite of, or rather, because of the fact that they all read the same biblical text. It is not that the Christians and the Jews read absolutely differently, but that Origen is obliged to construct the cultural myth of literalism in order to *make* an absolute difference between Jews and Christians and to accuse Jews of mistaken or wrong interpretations. Whatever element of spirituality there is in rabbinic interpretations, Origen and his followers would not allow it to be counted as spirituality. As de Lange reminds us, talks and echoes of "Jewish literalism," the sediment of a cultural myth over the centuries, are "still heard even today."[47] The persistence of cultural myths is a sad testimony to the inertia of thinking, the tenacious grasp of our minds on facile generalizations and stereotypes that enable us to categorize human beings and realities cleansed of their complexity and individuality, and pigeonholed in clearly labeled boxes of collective identity. Thus to expose the construction of a cultural myth, to recognize the tendentiousness of polemical talk of "literalism," may remind us of the danger of exclusion and repression, and help set us free from thinking in rigid binary opposition and collective categories.

Sinology in a Historical Perspective

In secularized modern times, in which religion as a system of beliefs or articles of faith is discreetly separated from scholarship as disinterested pursuit of knowledge, the influence of Christianity on Western views of China and Chinese culture is perhaps seen by many as an embarrassing legacy at best and thus often forgotten and largely unacknowledged in the academic field of sinological studies. Nevertheless, the Jesuit missionaries were the first Westerners who made a serious effort to study the Chinese language and culture, and many problems and debates in si-nological studies today often recall, albeit in a rather different context, some of the earlier debates among Christian missionar-ies, especially the so-called rites controversy in the seventeenth and eighteenth centuries. The crux of the matter in that contro-versy is the compatibility, or lack of it, of Chinese culture with Christianity, that is, whether the Chinese converts should be al-lowed to continue their ancestor worship, whether they could possibly have any understanding of the spiritual truth and con-cepts like God, angels, or salvation, and whether their language is capable of expressing such spiritual truths and concepts. Com-menting on the rites controversy, George Minamiki observes that the controversy has two aspects: one concerns the problem of an-cestor worship, and the other has to do with "the problem of how Western man was to translate into the Chinese language the concepts of the divinity and other spiritual realities," namely, the issue of terminology or language.[48] David E. Mungello also re-marks that besides historical chronology, "a second significant area of proto-sinological concern was in the assimilation of the Chinese language," that the seventeenth-century fascination with language looked to Chinese "as a possible candidate for *lingua universalis* status."[49] Western views of Chinese culture and the Chinese language are thus closely intertwined from the very start. Matteo Ricci (1552–1610), head of the China mission, and his followers among the Jesuit missionaries spread the idea that Chinese culture, especially Confucianism, had reached a perfect state of natural religion and had thus paved the way for receiv-ing the light of revealed religion, namely, Christianity. That idea is often referred to as the Jesuit approach of "accommodation," the ways in which Ricci and the Jesuit Fathers immersed them-selves in the native language and culture and made concessions to the Confucian tradition in order to win over members of the cultural elite, the literati-officials at the imperial court of late Ming China. The sympathetic view of Chinese culture that Ricci and his fellow missionaries advocated had a notable impact in Europe and provided philosophers like Leibniz and Voltaire with ideas and information for their enthusiastic praise of Confucius and Chinese culture. By the end of the seventeenth century, as Arthur Lovejoy observes, "it had come to be widely accepted that the Chinese—by the light of nature alone—had surpassed Christian Europe both in the art of government and in ethics."[50] Filtered through Jesuit interpretations, the political and moral philosophies of ancient China set up an ideal example for many European thinkers, and the Chinese sage Confucius, as Reichwein puts it, "became the patron saint of eighteenth-century Enlightenment."[51]

In presenting a positive image of Chinese culture as essentially compatible with Christian values, however, the Jesuit missionaries were following their religious agenda and patiently working toward the eventual conversion of China. Instead of directly debating on matters of religion, the Jesuits worked as scholars, astronomers, mathematicians, and the battle was often fought on the front of scientific and philosophical debates. As Lionel Jensen argues persuasively, Confucius, the image of a Chinese philosopher who preached the gospel of monotheism among the ancient Chinese like a prophet or a Christian saint *avant la lettre*, was a Jesuit *invention* constructed in the narrow passage between their accommodationist program to convert the Chinese through enculturation and their awareness of the grave concerns of the higher authorities in the Vatican, who would not allow any concession to a pagan culture. "As the Italian Padres imagined him," says Jensen, "this Chinese saint and his teachings on the one God, *shangdi*, had presaged their arrival and it was with this presumption that they undertook a restoration of what they termed his 'true learning' (*zhengxue*)." In upholding Confucius as the ancient Chinese saint who shared some basic ideas with the Christians, the Jesuits were able to claim him as their own and, more

important, "to represent themselves to the natives as the orthodox bearers of the native Chinese tradition, *ru*."[52] As Ricci wrote
in a letter to the General of the Jesuits in 1604, he tried to interpret the Confucian classics and traditional commentaries *"in such
a way that it is in accordance with the idea of God*, so that we appear
not so much to be following Chinese ideas as interpreting Chinese authors in such a way that they follow our ideas."[53] In a peculiar way, this subtle appropriation of the Confucian tradition
reminds us of the Christian typological reading of the Hebrew
Bible, because in both cases, the true meaning of an ancient tradition, either Jewish or Chinese, is said to have been lost among
the native inheritors but is accessible to Christian interpreters
through a more adequate understanding that transcends the letter of their ancient books and the literalism of the native exegetical tradition.

Thus Ricci and the Jesuit Fathers presented themselves as the
legitimate bearers of the Confucian legacy, as Confucius's true
interpreters who understood the Chinese philosopher's teachings
better than the Chinese themselves. Not only did they attack the
Buddhists and the Taoists for exerting a devilish influence on the
Chinese, but they also dismissed much of the native tradition of
what sinologists now call neo-Confucianism as deviating from
Confucius's original teachings. Joachim Bouvet (1656–1730), a
Jesuit who served as an important contemporary source of Leibniz's knowledge about China, can be taken as an interesting example.[54] Bouvet gave a most imaginative interpretation of Chinese classics, especially the *Book of Changes*, in which he saw the
sixty-four hexagrams as organized on the same principle as
Leibniz's binary system of numerical progression. In his letters to
Leibniz from Beijing, he maintains that the hexagrams invented
by the Chinese sage Fu Xi contain the same "true ideas of the ancient hieroglyphs and the cabbala of the Hebrews."[55] Fu Xi's system, and ancient Chinese books in general, he argues, exhibit
deep affinities with Christian ideas and "open a way both natural and easy to guide the spirit of China not only to the knowledge of the Creator and natural religion, but also to His only son

Jesus Christ, and to those most difficult truths of Christianity."[56] In another letter, Bouvet cites Clement of Alexandria as saying that God gave the Jews the law and gave the Gentiles philosophy in order to lead them to Jesus Christ. "The philosophy which God gave to the Chinese for that purpose and which is contained in their canonical books," says Bouvet, "is then not an atheistic philosophy, . . . but a philosophy like the Christian one."[57] Just as Christian allegorists see the advent of Christ prefigured in the Old Testament, Bouvet assures Leibniz that "almost the entire system of the true religion is hidden in the classic books of China, and that the principal mysteries of the incarnation of the Word, the life and death of the Savior, and the main offices of his sacred Ministry are contained, in a prophetic manner, in these major monuments of Chinese antiquity." In a word, the Chinese classics contain "nothing but a continuous texture of shadows, figures, or prophecies of the truths of the new Law."[58] In Bouvet's allegorical reading, the ancient books of China, like the Hebrew Scripture, become anticipations of the Christian doctrine.

The use of typological language can hardly be more explicit than in these comments, and the consequence of such a typological reading is just as unavoidable. The hidden affinities of the Chinese classics with Christianity, Bouvet claims, are all lost in China, where "the various commentaries done in different times, even before Confucius, had only served to render the understanding more obscure." The Chinese sage Fu Xi, "whose physiognomy has nothing Chinese about it," turns out to be not Chinese at all, but is identified by Bouvet as one of "our ancient authors," either Zoroaster, or Hermes Trismegistus, or Enoch.[59] Here we have a familiar list of names in the Hermetic tradition that identifies certain pagan writers as "ancient theologians" whose writings contained vestiges of the true religion. "By 1650," as David Mungello observes, "a list of the Ancient Theologians included: Adam, Ennoch, Abraham, Zoroaster, Moses, Hermes Trismegistus, the Brahmans, Druids, David, Orpheus, Pythagoras, Plato and the Sybils. By 1700 the list had grown to include Fu Hsi."[60] Once those ancient writers were listed as "ancient theologians," they could be treated as proto-Christian and separated from their own native traditions. Thus in the Jesuit interpretation of the Chinese classics, typological reading is predicated on a strict distinction between what the Jesuits called the true Confucianism of antiquity, which accorded with Christianity, and the later ideas of the native neo-Confucian scholars, who had allegedly misunderstood and betrayed the ancient teachings of Confucius. That is indeed how Leibniz understood the matter, in which he was obviously influenced by Bouvet's letters. "It is not absurd for discerning Europeans (such as Ricci)," says Leibniz, "to see something today which is not adequately known by the Chinese erudites, and to be able to interpret their ancient books better than the erudites themselves. Who does not know in our own day," he goes on to add, "that Christian scholars are much better interpreters of the most ancient books of the Hebrews than the Jews themselves?"[61] It is thus as authoritative interpreters of the Confucian tradition that the Jesuit Fathers installed themselves among the Chinese, competed with the Buddhists and the Taoists for religious influence, and argued for the fundamental compatibility of ancient Confucianism with the teachings of Christianity.

Though ultimately aiming at the Christian conversion of the Chinese, the Jesuit accommodation as a strategy clearly recognized the powerful tradition of a non-Western culture. The great antiquity of that tradition, its emphasis on moral principles, its highly developed philosophical teaching or what the Jesuits called "natural theology"—all these were fully acknowledged, and the effort to find similarities or convergences between Confucianism and Christianity was in itself a necessary step on the part of the Jesuit missionaries toward cross-cultural understanding. In a way, accommodation was also the strategy that the Buddhists had used centuries earlier, and when Buddhism became successfully engrafted into Chinese culture and society, it was itself sinicized and produced Chan Buddhism, whose influence spread far and wide in China and the other East Asian countries. Many Chinese scholars understand Ricci's accommodation with great sympathy and respect, and they see the Chinese rites controversy as reflecting "the intolerance of the Catholic Church that followed an absolutist and exclusionist Christian doctrine and could not stand a sinicized religion of compromise and toleration."[62] Again, it was Leibniz who clearly understood the significance of the Jesuit accommodation and may be said to have given an apposite expression to its reason and basic ideas, which agreed well with his own vision of universal harmony among different peoples and nations:

China is a great Empire, no less in area than cultivated Europe, and indeed surpasses it in population and orderly government. Moreover, there is in China a public morality admirable in certain regards, conjoined to a philosophical doctrine, or rather a natural theology, venerable by its antiquity, established and authorized for about 3,000 years, long before the philosophy of the Greeks whose works nevertheless are the earliest which the rest of the world possess, except of course for our Sacred Writings. It would be highly foolish and presumptuous on our part, having newly arrived compared with them, and scarcely out of barbarism, to want to condemn such an ancient doctrine simply because it does not appear to agree at first glance with our ordinary scholastic notions. Furthermore, it is highly unlikely that one could destroy this doctrine without great upheaval. Thus it is reasonable to inquire whether we could give it a proper meaning.[63]

If understanding of a different culture is always a fusion of one's own horizon with that of the Other, then for the Jesuit missionaries that fusion certainly took the form of appropriating ancient Chinese classics in terms of the Christian doctrine. In trying to find possible convergences of Chinese culture with Christianity, however, the Jesuits were themselves subjected to the danger of being "converted" or infatuated by the very myth they created about a Chinese natural religion, forgetting the expedient nature of their enculturation. In his study of the Christian mission in China, Jacques Gernet repeatedly emphasizes that the spirit of Christianity is absolute and exclusive, and he blames Ricci and his followers for losing sight of this spiritual exclusiveness and overdoing it in cultural accommodation. To be sure, the Jesuits aimed at the eventual conversion of the Chinese, but, Gernet complains, "many missionaries truly held the naive belief that the most ancient Chinese ideas were identical to those of the Bible."[64] In reading the Chinese classics as though they could, like the Old Testament, be allegorized to appear compatible with Christian concepts and values, Ricci and the Jesuit Fathers, Gernet argues, misunderstood and misrepresented a non-Western culture as if it could have anything in common with the Christian West.

The rites controversy was basically the doctrinal purists' reaction against cultural accommodation or Ricci's "error" of making concessions to a pagan tradition. It also has a complicated background of rivalry, professional jealousy, and principled differences among individuals as well as different religious orders; moreover, there were different political and cultural influences at work. While most Jesuits followed Ricci's approach of accommodation, as Mungello observes, "Portuguese and Spanish cultural factors converged with the outlooks of the Franciscan, Dominican and Augustinian orders to foster somewhat rigid and Europocentric attitudes and approaches among their missionaries."[65] Against Ricci's argument for the compatibility of Chinese culture with Christian doctrine, the purists emphasized the fundamental difference between the East and the West and reaffirmed the spiritual exclusiveness of the Christian faith. The Chinese classics are not Old Testament, after all, so why bother to interpret them as though they were congenial to Christian values? The Franciscan Father Antonio de Caballero, alias Sainte-Marie, makes the point most clearly: "What does it matter whether or not the ancient Chinese knew God?" he asks. "We are here to proclaim the Holy Gospel, not to become apostles of Confucius." The Chinese, including those converted men of letters, have no understanding of spiritual truth. "In the passages where they appear to speak of our God and his Angels," he continues, "they are merely aping the Truth or, if you like, they resemble the peacock whose feet are a disgrace to its splendid rich plumage."[66] Niccolò Longobardi, Ricci's successor in the China mission, held completely different views from Ricci's. "Their secret

philosophy," Longobardi says of the Chinese, "is pure materialism," for they "have never known any spiritual substance distinct from matter." Father Sabatino de Ursis concurs: "According
to the principles of their philosophy, the Chinese have never
known any spiritual substance distinct from matter. . . . And consequently they have never known either God or the Angels or
the Rational Soul."[67] This Chinese materialism is soon related to
the limitations of the very language with which the Chinese express themselves. If God, angels, and the other spiritual realities
can be expressed only in a Western language as a vehicle for
Western thinking, then the Chinese language, as expression of
Chinese thinking, is concrete and materialist, with no spiritual
value whatsoever. The use of Chinese expressions like *shangdi*
(Sovereign on High) to mean God and the word *tian* as Heaven
were officially condemned by Pope Clement XI in 1704 and 1715.
The problem persisted, however. "Is there any convenient method of stating the doctrine of the Trinity which does not imply the
grossest materialism?" asked C. W. Mateer, a Protestant priest, in
1908. "Who has been fortunate enough to discover a name for sin
which does not dash us on the Scylla of civil crime or engulph
[*sic*] us in the Charybdis of retribution for the faults of a former
life?"[68] In the eyes of the Christian spiritualists, the Chinese culture is materialist, and the Chinese language is concrete, material, utterly incapable of conveying any spiritual truth, abstract
ideas, transcendental notions, or metaphysical concepts.

The translation of terminology, or more generally the problem
of language, is always crucial in cross-cultural interrelations. It is
in this regard that we find the old view of the Chinese language
in the rites controversy, the emphasis on cultural difference and
the *untranslatability* of terms, still influential and reemerging
from time to time in some modern sinological works. In a well-
known essay, "The Chinese Language and Foreign Ideas," Arthur Wright basically agrees with the many missionaries he cites
and comes to the conclusion that "the Chinese was relatively
poor in resources for expressing abstractions and general classes
or qualities. 'Truth' tended to develop into 'something that is

true.' 'Man' tended to be understood as 'the people'—general
but not abstract. 'Hope' was difficult to abstract from a series of
expectations directed toward specific objects."[69] Noting the ideas
of Longobardi and the other doctrinal purists, Jacques Gernet
maintains that the conflict between Christianity and Chinese
culture ultimately comes from a fundamental difference: "not
only of different intellectual traditions but also of different mental categories and modes of thought." Seeing language as indi-
cator of a certain "mode of thought," Gernet finally traces all the
difficulties the Christian missionaries had in China to the fundamental difference in language, to the problem of expressing
abstract ideas in Chinese, the embarrassing failure "to translate
into Chinese concepts formed in inflected languages such as
Greek, Latin or Sanskrit."[70] Presumably all Chinese translations
of foreign works are, for Gernet, little more than embarrassing
corruptions of the original Indo-European ideas. "Of all the languages in the world," he writes with the assurance of an expert,
"Chinese has the peculiar, distinctive feature of possessing no
grammatical categories systematically differentiated by mor-
phology: there appears to be nothing to distinguish a verb from
an adjective, an adverb from a complement, a subject from an
attribute." From this supposed lack of grammar in the Chinese
language, Gernet arrives at the idea of a corresponding lack of
the notion of *being* in Chinese philosophy:

Furthermore, there was no word to denote existence in Chinese, nothing to convey the concept of being or essence, which in Greek is so con-
veniently expressed by the noun *ousia* or the neuter *to on*. Consequently,
the notion of being, in the sense of an eternal and constant reality,
above and beyond that which is phenomenal, was perhaps more difficult to conceive, for a Chinese.[71]

In this ex cathedra pronouncement of cultural difference between China and the West, a sharp antithesis is set up by evoking the Greek notion of being, the concept of metaphysical ontol-
ogy, the transcendental *ousia*. It is no use to protest that the Chinese may also possess general and abstract notions such as *li*

(principle, reason), *qi* (universal energy, vitality), *yin* (the feminine principle), *yang* (the masculine principle), *you* (being, having), *wu* (nonbeing, nonhaving), *dao* (Tao, the Way), and so forth. Once it is decided that the Chinese language cannot express abstract notions, it follows that whatever notion there is in Chinese, it cannot be counted as abstract. That is the logic Longobardi articulates, which we still often encounter in discussions of the nature of the Chinese language and thinking. According to Longobardi, *li* is "nothing other than primary matter," and *qi* is only "the primeval air."[72] Gernet very much agrees. The Chinese have neither grammar nor logic because, says Gernet, "logic comes from *logos*."[73] The contrast between the Chinese and Western languages proves, he concludes, that "the structure of Indo-European languages seems to have helped the Greek world—and thereafter the Christian one—to conceive the idea of realities that are transcendental and immutable as opposed to realities which are perceived by the senses and which are transitory."[74]

Such a line of argument runs consistently in a number of sinological works that explain the Chinese language, literature, and culture as the opposite of whatever they believe the unique nature of Western language, literature, or culture to be. Thus some have argued that the Chinese see the world as an accumulation of stuff or substances marked by "mass nouns" in their language,[75] that the Chinese hold a "wholly immanent vision" expressed in "a language of concreteness,"[76] that Chinese as a language of natural signs or concrete things does not point to anything beyond its bodily sense, its materiality or literality, to represent things in an imagined fictional world, that there is no metaphor, allegory, or fictionality in Chinese, and that what is called Chinese literature is really literal records of unmediated experiences at a particular time and place, or autobiographical accounts in the world of empirical events and concrete phenomena.[77] In such a view, the Chinese language, thinking, and culture remain firmly grounded in matter or materialism, and ideas first articulated by the doctrinal purists in the Catholic Church two or three centuries ago are transformed into modern scholarly pronouncements. Formulations like these cover a large ground of religion, philosophy, and literary criticism, and they may differ in motivation, theoretical orientation, and details of argument, but when put together, their similarities become most striking as they show an unmistakable point of convergence, namely, the conceptualization of cultural difference between China and the West in a mutually exclusive opposition that recalls the Christian orthodox view in the seventeenth-century rites controversy.

The significance of the rites controversy for understanding modern debates is just beginning to unfold in recent scholarship. Lionel Jensen's discussion of the "invention of Confucius," as cited above, discloses the nature of the Jesuit accommodation as the subtle appropriation of a native Chinese tradition. Haun Saussy's book *The Problem of a Chinese Aesthetic* challenges the presumption of radical immanence by showing the close relations of current debates in the study of Chinese literature with "the missionary beginnings of European sinology."[78] Put in the perspective of historical connections, we can see that it is a similar will to differentiation that makes Longobardi and some modern scholars emphasize the fundamental difference between China and the West and advocate the idea that the Chinese do not have any notion of transcendence or know any distinction between the spiritual and the material, the abstract and the concrete, the figural and the literal, and so on, and so forth. If Ricci's effort to understand Chinese culture in Christian terms was, for a sixteenth-century Jesuit missionary, the necessary and indeed commendable first step in cross-cultural understanding, Longobardi and Bouvet, though nearly opposite in their views concerning the Chinese, actually retreated from such a step. Not only does Longobardi's dismissal of Chinese culture as totally materialist come from the will to differentiation, but so does Bouvet's idealization of Fu Xi and ancient Confucianism as a precursor or shadow of true Christianity, one that can be truly understood only by a Christian interpreter, not a native Chinese scholar. Whether manifested as a negative dismissal or a positive idealization, the will to differentiation is bound to produce an image of China that is nothing but a cultural myth of difference. In some peculiar ways, such an image still emerges from time to time in the modern Western discourse on China. Given the pervasive antithetical structure in formulating the cultural difference between China and the West, the importance of a historical perspective cannot be overemphasized, because it is such a perspective that will allow us to recognize the often unacknowledged and insufficiently theorized connections between missionary debates and scholarly arguments today, and challenge us to reconsider some of the basic assumptions of modern sinological studies in a critical examination.

Degrees of Difference

Now what do we find in common in the polemic against Jewish literalism and in the presumption about Chinese language and culture as totally concrete, materialist, without notions of transcendence, and so forth? There seems to be a difference of emphasis in the two versions of literalism, for in Origen's attack against rabbinic interpretation, the focus was on the reading of Scripture and thus on matters of textual interpretation, while in Longobardi's disparagement of Chinese philosophy and language, the concern was with a materialist outlook and a practical orientation in life, and in some modern scholarly views on the Chinese language and writing, the version of literalism is also related to the alleged immanence of a materialist and monistic Chinese weltanschauung. That is to say, as a polemical object, Jewish literalism was perceived to be of a textual nature, as the inadequate interpretation of the Scriptures, while Chinese "literalism" was more a matter of life and the world. Text and the world, however, are not mutually exclusive, and it would be a mistake to set up a rigid dichotomy between the two. The reading of the Torah or the Christian Bible has always borne a close relation to the religious and social life of Jews and Christians, while arguments about the Chinese outlook on life and the world are often based on the interpretation of ancient Chinese books, especially the Confucian classics. Moreover, insofar as they are constructed to be "literalistic" in a broad sense, the Jewish and the Chinese traditions have both been conceived of as a foil to the spiritual values of Christianity, and they are both seen in that context as totally immanent, without the capacity to go beyond the bodily, the literal, the mundanely historical. In other words, the exclusive Christian claim to spirituality, the Christian orthopraxy operates as a form of "reading" that reduces Jewish and Chinese traditions to a kind of literalism. At the other extreme of the dichotomy, against the literal and the immanent, stands the spiritualist notion of transcendence understood in narrowly defined Platonic terms. Thus against Hebraism or the Chinese "radical immanence" is posed not just Hellenism, but an etherealized Platonism.

But, one may ask, aren't all these contrasts and oppositions built on badly exaggerated generalizations? Isn't Hellenism more than a spiritualist Platonism? And, indeed, isn't Plato a philosopher who cannot simply be reduced to an abstract, bodiless specter? To reduce Platonism to an overweening intellectualism or spiritualism is to ignore much of what Socrates teaches about man and society, the deeply moral concerns of the Socratic philosophy. "Plato's *Republic*, that most influential of ancient works," as Louis Feldman notes in a critique of the old dichotomy between Hellenism and Hebraism, "while identifying virtues with knowledge, proceeds to stress the practical applications of these virtues."[79] Plato is certainly different from Moses or Confucius, but that difference cannot be taken for an absolute one between intellectual values and practical concerns, or between transcendence and immanence. All these values, concerns, and categories are present in all these philosophical and cultural traditions, among which difference is a matter of degree, not of kind. To realize that languages and cultures differ from one another to various degrees is one thing, but to exaggerate their difference to the absolute degree and polarize them in an either/or dichotomy is quite another. Moreover, when the polarization of cultural difference is connected with racial, religious, and other factors—and it usually is—the consequences of cultural dichotomy are either absurd or dangerous, or both.

Insofar as the Hellenic and Hebraic traditions have long been recognized as the great fountainheads of Western civilization, the dichotomy between Hellenism and Hebraism cannot, logically and in theory at least, be considered absolute. It seems much easier, on the other hand, to exaggerate the cultural differences between the East and the West and set them up in a rigid and total antithesis. An implicit Eurocentric prejudice manifests itself in the negative way in which the Chinese language, literature, and culture are defined as the lack of something uniquely Western, typically expressed in such formulations as "there is no word in Chinese for [such and such a concept or term]." Expressions like these do not just register the presence of cultural differences, but they tend to set differences in a hierarchical relation. "If the Chinese imagination is literal and the Western one figurative," as Saussy remarks, "their relation cannot be symmetrical; comparing the two will only reduce one to the other, make it the other's moon. . . . The figurative has a place for the literal (as tenor or vehicle), but the literal cannot account for the figurative except by abandoning the literal position."[80] In other words, since the literal by definition cannot know the meaning of the figurative and thus cannot tell their difference, it is only the figurative that can fully realize the nature of literalism as its inadequate opposite. Here again we recognize the familiar strategy of typological appropriation, for the imbalance between Chinese literalism and Western allegorism means that the Chinese will invariably mistake shadows for transcendental reality that they cannot know, and that only the West or Western scholars have the concept, the language, and the analytic wherewithal to understand the nature of Chinese language, literature, and culture. Isn't this reminiscent of the opposition between the letter and the spirit in Christian allegorical interpretation and the ways in which Origen dismisses what he considers to be the limitations of Jewish literalism?

And yet, the letter and the spirit, literalism and allegorism, Hebraism and Hellenism, or Chinese immanence and Western transcendence, as I have tried to show, are all cultural constructs rather than representations of the reality of different traditions. To the extent that differentiation is prerequisite for the establishment of any identity, the desire for difference is natural enough, and the recognition of difference is crucial for the very notion of cultural identity and tradition. That is to say, difference is necessary and necessarily ubiquitous, but we find difference in our daily life as much as we do in encountering other cultures and other traditions, and indeed there is always, in some form or other, the presence of other cultures and other traditions in our daily life. Difference exists everywhere, between and among individuals in the same culture as well as between and among cultures and societies. Thus to recognize difference means to acknowledge it *within* cultures as well as between cultures, and to see it as a matter of degree, not of kind. The problem of the talk of literalism and the construct of radical dichotomy of cultures, either Hellenic-Hebraic or Chinese-Western, lies in the willful tendency to see only difference between cultures, and to do so at the expense of ignoring internal differences, and consequently overlooking the very richness of a cultural tradition. In other words, the problem is not the recognition of difference as such, but the construction of a rigid and absolute dichotomy of differences along the lines of race, nation, religious beliefs, and cultural traditions.

What we recognize as the Chinese cultural tradition is by no means a singular or monolithic body of knowledge or codes of behavior, nor does it provide one unified perspective or one way of thinking. To speak only of the most influential trends of thought in traditional China, there are at least the three major religious and philosophical orientations, the Confucian, the Buddhist, and the Taoist, of which the Buddhist culture originated in India and began integrating into the Chinese tradition at a relatively early time in history. If Confucianism is mostly concerned with moral behavior and political action based on a set of principles of interpersonal relationships, Taoism and Buddhism often delve into metaphysical questions about man and nature in religious and mystical terms. All three teachings (*san jiao*) interact with one another and offer certain views about the universe and its basic elements, about nature and human nature, about man and society and the forces above, but they also differ significantly in many ways. In Chinese antiquity, before the unification of the various small states into the first big empire of Qin (221 B.C.E.), many philosophical schools contended with one another in lively debates. The different pre-Qin philosophical schools, as the Taoist philosopher Zhuangzi (369?–286? B.C.E.) observes, "all affirm what others negate, and negate what others affirm."[81] The Confucian thinker Xunzi (300?–237? B.C.E.) also remarks: "All the princes today differ in their ruling policies, and all the hundred schools differ in their philosophies. Therefore some must be right and some wrong, some result in stable condition and some bring about chaos."[82] The great diversity of philosophical ideas and views within the larger context of ancient Chinese culture is often referred to as a hundred flowers in full bloom and a hundred schools contending in argumentation: a picture of rich colors, changing shapes, and very different contrasting and complementary forms. If it makes any sense at all to speak of a Chinese cultural identity, it cannot be reduced to any one of these different trends of thought or philosophical orientations, but must allow all these views to assume a place and contribute to this rich tradition.

Likewise in rabbinic Judaism, diverse opinions and multiple interpretations of every law are all preserved as articulating the will of God. The proclivity toward different interpretations can be said to characterize midrash and rabbinic exegesis in general, and if the interpretation of the Law was decided according to the opinion of the famous House of Hillel in their debate with the House of Shammai, both of which are important first-century schools of Pharisaic sages, it was because the House of Hillel respected their opponents and taught the teachings of the House of Shammai before they taught their own.[83] That is to say, in both Chinese and Jewish cultures, a great number of different views and ideas about a great number of things exist side by side, which cannot be reduced to a single "literalistic" or "immanent"

outlook to contrast with an equally reductionist view of the Hellenic or Christian tradition. To do so would produce only what
Daniel Bonevac calls "a cartoon version of foreign thought, contrasted with a cartoon version of the West."[84] In such cartoon
versions, differences between cultures are exaggerated to the
extreme, while differences within cultures or similarities across
cultures are totally suppressed. And that, as we have seen, is
how cultural constructs are made. Such cartoon versions of culture would fit in the dichotomous frame dictated by the will to
differentiation, the either/or presumption of the contrastive
principle, but they cannot help understand the richness, the variety, and the complexity of different cultures and their dynamic
interactions.

   To the extent that differences are necessary for the very conceptualization of culture and identity, they must be fully recognized where they function in the world's different languages, religions, histories, social and political institutions. All the concepts
and names we use to speak of cultures—the Hellenic, the Hebraic, the Western, the Chinese, and so on, and so forth—depend
on the recognition of such differences. In the study of cultures,
however, and especially in cross-cultural understanding, the recognition of difference means first of all a careful and patient differentiation of real as opposed to imaginary differences, that is,
differences that can be found in the reality of languages, histories, social and political institutions, as opposed to differences
that are constructed or fabricated outside these by applying the
contrastive principle, by pushing difference of degree to the absurd extreme, by imagining cultural values as uniquely one's
own and the essence of an alien culture as whatever stands at the
opposite from oneself. Perhaps owing to the deeply conservative
and ethnocentric nature of cultural systems in isolation as well as
to the attractiveness of exoticism, all cultures tend to engage in
the construction of such myths of cultural difference, but that
makes the differentiation of reality from fabrication all the more
important. In this regard, the difference in language is not only
the most basic and most obvious, but also the most paradigmatic,

and therefore the translation of a foreign language can serve as a model for cross-cultural understanding. One has no difficulty in knowing the foreignness of a foreign language, where the difference is an undeniable reality, as communication is blocked by an alien system. In trying to understand a foreign language, one cannot simply imagine its meaning, but must acknowledge its meaning as determined by that foreign system, and then make comparisons with one's own language and find equivalent ways of expression. Linguistic purists, like cultural purists, always emphasize the uniqueness of a language and its untranslatability into any other, but communication is and has always been made possible by negotiating a common ground between the foreign and the familiar, a ground on which we find not the identical, but the equivalent, which nevertheless makes the expansion of our knowledge and vision possible. "The very aim of translation—to open up in writing a certain relation with the Other, to fertilize what is one's Own through the mediation of what is Foreign," as Antoine Berman puts it so astutely "—is diametrically opposed to the ethnocentric structure of every culture, that species of narcissism by which every society wants to be a pure and unadulterated Whole."[85] What we get in translation is not the original, certainly not the myth of a pure linguistic essence; likewise in cross-cultural translation of ideas and values, what we get is not the myth of an unadulterated cultural essence. What translation allows us to gain, however, is invaluable linguistically and culturally, that is, understanding, knowledge, and communication, for which every effort of ours is worthwhile and richly rewarding.

CHAPTER 4

Out of the Cultural Ghetto

The study of Chinese literature as a scholarly pursuit is something of a very special specialty in the West, a specialized realm in the already small field of sinology or Chinese studies. Such a special realm, however, is not completely isolated from the other disciplines in the academic world, but is influenced by the changes that are taking place in them as well as in society at large. The changing climate in international politics and economy, the often talked-about potential, real or imagined, of East Asia or the Pacific Rim in the next century, and the challenge to the traditional Eurocentric worldview—all these have bearings in different degrees on the way Chinese literature is studied in the United States. This can be seen in a number of controversial essays that have appeared in recent years, because these essays, when brought together and examined in a concentrated manner, may well signal a crucial moment of fundamental change in the study of Chinese literature in America. Judging from the polemical intensity of these essays, it seems indisputable that the change has made its impact felt in the relatively narrow circle of specialists, and that it is precisely the self-enclosure of this very circle, with which many scholars in this field have become discontented, that is being broken and changed. The advent of this transformative moment is of course not without the anxiety and agony that typically mark the contingencies and ambivalence of a turning point, but the controversies and debates deserve our careful examination not only because they manifest a sense of disorientation as well as paradigmatic change, but also because the contested issues force us to rethink the underlying assumptions of literary analysis and criticism. A sober understanding of these issues thus promises to carry implications that will go beyond the study of Chinese literature as a specialized field. To the extent that it does not participate in a dialogue with studies of other literatures and does not address critical issues of interest to a wide range of audiences beyond the boundary of local specialties, the study of Chinese literature, despite the long history of that literature and its rich content, is likely to remain a narrow and marginal field as compared with the study of English or French, something of a cultural ghetto, one might even say, closed and of little interest to outsiders in the academic environment of the American university.

The Challenge of Theory

In order to understand the recent debates in the study of Chinese literature, I shall first mention the pressure for change coming from two different directions, to which the recent signals of change may be seen as a response from within the field of Chinese literature studies. It is undeniable that literary studies in America since the 1960s have been heavily influenced by a plethora of critical theories grounded in European Continental philosophy, especially its French variety. There has been a pervasive infusion of critical theory into all the areas of literary studies, a situation Gerald Graff has characterized as a "theory explosion."[1] As Western literary theories—structuralism, deconstruction, psychoanalysis, reader-response criticism, new historicism, feminism, Marxism, Orientalism, postcolonialism, and a number of others—have mainly been concerned with reading texts of the Western canon in different ways so as to question, challenge, or subvert a humanistic tradition of Western culture, it is not surprising that the study of English and other European literatures has been the first to bear the impact of this "theory explosion." The recent debates I shall soon examine, however, seem to suggest that the study of Chinese literature is now also confronted with the challenge of theory that other literatures have already faced.

Some more than symbolic gestures of this challenge have appeared when theorists in the West begin to reflect on non-Western or Third World culture in relation to that of the Western world. Although their reflections on the non-Western often serve to set off what they understand as the Western tradition, their comments on the language, literature, and culture of China present a real challenge that often has a notable impact on modern Chinese writers and critics. I shall cite as an example the works of Fredric Jameson, America's foremost Marxist critic and one of the most influential theorists, who has not only written extensively on Western theory and culture, on postmodernism and late Marxism, but has also made some intriguing and provocative remarks specifically on modern Chinese literature. Jameson first interposed himself in Chinese literature studies in the form of a commentary in 1984 when he joined William Tay, Edward Gunn, and Sungsheng Chang in the discussion of a number of important texts. As we can expect of Jameson, his critical commentary is at the same time a highly theoretical analysis based on Marxist ideas he has himself developed concerning the modes of production and the expansion of capital and market economy in postmodernity. In his analysis of Lao She's *Camel Xiangzi* as a complex narrative in which there is "a superposition of two distinct narrative paradigms," Jameson clearly tries to read this Chinese novel as in some way disclosing the problems of an incipient capitalism in a non-Western context, in which the coexistence and interaction of different modes of production, and the mixture of precapitalist and capitalist mentalities, become, in the fictional world of the novel, the tension between two narrative paradigms or two forms.[2] Jameson argues that Xiangzi's passion, his precapitalist fixation on the desired object itself (the rickshaw), and the old narrative paradigm of the wheel of Fortune (Xiangzi's necessary failure) are brought into conflict with a properly "petty bourgeois wisdom," "the wisdom of capital and the market" as represented by his wife, Tigress, who would have Xiangzi climbing up the social ladder to join the small-business class.[3] In Lao She's novel, says Jameson, this conflict is not solved but remains "an ideological double-bind, an ideological binary opposition which cannot be resolved in its own terms," and yet the very effort to reveal and dramatize such a conflict is already a significant act with "genuine political resonance of a progressive kind."[4]

Jameson maintains that the interaction of two narrative paradigms, the tension between an inner and an outer form, are characteristic of realist literature in general, to which Lao She's novel properly belongs, while the more recent works of Wang Meng and Wang Wenxing (Wang Wen-hsing) can be read as indicative of the modernist and postmodernist moments in Chinese literature, respectively. Jameson's reading of the three Chinese writers in terms of modes of production and their cultural expressions implicitly forms a narrative in its own right, a narrative with its specific notions of temporality and spatiality that specifies modernism (and its cognate socioeconomic term, modernization) as a Western import, while making the definitive pronouncement that postmodernism "which articulates the logic of a new global and multinational late capitalism can no longer be considered a purely Western export but may be expected to characterize at least certain other local zones of reality around the capitalist world."[5] As Jameson acknowledges, his periodization of the three stages of realism, modernism, and postmodernism is inspired by Ernest Mandel's notion of the tripartite evolution of machinery under capitalism, and he sees the third stage in this cultural periodization, that is, postmodernism, as inextricably related to the last stage in the evolution of capital itself, which has now become a global totality expansive enough to include the Third World. This is "a new and historically original penetration and colonization of Nature and the Unconscious: that is, the destruction of precapitalist Third World agriculture by the Green Revolution, and the rise of the media and the advertising industry."[6] Jameson's reading of modern Chinese literature is thus grounded in his conceptualization of modernism and postmodernism, in his "ideological mapping" of global economy and politics, in which the Western World and the Third World are posed in constant tension with one another, a tension that opens up a critical perspective on the future of human history.

Some of these ideas, and especially the cultural difference Jameson detects between First World and Third World literature, are further elaborated in a seminal essay published in 1986, where Jameson proposes to read Third World texts as "national allegories" and offers Lu Xun's stories as "the supreme example of this process of allegorization." Conceding that what he puts forward is "a sweeping hypothesis" and "grossly oversimplified," he nonetheless argues that Western realist and modernist novels and their reading are predicated on "a radical split between the private and the public, between the poetic and the political, between what we have come to think of as the domain of sexuality and the unconscious and that of the public world of classes, of the economic, and of secular political power: in other words, Freud versus Marx." Third World texts, on the other hand, do not separate the two domains, and, by telling the story of a seemingly private and even libidinal nature, they simultaneously tell another story of a public and political dimension, and therefore a story of "national allegory: *the story of the private individual destiny is always an allegory of the embattled situation of the public third-world culture and society.*"[7] For Jameson, Lu Xun's stories, even though they may appear intensely personal and psychological, are exemplary of such Third World "national allegories."

Western readers may take Lu Xun's "Diary of a Madman," the story of a lunatic's morbid fear of being eaten up by everyone around him, to be an interesting study of paranoid delusions, but in so doing they completely neutralize the force of this political allegory by psychologizing it and consigning it to the private domain of a pathological self. The central metaphor of cannibalism in "Diary of a Madman" as well as in "Medicine," Jameson remarks, clearly points to a different direction, in which we must read Lu Xun's stories allegorically as revealing "a social and historical nightmare, a vision of the horror of life specifically grasped through History itself."[8] Not only does "The True Story of Ah Q" tell an allegorical story of the humiliation of China by foreign powers, but its complexity also "shows the capacity of allegory to generate a range of distinct meanings or messages, simultaneously, as the allegorical tenor and vehicle change place," since both Ah Q and his persecutors are, allegorically, China itself, the self-cannibalistic China we have seen in "Diary of a Madman."[9] Allegorical structures, according to Jameson, are not so much absent as unconscious in modern Western texts, where they can be deciphered only through allegorical interpretations, but "third-world national allegories are conscious and overt: they imply a radically different and objective relationship of politics to libidinal dynamics."[10] For Jameson, Third World literature and especially the engagement of Third World intellectuals in political life and social change can offer important lessons to Western intellectuals who have, precisely in separating the private from the public, the poetic from the political, lost contact with social reality and become politically ineffective. In this connection, Jameson calls for "the reinvention, in a new situation, of what Goethe long ago theorized as 'world literature,'" in which Third World literature, a literature of vitality and social relevance, must occupy an important place, and its value and significance must be fully appreciated in the West, through the mediation of cultural studies.[11]

Whatever one may think of Jameson's reading of the various Chinese works, it would not be the most interesting and productive response just to dismiss it too hastily as either a heavy-handed theoretical imposition or uninformed amateurism. In fact, embedded in a nexus of ideas that constitute a complicated theory of Marxism and postmodernism, Jameson's reading of Lao She and Lu Xun seems to me at times remarkably sophisticated and insightful. The concept of "national allegory," for example, highlights the vision of history and the urge for social and political change that literary texts like Lu Xun's stories themselves unfold and advocate. This concept can indeed be somewhat useful in analyzing any—that is, not just a Third World—literary text that discloses some sort of utopian desire, either positively as a dream of its fulfillment or negatively as its nightmarish distortion and inversion. At the same time, however, the idea that this kind of allegory is somehow related to Third World "nationalism" seems to me singularly ill-informed, and it serves only to build up a very limited and limiting framework, especially in the Chinese context, for understanding literary works, those of Lu Xun in particular. Lu Xun and many other writers of the May Fourth new literature clearly saw it as their vocation to mold a sense of the independent and responsible individual against the effacement of the self in a repressive moral and political totality, whether the patriarchal family or the authoritarian society, and therefore they were very far from championing the cause of any "nationalism," and indeed far from promoting the interest of any organized collectivity. Moreover, I would hesitate to concur with Jameson when he declares in absolute terms that *"all* third-world texts are *necessarily* . . . allegorical."[12] Not only would such a totalizing statement fail to do justice to the rich variety of heterogeneous texts worthy of the name of a literary tradition, but the very emphasis on the allegorical, that is, on the public and the political domain, is likely to prove, in the specific context of reading modern Chinese literature in general and reading Lu Xun in particular, self-defeatingly counterproductive.

This is not a casual remark but an observation made on the basis of copious evidence, because crude politicization has been normative in much of Lu Xun scholarship in mainland China; it has made Lu Xun a saint of communist revolution and his texts *nothing but* political allegories subservient to whatever ideological directives of the Communist Party are in place at any given time.[13] While Jameson sees "national allegories" as the Third World intellectuals' voluntary participation in politics, politicization in China is not a voluntary choice but a mandate laid upon all by the state apparatus, and allegorical interpretation of literary works is tightly controlled by the Party's ideological establishment. It is against the backdrop of such a uniform and uniformly allegorical reading and deification of Lu Xun in mainland China that some of the most innovative critical studies, notably Leo Ou-fan Lee's *Voices from the Iron House*, have attempted to restore this great Chinese writer to his multidimensional integrity and complexity, emphasizing precisely the personal and individual side, seeing his intellectual growth as "a series of psychological crises marked by quandary, frustration, failure, and spells of soul-searching," and his chosen goal in life unfit for "the utilitarian temper of nationalism as promoted by such luminaries as Liang Qichao, Yan Fu, and Sun Yat-sen."[14] The personality of Lu Xun as revealed in his letters, essays, and prefaces bears a thematic resemblance to the protagonist in many of his stories. Like his own creations, this great writer impresses us as fiercely individualist, an isolated and alienated loner, sharply critical of the society and tradition he was living in, and deeply suspicious of the self-righteous rhetoric of any collectivity, let alone the entire nation.

The ambiguous final tableau of the short story "Medicine," for example, can be seen as an indication of Lu Xun's sense of the tragic fate of an individual who is the isolated loner with his eyes open but trapped in the midst of the unawakened multitude. The tragedy in the story is not so much the death of a revolutionary, but the complete lack of understanding on the part of the common people for whom the revolutionary gave his life. In the final scene, we find a flower wreath mysteriously placed on the grave of the revolutionary martyr, but the solitary crow perched on a nearby tree does not answer the solicitation of the grieving mother for a premonitory sign of just retribution. Focused on the textual ambiguity, Leo Lee's reading of this graveyard scene definitely aims at dissipating any effort to eliminate the indeterminacy or to explain away Lu Xun's own ambivalence toward revolution, his anxiety about being caught, one might say, in the very split Jameson evoked in his essay, the split between the private and the public, the libidinal and the political dynamics. "The crow," Lee argues, "flies in the face of any human attempt to find easy solutions and comfort, including that of the ever-eager ideological reader. The crow's message . . . is ultimately indeterminate, but it certainly cancels out the mundane optimism that the flower wreath has forced upon the ending."[15] Such a reading becomes more persuasive, and perhaps more true to the spirit of Lu Xun's own sense of history at that particular juncture of revolution and repression in early Republican China, when we recall his capsule allegory of writing, his well-known fable that depicts the writing and publication of his social satires and political allegories as a pointless and cruel act, as awakening a few light sleepers only to make them aware of the agony of death in an indestructible and suffocating "iron house."

The argument above does not, however, necessarily contradict Jameson's claim that Lu Xun's "Medicine" and the other stories are all allegories and that their writing was an activity with profound political ramifications. Jameson's is a powerful claim based on a powerful ideology, and to argue for or against it one must engage his position on many different issues about modernism and postmodernism, about literature and politics, about the Third World and global or multinational capitalism. Jameson's reading is formulated from his particular theoretical perspective and put to the students of Chinese literature as a question or challenge. To meet that challenge, whether one agrees with him or repudiates his views, is already to participate in a theoretical discussion. The challenge of theory is, as I see it, a welcome one, because it offers at the same time an opportunity for us to open up the self-enclosure of specialization and to make the study of Chinese literature relevant to the interest and concerns of people outside the narrow circle of China specialists. In reading literary texts, we all have our critical assumptions and theoretical perspectives; even the decision to resist and reject a certain theory is in itself a theoretical position. To engage in theoretical discussion is thus important because it will make us critically aware of our own assumptions and positions, which, if left implicit, unconscious, and simply taken for granted, will operate like some invisible force that would leave us in the dark.

But it would be an error to assume that the challenge comes only from Western theory as some sort of external pressure, because writers and critics in post-Mao China are producing literary and critical texts that are increasingly "modern" or even "postmodern," while talk of theory and postmodernism has been going on in Taiwan for quite some time.[16] That is to say, the pressure for change also comes, as it were, from the inside as the very object of study is changing and calls for new concepts, new approaches, and new interpretive strategies that can hardly be immune from some consideration of Western theory. In fact, insofar as the study of modern Chinese literature is concerned, it is extremely difficult not to put a literary text in a context that somehow includes the West or Western literature. What that means for the study of Chinese literature, however, is not simply to accept whatever concepts and methodologies Western theories have to offer and mechanically apply them to the reading of Chinese texts. To take a truly theoretical position, I would suggest, means first and foremost to think critically of theory itself. One does not, however, arbitrarily take a position outside theory to think critically of it, for there is no theoretical position available outside theory like a fulcrum on which one could, as it were, move the mental lever of critique. The critical thinking I would recommend is not based on pure thinking, on some first principle, some ultimate explanatory power that claims to account for the real and the material exhaustively; neither can it be based on some sort of a Chinese essence that denies commensurability between Chinese and Western traditions. To think critically of Western theory thus means to rely on the aesthetic experience of reading a Chinese text and, in a broader context, to rely on the experience of real life in China, the experience of that economic, political, and cultural environment we call China. In our lived experience, there is a certain recalcitrance, certain things that cannot be fully accounted for in neat theoretical formulations and principles, things that may provide the basis for a position from which we can think independently and critically. And that, I believe, should be the basis of a properly theoretical position.

In stressing the importance of lived experience for critical thinking, however, I am certainly not suggesting that to theorize about China or Chinese literature and culture one needs to be ethnically Chinese, living in China, or speaking from inside some special enclave of knowledge in which only the initiated have the privilege of admission. First of all, experience of reality is always concrete and diverse on the personal level, and no one can speak for all others on the basis of one's own experience. That is to say, I am not at all trying to appeal to a unique collective Chinese experience, nor to set up a dichotomy of some intuitive knowledge between the Chinese and non-Chinese based on racial, ethnic, or cultural differences. I would as quickly disregard the extreme nativist's claim that "only Chinese can understand China," as I reject the Christian spiritualist's claim that only a typological reading can unfold the true meaning of Scripture or the Confucian classics beyond the limitations of a Jewish or Chinese "literalism." Knowledge as self-conscious understanding gained by experience is not inborn or intuitive, but acquired, and anyone can acquire knowledge, including that of other cultures and other traditions, as long as one is willing to make the necessary and painstaking effort. In our effort to know and understand, we do want to take seriously what the native informant has to say, though we should never assume that information to be a representation of the reality of an entire culture. Nevertheless, having dissolved the myth of collective experience or intuitive knowledge defined in ethnic terms, I do want to reaffirm the significance of personal experience in critical thinking. While knowledge about China can be acquired by anyone, those who have experienced the reality of China in their personal lives do have the opportunity to turn their personal experience into something valuable in terms of critical thinking: they do have a special advantage—and I may even say a special responsibility—of checking theoretical statements about China, Chinese literature, and Chinese culture with their own experience and their insights gained by experience, and thus measuring theoretical arguments by things in real life and by the consequences of theory in practice. It is from a theoretical position thus understood that I shall comment on the recent debates in Chinese literature studies.

Cultural Difference and the Ghettoization of Culture

Perhaps few can match the forthrightness of a short piece by Jonathan Chaves, published in 1991, in which he laments the crisis of "ideologization" of the humanities, and imputes this to the bad influence of literary theory, the coming to the field of Chinese literature studies "of the same approaches to literature that have shaken the study of English and other traditions."[17] Literary theory, especially deconstruction, seems to be the chief culprit responsible for the deterioration of scholarship, and Chaves singles out Stephen Owen as some sort of fifth-column sinologist who has, with his recent book *Mi-lou: Poetry and the Labyrinth of Desire*, "thrown open the portals of Chinese poetry studies to the gremlin progeny of Derrida's febrile brain."[18] Though the tone of Chaves's article is that of an angry jeremiad, the image of an invasion by alien forces and the strong sentiment of resistance to theory have made it quite clear that the study of Chinese literature is now experiencing the effect of the "theory explosion." Chaves has unintentionally proved that Paul de Man was truly prophetic when he declared, more than a decade ago, that "the whole of literature would respond" to the strategy of deconstruction because there is no reason why the kind of deconstructive analysis he applied to the text of Proust "would not be applicable, with proper modifications of technique, to Milton or to Dante or to Hölderlin."[19] Or to Chinese literature, one might add, sadly or gleefully, depending on where one stands with regard to deconstruction. It is arguable whether Owen is a hard-core deconstructionist, but surely we should admit that Owen and Pauline Yu (who is also criticized in Chaves's article) are influential in Chinese literature studies because they do not, in their works on Chinese poetry, shy away from considerations of theoretical issues. In fact, most scholars in this field are not against theory, and the important critical works that command our attention and respect, whether of ancient or of modern writers, whether textual studies or studies of a genre or a period, often make contributions to the understanding of Chinese literature through some comparison between works of the Chinese and other literary traditions, including that of the West, leading from a discussion of particular texts to a consideration of larger issues of theoretical or philosophical interest.

For all the angry alarms and denunciations, however, the crisis Chaves depicts is largely an exaggeration, and if there is anything close to a crisis, it is not that Owen or anyone else has opened the portals of Chinese poetry studies to deconstruction, but that the opening is not yet wide enough to let Chinese literature out of the cultural ghetto. In fact, as we shall see in another controversy, Owen himself is perhaps not particularly happy to let those portals open when contemporary Chinese poets themselves try to walk out of the shadow of tradition and to speak in a modern idiom. I am referring to Owen's review of *The August Sleepwalker*, a collection of poems by the young Chinese poet Bei Dao, and the protest that review has elicited from other scholars of modern Chinese poetry. Like Jameson, Owen is also talking about Chinese literature as a specimen of Third World literature, but while Jameson appreciates and calls for a reinvention of "world literature,"[20] the invented or reinvented "world poetry" is for Owen a creature with no value or significance, a commodity poets in the Third World try to sell to an international, that is, Western, market by putting together clichés, sentimental language, and universal images peppered with a certain amount of exotic local color. One of the hot commodities on the market is politics or the suffering of oppression, for "the struggle for democracy in China is in fashion," but to write about oppression, Owen warns the Third World poet, "does not guarantee good poetry, anymore than it endows the victims of oppression with virtue. And there is always a particular danger of using one's victimization for self-interest: in this case, to sell oneself abroad by what an international audience, hungry for political virtue, which is always in short supply, finds touching."[21] The warning may sound a little harsh to the ears of modern Chinese poets and their sympathetic readers, and the metaphors of selling and commodity are deliberately used to shatter any illusion or pretension of literary quality in this poetry, but Owen is surely right to point out that poetry is not a kind of intellectual prostitution and that there is nothing inherently good about political poetry.

The problem with this "world poetry," however, does not end with its cashing in on Third World victimization. As "new poetry" without history and tradition—here Owen mentions modern Chinese, Hindi, and Japanese poetries as examples—"world poetry" turns out to be nothing but English translations of poor Third World imitations of poor translations of Western poetry. "Which is to say," Owen explains, "that we, the Anglo-American or European part of the international audience, are reading translations of a poetry that originally grew out of reading translations of our own poetic heritage."[22] This sounds very much like the typical Western reader's experience of Third World literature as Jameson also describes it, the sense that what is being read is not new and original, "but as though already-read." For Jameson, this sense of *déjà vu* only disguises the Western reader's "fear and resistance," the sense that to understand the alien text as a native Third World reader does, "that is to say, to read this text adequately—we would have to give up a great deal that is individually precious to us and acknowledge an existence and a situation unfamiliar and therefore frightening—one that we do not know and prefer *not* to know."[23] But Owen is a distinguished scholar of classical Chinese poetry, to whom no Chinese text would seem alien, unfamiliar, or frightening. Thus the problem can only be with the modern Chinese text, which has eschewed history and "the intricate learning presumed in traditional poetries."[24] Reading Owen's elegantly written review, one may have the strong impression that Chinese history has somehow ended with classical poetry, and that scholars like Owen himself are now the true custodians of "the intricate learning" that is lost and absent in modern Chinese literature.

Perhaps that is one of the reasons why Owen's review has left some other scholars unpersuaded. In her rejoinder to that review, Michelle Yeh questions the possibility of drawing a line between national and international poetry and argues that Western influence on modern Chinese literature "involves a far more complicated process than the simple transmission of a literary model from one culture to another; that reception of influence is frequently predicated on intrinsic conditions and needs; that an influence cannot take place unless there is preexisting predisposition."[25] But once the fact is acknowledged that there is some foreign influence—and that is a fact no one can deny—modern Chinese poetry, according to Owen, has lost that which makes it distinctly Chinese; it is no longer Chinese poetry but mere "world poetry." "National poetry had a history and a landscape," says Owen. "The international poem, by contrast, is an intricate shape on a blank background without frontiers, a shape that undergoes metamorphoses. It achieves moments of beauty, but it does not have a history, nor is it capable of leaving a trace that might constitute a history."[26] Notice the past tense used in speaking about the history of "national poetry." The inference we are encouraged to draw from Owen's comment seems to be that modern Chinese literature has no history and that modern Chinese poets, doomed to speak an idiom not their own, are writing words "without having won them, without having earned the right to say them."[27] This is not just a critique of the worst of contemporary Chinese poetry, for Owen clearly thinks that Bei Dao may well be one of the best, and that *The August Sleepwalker* contains "the only translations of modern Chinese poetry that are not, by and large, embarrassing."[28] In Owen's view, then, the weaknesses of Bei Dao's poems may represent those of modern Chinese poetry as a whole. Having quoted some lines from Bei Dao's poems and dismissed them as empty clichés, Owen asks: "Is this Chinese literature, or literature that began in the Chinese language?" The implication is that this literature, though originally written in Chinese and exemplary of the less embarrassing part of modern Chinese poetry, has nothing Chinese about it and is intended all along to be translated into English for an international audience. Hence the next question: "For what imaginary audience has this poetry been written?"[29]

Many of Bei Dao's poems were written in the difficult years of the Cultural Revolution, when conditions for writing poetry in China were far from propitious. According to Bonnie McDougall, Bei Dao "wrote only for himself and a close circle of friends. Since open publication was so restrictive and potentially dangerous, there was scarcely any temptation for would-be writers to join the sparse ranks of official writers."[30] Owen would have none of this romantic myth of a lonely poet writing in solitude against a repressive and hostile society, though that particular myth is perhaps a most persistent one in the Chinese tradition as well, a myth promoted, since Qu Yuan if not earlier, by Chinese poets and critics for thousands of years. At the beginning of his review, Owen has already posited a principle, what he calls "a gentle heresy, that no poet has ever made a poem for himself or herself alone. Poems are made only for audiences."[31] So Bei Dao must have written for an audience, and—so we gather from Owen's review—with an eye to future profit, an uncanny presentiment for future success, but no real talent, he wrote for an imaginary international audience who would, ten years down the road, read him in English translation. "If this had been an American poet writing in English," Owen wonders about this literary commodity, "would this book have been published, and by a prestigious press?"[32] The implied answer is unmistakable: the so-called world poetry is a fraud, its publication scandalous, and Bei Dao is one of those moral and intellectual weaklings Owen feels himself appointed to chastise.

Some have expressed dissent, however. Michelle Yeh believes that Owen, while calling attention to the cultural hegemony of the West, is himself "imposing another hegemonic discourse, one that is based on traditional poetry, on modern Chinese poetry."[33] While Owen dislikes the fungibility of universal words and images in the translated "world poetry," Leo Lee notes that the wording of Bei Dao's Chinese original registers a specific Beijing accent, to which one must listen before one can appreciate those poems. "Homeland is a universal image; home accent may be another one," says Lee. "But you can experience the fear that reality brings to the poet only when you 'hear' in your heart the accent of the local people in Beijing while reading the poem." Poems, at least some poems, Lee continues to argue, are made for listening, and he wonders how Owen would describe the effect of listening to Tang poetry when it was chanted, presumably in the ancient accent.[34] Another critic charges that Owen "has too indiscreetly taken some 'non-realistic' Chinese works for evidence of the 'globalization' of West-centered discourse."[35] But are these dissenters making too much fuss about a short and occasional piece? The review is, after all, written by an authority on classical Chinese poetry as one of his intellectual excursions outside his usual turf. It would indeed be most fortunate if a scholar of classical Chinese literature were willing to step into the area of modern studies, for the willingness to pull down the usual barriers between fields of scholarly pursuit is a prerequisite for success in the attempt to get out of the cultural ghetto. The problem with Owen's review, however, is not that he likes or dislikes a particular poet or some particular poems, but that his views tend to ghettoize Chinese literature, and to define China and the West, "national" and "international" poetry, "as mutually exclusive, as closures."[36] Parodying Owen's witty title, "The Anxiety of Global Influence," which parodies the title of Harold Bloom's famous book *The Anxiety of Influence*, Yeh describes Owen's own view as also filled with anxiety, both the "anxiety of the dissolution of difference (between China and the world)" and "the anxiety of difference (between tradition and modernity)."[37] In his study of Chinese poetry, as we shall see, Owen does have a predilection for cultural differences.

Chinese and Western, or "national" and "world" poetries, Owen maintains, are incommensurable, and their incommensurability is grounded in the fundamentally different ways in which the very notion of poetry is understood in China and in the West. The intertwining of poetry with history, which is reiterated in Owen's review and used as the most important criterion to disqualify Bei Dao's work, has a specific meaning in his conceptualization of Chinese poetry. In that conceptualization, poetry in premodern China was itself history or true historical record, and the Chinese reader always approached a poem with the "faith" that poems were "authentic presentations of historical experience."[38] Western poetry is fictional and detached from history; Chinese poetry, on the other hand, remains in a fundamental continuum with historical actuality. "The Western literary tradition has tended to make the boundaries of the text absolute, like the shield of Achilles in the *Iliad*, a world unto itself," says Owen. "The Chinese literary tradition has tended to stress the continuity between the text and the lived world."[39] The curious thing about the much-prized "history" and "lived world" is that they exist only in the past and can be recuperated only by scholars in possession of "intricate learning." History is always something gone and done with; it is thus by definition unavailable to modern Chinese literature. When modern poets write, for example, about oppression or the struggle for democracy, which are very much part of their experience in the lived world, they are sternly rebuked for writing inherently uninteresting political poetry and for selling themselves as literary commodities. But when they write poetry "as poetry" with the conscious effort to escape the grip of political determinism, they can be chided for "sentimentality (or, perhaps, self-conscious posing)," which is, in Owen's diagnosis, "the disease of modern Chinese poetry."[40]

The idea that the difference between Chinese and Western literature is one between historical fidelity and creative fictionality is expressed more clearly in Pauline Yu's works. In the Western tradition, she argues, the notion of literature is "predicated on a fundamental ontological dualism—the assumption that there is a truer reality transcendent to the concrete, historical realm in which we live, and that the relationship between the two is replicated in the creative act and artifact."[41] Metaphor and especially allegory are possible in Western literature precisely because of the presence of this "fundamental ontological dualism," but they cannot exist in Chinese literature, because Chinese thinking is supposedly not dualistic, because there is no notion of transcendence in Chinese philosophy, and because poetry in China is not metaphorical or fictional, but "a *literal reaction* of the poet to the world around him and of which he is an integral part."[42] Chinese poems are read "not as fictional works composed ad hoc to create or correspond to some historical reality or philosophical truth, but as literal vignettes drawn from that reality."[43] Even though one can cite numerous examples from the corpus of classical Chinese poetry to contradict this alleged Chinese literalism, the radical difference between Chinese and Western tradition set up in Owen's and Yu's works has a tremendous appeal because some Western scholars are eager to see the non-Western world as a world of irreducible difference, an intriguing heterotopia with a totally different mode of thinking and speaking, more romantic and more fantastic than anything they can hope to find in their ancient myths or medieval romances. In a sense, Jameson's appreciation of Third World "national allegories" and their "radically different and objective relationship of politics to libidinal dynamics" is also a manifestation of the same romantic desire to find a different non-Western world that would display just the kind of difference one desires and appreciates. The difference *within* Chinese culture is largely ignored so that the relevant difference *between* the Chinese and the Western can be highlighted. Thus only in the West can one find the "radical split between the private and the public, between the poetic and the political,"[44] and only in Western poetry and poetics exists this "fundamental disjunction" between "two ontologically distinct realms, one concrete and the other abstract, one sensible and the other inaccessible to the senses."[45] Such formulations, as we have seen with regard to Jewish or Chinese "literalism" and other such oppositions, articulate a strong desire for difference, the will to differentiation, and tend to construct the East and the West in a mutually exclusive dichotomous relation.

For those who read classical Chinese poetry in the original and believe that great Chinese poets like Li Bo and Du Fu are no less creative and imaginative than Western poets like Dante or Milton or Hölderlin, that is, equally capable of making a fictional world all their own in poetry, it may be somewhat disconcerting to learn that Chinese poets could only write poetry "based on a stimulus-response method of poetic production rather than a mimetic one."[46] A stimulus-response method? This sounds more like the predictable reaction of dogs in the Pavlovian study of conditioned reflex than any imaginable process of "poetic production." Although I do not share Chaves's strongly antitheoretical sentiment, I do believe that he has made a valid and important point in his critique of Owen and Yu when he remarks that in this "dichotomy—Chinese monism vs. Western dualism—together with its implications for metaphor and allegory . . . there appears to be a *denial* of something to Chinese language and thought: an ability to express abstraction."[47] Here I am not concerned with presenting a fully developed counterargument to the conceptualization of Chinese poetry Owen and Yu have advanced in their works, but I do want to indicate that in drawing a rigid line between China and the West, Chinese literalism and Western transcendentalism, they may have done a disservice to the study of Chinese literature, that they may have closed its portals and pushed it further into the cultural ghetto, and that they may have made Chinese literature as the West's culturally exotic Other more strange than it really is. The irony is that they have apparently done this out of their genuine love of Chinese literature, their real interest in literary theory, and their hope to find and grasp the distinctly Chinese nature of classical Chinese poetry. They have attempted, in a word, to focus on the fundamental difference that would distinguish the Orient from the Occident, the Chinese from the Western. If the predilection for difference is indeed the mandate of contemporary Western theory, then the problematic formulation of cultural differences between the Chinese and the Western tradition we find in the works of these respectable scholars may force us to rethink the relationship between Western theory and the study of Chinese literature, and to explore alternative ways in which our study may contribute to the ongoing discussion of literary and cultural issues beyond the boundaries of national or linguistic enclosures.

First World Theory and Third World Experience

In an essay published in *Modern China*, "Politics, Critical Paradigms: Reflections on Modern Chinese Literature Studies," Liu

Kang argues forcefully for the pervasive presence of politics in all literary and cultural expressions by disclosing the underlying political agendas or assumptions in the works of three influential scholars, namely, C. T. Hsia's formalist, Leo Lee's historicist, and Liu Zaifu's humanist paradigms in the study of modern Chinese literature. All three scholars, he claims, fail to disengage themselves from political concerns or to escape from politics in spite of their intention or overt protestation. Liu Kang's emphasis on the permeation of politics in all literature and literary criticism, as he acknowledges, is informed by contemporary literary theory and postmodernist debates on cultural issues. An interest in theory for Liu Kang thus also means an interest in politics, and his essay ends with a clarion call for "a certain cultural and political affiliation and involvement."[48] Politics seems to be his key word, and one thing he tries to accomplish is to bridge the gap between politics as a concept in Western theoretical discourse and politics as social practice in China. The former can be represented by what he calls "the Foucauldian revelation concerning the complicity of power and knowledge," and the latter, by Chairman Mao Zedong's views and the political reality in China. Though the two seem to have very different reputations in the West, Liu Kang reminds us that "Mao's conception of the relationship between politics and aesthetics might in fact have inspired Foucault's radical critique of western liberal humanism."[49] This is meant to confirm the validity of Mao's views by connecting them with Foucault's, and once that is done, Liu Kang is able to demonstrate the truth value of Mao's and Foucault's views about the permeation of politics by arguing that the very rejection of Mao's views by writers and critics in post-Mao China, despite their professed purpose of depoliticizing literature and culture, is in itself a political act, which "attests to Mao's view of the political nature of cultural and literary activity, rather than undermining that view."[50] In other words, depoliticizing is, like everything else, political, and the very attempt at undermining Maoism proves, according to Liu Kang, Mao's correctness. It is true that all sides engaged in a political struggle are political in their own ways, and that the effort to depoliticize literature in China is indeed political in the sense of setting it free from the control of state power. But what is to be gained, one may wonder, by asserting that all and everything in literature and culture are political? If the assertion is indeed equally applicable to all views and activities, is it then saying nothing about the *specific political nature* of anything in particular? If critical activities are all political, one may then ask whether it is for their apolitical views (which would be an impossibility), or for their failure to share the politics Liu Kang holds as the right kind, that he has taken the other critics to task.

Despite the apparent complexity, Liu Kang's argument actually rests on a simple premise: contemporary Western theory with its rhetoric of politics is accepted as an absolute value with the power of legitimation in literary and cultural studies, so once Mao (that is, a local political theory and practice) is seen as in conformity with, and even anticipation of, Foucault (that is, Western theory), Mao's views can be thought to have been validated through this connection. For me, however, the premise of this logic is not axiomatic, so the connection of Foucault with Mao does not lead me to the conclusion that we should therefore accept the truth of Mao's views via Foucault, but rather that we should think twice of Foucault because of our experience of the political reality in China. Foucault, as Stanley Rosen also observes, indeed "lapsed into a flirtation with Maoism during his later years."[51] Insofar as I can tell, the outcome of this flirtation is more likely the contamination of Foucault than the sanitization of Mao. This is, I believe, a good place to make clear what I mean by taking a theoretical position, which requires thinking critically of the theoretical premise itself on the basis of our recalcitrant experience. While fully acknowledging the importance and the special intellectual gratification of critical theory, I nevertheless want to reiterate the necessity of testing theory with concrete experience—the experience of reading as well as the experience of social and political reality. Theory and practice are not necessarily contradictory to one another, but neither are they always in conformity, and it is through an examination of their problematic relationship that we can arrive at a position beyond the limitations of pure empiricism and the scholasticism of pure theory.

If we accept Liu Kang's statement that "politics always permeates, in various forms, every cultural formation and institution," the very ubiquitous permeation of politics will make his statement a truism so obvious that it becomes, without further attention to the "various forms," completely useless in literary and cultural studies.[52] To proclaim that politics inhabits every cultural formation, like the assertion that every poem is made of words, hardly promises a better understanding of any particular cultural formation or any particular poem. The problem with Liu Kang's argument, however, is not only a useless truism about the omnipresence of politics, but also the positive danger of collapsing the crucial difference between politics in the Western academy on the one hand, where the autonomy of cultural and literary activities is vouched for by a civil-society tradition, and state politics in China on the other, where such a civil society and its corollary pledge of individual freedom are not a political reality.[53] The confusion of these two different kinds of politics has made Liu Kang's essay typical of a certain American discourse of "multicultural" studies, in which, as the Chicago Cultural Studies Group points out in a sobering argument, there are a number of "weaknesses in its own rhetoric: an overreliance on the efficacy of theory; a false voluntarism about political engagement; an unrecognized assumption of civil-society conditions; a tendency to limit grounds of critique to a standard brace of minoritized identities (for example, race, class, and gender); and a forgetfulness about how its terms circulate in 'Third-World' contexts."[54]

The "forgetfulness" mentioned last seems to me the most unfortunate mistake that can be made by those of us who do have some experience of living in a "Third World context," that is, in a society where politics is never subject to analysis and discussion in the academic sense but is defined by the state authority alone. In China, politics used to permeate everything from the Party organization and state institutions down to the minute details of individual life, and its grip has just recently begun to relax a bit and become more subtle and selective. For most Chinese, the result of such total politicization is disastrous. The claim that politics permeates everything has led to an openly declared primacy of politics, to the monopoly of state power that makes everything, literature and criticism included, subservient to the interest of the ruling few, the command of totalitarian politics. In such a situation, literary works produced to promote a certain Party line or policy and to illustrate the truth of its claim, works that accept the job of dramatizing the Party line as the very justification of their own being, are little more than political propaganda of the dullest kind. The dreary experience of reading a novel or watching a play made solely to indoctrinate is also, in its own distasteful way, unforgettable. Liu Kang castigates C. T. Hsia for his "modernist biases" in canonizing the works of Shen Congwen, Qian Zhongshu, and Zhang Ailing, and for his "favorable readings of 'symbolist' works of [these] non-leftist writers."[55] To be sure, aesthetic taste is personal, but given the social and political conditions under which aesthetic taste is shaped in mainland China, I suspect that Liu Kang's preference for "the communist novel *A Thousand Miles of Lovely Land* by Yang Shuo" over the works of Shen Congwen, Qian Zhongshu, and Zhang Ailing is built on something other than aesthetic considerations.[56] In the relatively open and relaxed atmosphere of the 1980s, it is precisely the latter group of writers that was rediscovered by Chinese readers and critics on the mainland, while Yang Shuo and the other Party hacks quickly fell into oblivion. That is a fact of the reading experience in a Third World context that simply cannot be ignored or discounted to accommodate one's affiliation with First World theory. On the contrary, it is precisely such an unforgettable experience, the result of total politicization we have known in our own world, that ought to give us pause in accepting and celebrating the influential "Foucauldian revelation" and applying it to the situation in China.

Indeed, our Third World experience may sometimes appear to

impede our total absorption or endorsement of First World theory, but that experience is part of our own being, our identity or historicity, which cannot be truly suppressed or separated from our historical consciousness. Moreover, that experience forms the very basis of our ability to know, to understand, and to gain some valuable insight: valuable because it is obtained from a perspective not wholly contained by Western theory. Perhaps our insight is valuable not just for ourselves but for Western critics as well. "When Western academic intellectuals announce a plan to intervene politically," again as the Chicago Cultural Studies Group observes, "that desire is enabled by a civil-society matrix, which is not often reflected in the plan."[57] Perhaps our sensitivity to politics may help make that matrix more visible, and our experience of total politicization may help forestall any unwanted consequences of politicization in real life. That is to say, our experience may help Western critics realize that "if politicization erases the boundary between the academy and public discourse, the result will not be a gain in relevance but the loss of the very ideal sought by politicization: the ideal of multiple cultural spaces all protected from invasion by each other or by the state."[58] In that sense, then, our experience may prove to be an intellectual asset rather than an impediment to be eliminated, and the moment we feel that our "Chinese experience" is putting in question some concepts of Western theory that we are expected to confirm, that may indeed be a moment of possible insight. That is, I believe, what Gadamer means when he remarks that "every experience worthy of the name thwarts an expectation. Thus the historical nature of man essentially implies a fundamental negativity that emerges in the relation between experience and insight." "Thus insight," he continues, "always involves an element of self-knowledge and constitutes a necessary side of what we called experience in the proper sense."[59] Therefore, reliance on experience, I would argue, has a tremendous hermeneutic significance in literary and cultural studies; it has nothing to do with the antitheoretical position; on the contrary, it provides a basis for a truly theoretical position, namely, a position that is not blind to its own critical assumptions and that can make theory work not as dogma, but as a powerful instrument of analysis and criticism.

It may be edifying, in this connection, to examine the uneasy relationship between experience and theory as evident in the recent works of some Chinese critics. When contemporary Western theories of literature were first introduced to the Chinese readership in the early 1980s, most critics welcomed their arrival with unreserved support and enthusiasm, because they saw in the new theories not only the possibility of different approaches to the study of literature, but a virtual liberation, at long last, from the Maoist orthodoxy and its political determinism that had long crippled both literature and criticism in China. That was certainly how I myself felt when I began reading the various Western theories and writing articles to introduce them in a special column in *Dushu* [Reading], a monthly publication tremendously popular among intellectuals and students in mainland China. For about a year, from April 1983 to March 1984, I was filled with as much eagerness and excitement in writing those articles every month as my editors were in publishing them; I was constantly struggling to find equivalent Chinese expressions, often for the first time, for such novel terms as *fabula, sjuzhet, foregrounding, deconstruction, Rezeptionsästhetik,* and the like, and trying to make them intelligible to a very wide readership. The introduction of Western theories definitely contributed to what later is often called the "culture fever" (*wenhua re*) of the 1980s.[60] As the contact with Western theory deepened, however, especially when some of the critics came to the West in exile after the June 1989 crackdown on the Chinese democracy movement, the conflict between Western theoretical discourse and Chinese experience began to emerge. One debate, which had already started years ago, has to do with the question of influence and authenticity, that is, whether the experimental literature in post-Mao China is legitimately modernist or just poor imitations of Western modernist works. Many critics now see this debate as largely pointless, because it takes for granted a simple lineal route of influence and adoption, which always goes from a Western source to a Chinese receptacle. The more interesting question, as the critic Li Tuo now asks, is whether Westernization is the only choice for Chinese literature, a choice that excludes all other alternatives. We should not forget, he reminds us, that all the argumentation about "modernization" and "modernity" is, after all, "a discourse representing a certain concept of power," and therefore should not be seen as the only "truth" or "law."[61] Here we can detect a sense of discontent with the hegemonic discourse of Western modernism and postmodernism, or Western theory in general.

The situation is dramatized quite revealingly by Liu Zaifu, who had expressed his enthusiastic support of Western theory when he was director of the Institute of Literature in the Chinese Academy of Social Sciences and editor of the influential journal *Wenxue pinglun* [Literary Criticism]. But later, in an essay significantly entitled "Farewell to the Gods," Liu Zaifu clearly articulates his disenchantment with Western theory, which is apparently shared by some other Chinese critics as well. To some extent and in an interesting way, this essay is also a contribution to the debate on influence and authenticity. He argues that Chinese writers and critics throughout the modern period have always been "stealing" theoretical apparatus from foreigners—the Germans, the Russians, the French, the Americans—and have consequently lost their originality and lived "in a ubiquitous spiritual hell created by others in a variety of forms." Therefore, the task Chinese critics must now fulfill at the close of the twentieth century, says Liu, is "to walk out of the shadow of the hell of others."[62] The hellish shadow in Liu's essay turns out to be a huge one that consists of every radical social and cultural theory introduced into China since the 1920s, all of which, he contends, become one or another sort of "tyrant of aesthetics" and share the traits of "totalitarianism packed in the gilded wrapper of revolution."[63] In contemporary China, a Russian tyrant reigns over the literary scene, namely, the idea that literature should "reflect" life, an idea originated by V. I. Lenin and further developed into the principles of "socialist realism." It is against this tyrannic "reflection theory" that Liu Zaifu has himself proposed a theory of "literary subjectivity" in order to offer a new "philosophical foundation" for Chinese literary studies. From the vantage point of an intellectual in exile, Liu can now put it unequivocally that his theory of "literary subjectivity" ultimately aims to "transcend the limitations and the totalitarianism of politics and ideology."[64] In the works of Ah Cheng, Han Shaogong, and the other "nativist" writers, Liu argues, there is evidently a conscious effort to "return to our spiritual home" out of the shadow of "Europeanization," while in literary theory, the same tendency is embodied in a "return to subjectivity" and a "return to the text."[65] Conceived as a theoretical program to lead contemporary Chinese literature and criticism out of the spiritual hell of state politics, Liu Zaifu's theoretical effort is thus first and foremost an effort of depoliticization.

Since he came to America after the June Fourth crackdown and accordingly was able to have close contact with Western literary theory, Liu Zaifu quickly realized that political engagement rather than depoliticization is currently the respectable position for most Western critics to take. Moreover, a theory of "subjectivity," and indeed the very concept of "subject," are very much deconstructed and discredited in the West, no longer considered viable for critical thinking. If Liu Kang's call for "cultural and political affiliation and involvement" follows the tendency of mainstream Western theory, Liu Zaifu's program of depoliticization clearly represents a different mode of thinking, which may appear embarrassingly outmoded vis-à-vis much of contemporary Western theory. Liu Zaifu acknowledges that there is obviously "a serious time lag between the cultural needs of the East and the West." As a result, a number of questions constantly bedevil Chinese intellectuals: How should we overcome this time lag? How should we understand, from a cultural perspective in which subjectivity is still something lacking, the postmodernist theory that has "decentered the subject"? For Liu Zaifu, this constitutes "a kind of *fin de siècle* anxiety for Chinese scholars."[66] If he sees in China a "socialist realist" tyrant, in the West he sees a different one, "the tyrant of signifiers," one that has reduced subject to a meaningless abstraction.[67] Evidently, the "gods" to whom Liu Zaifu bids farewell are not just old ones like Plato and Aristotle, Croce and Spingarn, Freud and Darwin, Lukács and Brecht, Plekhanov and Chernyshevsky, but also the new post-modernist and poststructuralist "gods" like Barthes, Lacan, Derrida, and Foucault. What Liu Zaifu calls a "time lag" seems to indicate a unilinear view of historical progression, but we do not have to view the difference between China and the West in such temporal terms. What seems a time lag may be seen as some sort of reversal in spatial terms: what is valued by intellectuals in China may not be valued by postmodern theorists in the West, and vice versa.

The impulse to escape from the shadow of other people's hell reminds us, quite unexpectedly, of Owen's disapproval of or anxiety about what he refers to as global influence, for both wish to achieve some kind of purity, in thinking as well as in style, that would guarantee the authenticity or originality of something uniquely or distinctly Chinese. The desire for originality in critical thinking totally independent of any influence of the Other, as seen from the perspective of postmodernist theory, can only be a romantic and utopian desire that arises from the very condition of its own impossibility. In a critique of Liu's essay that appropriates some deconstructive terminology, Wu Xiaoming argues that Liu Zaifu's essentialist rhetoric, his "myth of originality" and his "dream of pluralism," belie his nostalgic desire for a "pure origin." The very idea of "farewell to the gods," Wu contends, is a Western metaphor, and Liu's sense of the *fin de siècle* already reveals a typically Western sensibility.[68] Wu is quite right to maintain that "it is possible to define the self only through the Other. The myth of the self can be generated only by forgetting or suppressing the conditions that make the self possible as self, by forgetting or suppressing the fact that the self is also an Other to the Other."[69] In this respect, his critique of Liu Zaifu does remind us not just of the impossibility of constructing an isolated

Chinese essence, but also of the danger of self-enclosure, the danger of locking oneself up in a cultural ghetto while imagining a critical space of one's own. In fact, given the condition of our own times, the interrelatedness of thinking in a global context is a pervasive phenomenon that no amount of desire for ethnic or cultural essence can overlook or deny. The first thing for Chinese critics to do, then, is not to get out of the shadow of others as so many alien and alienating "gods," but to see these "gods" as merely human, just like us. That is to say, the task is not so much to think independently of others as to think critically of what others have already thought, because, as I see it, it is only by working out the thought content of others that we may arrive at our own independent thinking and critical position. Insofar as thinking or knowledge is concerned, originality and true freedom can be achieved only by an accumulative effort and a constant interaction with others or other minds.

However, if we do not accept Western intellectual authorities as "gods," we may wonder whether Wu Xiaoming is giving Western theorists too much credit when he claims that "the concepts of 'man' and 'subjectivity' are themselves borrowed from Western philosophy," and when he further characterizes these concepts as "constructs in Western philosophical discourse since Descartes."[70] Didn't Chinese philosophers before the time of Descartes talk about the idea of "man" at all? Was there any possibility of their formulating an equivalent of the idea of "subjectivity"? Do we need to revisit the debate on terminology in the so-called Chinese rites controversy? Wu's argument wholly relies on the deconstructive metanarrative as told by Lyotard, Foucault, and Derrida, but if we do not accept deconstruction as the only Western theoretical discourse, we shall be able to see that the debate on subjectivity is by no means a dead issue, even within Western literary theory, and that the "time lag" Liu Zaifu imagined between the East and the West also inhabits the West itself. For the traditionally marginalized Other in Western societies, for women, for blacks, and so on, regaining subjectivity is as viable a project and ambition as it is for Liu Zaifu in the cultural context of China. While it is justifiable for Western critics to de-construct "the Western male subject" that has "long been con-stituted historically for himself and in himself," as Henry Louis Gates, Jr., argues, "to deny us the process of exploring and re-claiming our subjectivity before we critique it is the critical ver-sion of the grandfather clause, the double privileging of catego-ries that happen to be *preconstituted*." Thus Gates considers it an unpleasant irony that "precisely when we (and other third world peoples) obtain the complex wherewithal to define our black subjectivity in the republic of Western letters, our theoretical colleagues declare that there ain't no such thing as a subject."[71] In a truly pluralist spirit, then, we may say that there are subjects and then there are subjects, just as there are politics and then there are politics. The important thing for a theoretical consid-eration of these different phenomena and different positions is to be alert to the very plurality of categories in things and in theo-ries. To accept uncritically any category or any theoretical ap-proach as the only valid one is to give up one's responsibility to think and to criticize, while that responsibility is precisely what critical theory is all about.

A Plea for Openness

If there is anything that we can draw as some useful conclu-sion from this brief examination of the recent changes and de-bates in Chinese literature studies, the first and foremost that comes to my mind is a sense of openness. This at least means two things: first, it is to open the door of Chinese literature studies to more works (modern and contemporary as well as ancient and classical) and to more methodologies (including the various ap-proaches based on Western literary theory); and second, it also means to open up one's views to the challenge and revision of others. If scholars working on Chinese literature are more open in both these ways, their works are more likely to have a notable impact not only in their own special field, but also in the larger context of cultural studies and cross-cultural understanding.

Openness certainly implies tolerance and flexibility, and some of the polemical rhetoric and intensity would indeed seem unnecessary if we were more conscious of the limitations of our own specialty, our own political views and critical assumptions, and if we were at the same time more willing to engage other people's views and interpretations. The barrier that needs to be pulled down is the rigid opposition between China and the West, which is sometimes misconstrued as an even more dubious one between the old and the new, tradition and modernity. If we remember that Chinese culture in its long and complicated history has been never a monolithic but instead a heterogeneous and syncretic tradition, that a living culture has as much claim to the present as to the past, and that in our times it is neither possible nor desirable to separate China from the rest of the world, then to isolate and grasp a pure Chinese essence will appear as both pointless and impossible. Although every poem, every novel, and every work of art worthy of its name is unique in the sense of being new and distinct from all others, uniqueness is ultimately a matter of degree. No work of literature as a socially meaningful symbolic structure is so unique as to deny any comparison with other works, works in other mediums, other languages, and other traditions. The question is not whether comparison is possible but whether it is interesting, useful, and productive. To break through the enclosures of the study of classical as opposed to modern Chinese literature, the study of Chinese as opposed to comparative literature, and the study of literature as opposed to theory and criticism would be the first step in our effort to get out of the cultural ghetto.

Openness thus entails a willingness to face the challenge of theory, but at the same time it also calls for a critical spirit that renders theory itself open to scrutiny and examination. Openness is not a passive acceptance of all the claims Western theory makes about literature, culture, politics, and so forth; it does not acknowledge theoretical authorities as "gods," but treats Chinese critical positions as possibly theoretically viable or vulnerable on exactly the same grounds as Western ones. A critical dialogue can be carried out only among interlocutors who are equals with a genuine desire for mutual understanding, and only when the exchange of ideas is constantly recontextualized to make theoretical formulations intelligible in specific cultural and political situations and relevant to the reading of particular texts. The matter of difference and similarity, for example, always needs to be settled in a particular context. Though I think there is an over-emphasis on cultural difference in contemporary theory and have tried to argue for similarity and commensurability, I neither do nor want to obliterate all differences between China and the West, Chinese literature and Western literature. A critical position of openness ought to be a position that moves and changes in response to the present needs and circumstances, but it is at the same time a firm stance once the needs and the circumstances are clearly understood. It is from such a critical position that I have raised some questions about Jameson's notion of Third World literature as "national allegories" and Liu Kang's argument for political engagement and affiliation. I am perfectly willing to see the viability of their views, but when we consider the specific situation of Chinese literature and criticism, depoliticizing in the sense of setting literature and literary studies free from the ideological control of the state, at the present at least, seems to me a more effective strategy than the endorsement of politicization. It is also from such a critical position that I propose to reconsider the problem of "subjectivity" as a still meaningful theoretical problem in China. If women and blacks in America still need to constitute or reclaim their subjectivity, why should anyone deny the same to the Chinese in China? From a deconstructive point of view, this may appear to be a nostalgic falling back to old-fashioned humanism and metaphysics, but deconstruction should not be treated as the universal truth it has aimed to deconstruct, and a truly critical attention to difference should examine each particular problem in its own context.

The openness I have proposed to consider as an important critical attitude, both as the opening of the special field of Chinese literature studies and as the opening of one's own views and positions, comes as a result of lived experience, a Chinese experience of living in a claustrophobic enclosure, political and otherwise, which Lu Xun's impressive metaphor of the "iron house" may still be borrowed to describe. If in their attempt to destroy that "iron house" Lu Xun and the other intellectuals of the May Fourth generation had polarized tradition and modernity in radical but perhaps destructive ways, Chinese intellectuals seventy-odd years later still find themselves in largely the same situation and face many of the same problems our predecessors faced at the dawn of the twentieth century. Standing at the close of the century and with the hindsight of history, however, we may have the advantage of rethinking the strategies for dismantling that "iron house," and indeed of seeing the many cracks and fissures in that house, which is, after all, not built of such indestructible iron as we had thought. Perhaps by pursuing openness rather than polarization, we may finally be successful in opening up China to a new and promising future, and in achieving that goal, the openness in the study of Chinese literature may be seen as part of a general spirit, a vital part of a great vision that will lead us into a more hopeful future in the next century.

CHAPTER 5

Western Theory and Chinese Reality

Qing, the last imperial dynasty in China, did not have any office to deal with foreign affairs until 1861, the year when the General Office of Managing Affairs of the Various Countries (*Zongli geguo shiwu yamen*) came into being under Prince Gong, uncle to the young Emperor Tongzhi, and it did not begin to train its own personnel with any knowledge of a foreign language until 1862, when *Tongwen guan* or the Interpreters' College was set up in Beijing. That is to say, it took almost twenty years after China's defeat and humiliation by the British in the infamous Opium War for any such institutions to be established, which marked the end of self-enclosure of the Middle Kingdom and the historical moment when the Chinese started walking gingerly toward the outside world. What is known in China as "Western learning" (*xi xue*) thus began in some measure as a solution to the question of national survival under the pressure and threat of Western imperialism. The so-called foreign affairs movement (*Yangwu yundong*), the late Qing effort to strengthen the imperial rule by assimilating certain Western techniques, was limited to learning advanced Western technologies, and to acquiring weaponry and military equipment in particular. Despite Yan Fu's (1853–1921) elegant translation of Thomas Huxley, Adam Smith, Stuart Mill, Rousseau, Montesquieu, Herbert Spencer, and others, most literati-scholars in the late imperial era were conservative in matters of culture and philosophy. As Confucian scholars with a tremendous sense of pride in their own cultural heritage, they could not accept the idea that the foreign barbarians, though strong in brute force in warfare, could have anything comparable to Chinese, and especially Confucian, *cul-*

ture. They had neither the interest to learn Western ideas nor the intention to introduce them to a Chinese audience. In fact, every reformist attempt to acquire something Western in science and technology for China's own modernization would meet with ten-fold resistance to Western ideas from the conservative quarters in the Chinese government and society. Of course, things changed dramatically after the downfall of the Qing dynasty in 1911 and during the May Fourth movement in the late 1910s and early 1920s, but resistance to things foreign, especially to the Western ideas of a democratic society and individual freedom, have always been an important factor in Chinese political life.

The Cultural Environment for Traveling Theory

Lu Xun, fiction writer, essayist, and foremost iconoclast in modern Chinese history, whose observations of the Chinese national character strike us today as no less shrewd and insightful than they were half a century ago, once caricatured the Chinese resistance to anything "foreign." The Chinese, he wrote in 1934, developed a strong enmity against what they called an ostentatious "foreign air" (*yang qi*)—that is, things or attitudes that seemed un-Chinese and therefore should be shunned by all Chinese patriots.

> And because we have been suffering from aggression for years, we become inimical to this "foreign air." We even go one step further and deliberately run counter to this "foreign air": as they like to act, we would sit still; as they talk science, we would depend on divination; as they dress in short shirts, we would put on long robes; as they emphasize hygiene, we would eat flies; as they are strong and healthy, we would rather stay sick.[1]

This is, of course, exaggeration, but the antagonistic mentality sketched out here is not, for this still forms to a large extent the cultural and political ambience in which foreign ideas and theories must find themselves when they travel, transfer, or migrate to China.

Indeed, resistance, as Edward Said observes, is "an inevitable part of acceptance" that ideas and theories must encounter when they travel to a new cultural environment.[2] In Lu Xun's day, traditional Confucian mores formed the core of Chinese resistance to foreign ideas; in our time, that resistance is predicated by the ideological principles of the Chinese Communist Party, which, in the face of a disintegrated Soviet Union and a chaotic Eastern Europe, has attempted to hold out, in professed ideological terms at least, as the last bulwark of world communism and to guard jealously communism's ideological purity, even when the Chinese social fabric is quickly and irrevocably dissolved in capitalist commercialism and consumerism. In both cases, past and present, the resistance to foreign ideas and theories is propped up by the pretensions of a nationalism already bankrupt in ideas. In this we may find an explanation for the successive waves of political campaigns against Western "spiritual pollution" and "bourgeois liberalization," campaigns that punctuated, since the end of the Cultural Revolution in the late 1970s, a period of recent Chinese history that was also the period of an official policy of openness and economic reform. The spasmodic rhythm of these campaigns is symptomatic of a peculiar political situation, the circumstances of all literary and cultural activities in China, a situation dominated by the tension between the desire for a modern economy and the fear of any structural change in the distribution of power and in social hierarchy, between a sinicized Marxism as the official ideology of the Communist Party and any foreign, especially Western, ideas and theories. Without bearing this political background in mind, it would make little sense to talk about the "traveling" of Western theory to and in China, and it would be very difficult, if not totally impossible, to understand the significance of Western theory and its reception by Chinese intellectuals.

In Lu Xun's caricature, activeness and an emphasis on science, on physical and mental health—in other words, the positive qualities in those pairs of contrasting values—are all allocated to the side of the "foreign." Understood as mere exaggeration, as the satirist's incorrigible propensity toward irony, witticism, and hyperbolic language, this can be easily brushed aside with a knowing, tolerant smile, and thus does not touch off serious thoughts. Caricatures, however, always have a point; they always expose and highlight by their very distortion and exaggeration. Lu Xun's point, of course, is to goad the Chinese into a more reflective thinking about what it means to be Chinese, a critical consciousness that would not only abandon the simplistic antagonism to foreign ideas but would reclaim what may be inherently Chinese, or to "grab" from foreign cultures whatever is good for China. "Without grabbing, a man cannot automatically become a new man," says Lu Xun; "without grabbing, literature and art cannot automatically become new literature and new art."[3] The essence of this "grabism" (nalai zhuyi), as Lu Xun calls it, is an active effort to choose and take from foreign cultures what is good and useful to the Chinese, and it is this activeness that differentiates grabism from a passive acceptance of colonialist impositions that come with foreign gunboats: "opium from Britain, derelict guns from Germany, French perfumes, American movies, and all sorts of Japanese junk that says 'made in China.'"[4]

In this connection, then, perhaps the "traveling" of Western theory to China, with which I am concerned here, may be redefined as the Chinese "grabbing" of Western theory in an entirely different situation and for entirely different purposes from what Western theory may find at home. Friedrich Schleiermacher once remarked that the translator of a foreign work can either ask the reader to go to the foreign author or bring the foreign author to the reader back home.[5] Insofar as Western theory is concerned, Chinese translation is never motivated by a mere tourist interest of sight-seeing in a foreign culture but is rather determined by the need one feels in China, the need to "grab" the foreign author home through translation and to open a window onto the outside world in this suffocating "iron house"—to borrow yet another of Lu Xun's famous expressions.[6] Redefining the dissemination of Western theory in China as an exercise of Chinese grabism immediately shifts the ground and changes the horizon or

perspective from which we may ask questions and make evalua-
tions—not from the point of origin where Western theory em-
barks on a journey abroad, but from the point of its destination,
or rather the point of origin in reverse, where the need for the
translation and assimilation of Western theory is felt in the first
place.

The very fact that Lu Xun was able to advocate grabism, however, proves that there is always some intellectual space, even in
an "iron house," for the assimilation of foreign ideas and theories
right in the middle of resistance and antagonism. Indeed, his
grabism must be understood as an act of antagonism in itself—
that is, as an active choice in opposition to imperialist culture
and to the institutionalized official Chinese culture of his time.
What Lu Xun attacks in his caricature is thus not antagonism per
se but the specific kind of antagonistic mentality the official culture systematically inculcates and propagates across the entire
social spectrum. His grabism, on the other hand, advocates a different kind of antagonism, which redraws the lines between the
opposite sides and shifts both the Chinese and the foreign in a
new alignment, in which the foreign tends to aid the unofficial in
opposition to the official Chinese culture.

It is in the context of this official versus unofficial antagonism
that we must understand the introduction of foreign literary the-
ory to China. For his time, Lu Xun introduced, indirectly from
Japanese translations, the work of Anatoli Lunacharsky and
Georgy Plekhanov to Chinese readers, taking these Russians to
be the leading Marxist critics and theorists.[7] After the Cultural
Revolution, it was Western theory of all kinds—from formalism,
New Criticism, and structuralism, to hermeneutics, reception
theory, deconstruction, reader-response criticism, feminism, and
Western Marxism—that generated a great deal of attention and
enthusiasm among Chinese scholars and students of literature.
In a short span of five or six years, roughly fifty or sixty years'
worth of Western theories were introduced to Chinese readers,
and all these theories willy-nilly found themselves to be both
"foreign" and "Western" and thereby acquired an oppositional

status with radically subversive implications—that is, potentially dangerous as "spiritual pollutants" in the Chinese political atmosphere.

In a totally alien environment shaped by very different courses of events, Western theories tend to lose the urgency of their internal distinctions and become strange bedfellows in spite of themselves. For example, the Chinese translation of *Theory of Literature* by René Wellek and Austin Warren appeared in Beijing in 1984, and its emphasis on the "intrinsic" study of literature as opposed to "extrinsic approach" was extremely welcome to Chinese literature and criticism, which were desperately trying to break away from the grip of political determinism, the tenets of the official cultural policy based on Mao Zedong's 1942 Yan'an talks and his theory of class struggle. At the same time, Fredric Jameson's series of lectures given at Peking University in 1985, translated and published in book form in 1986 as *Houxiandai zhuyi yu wenhua lilun* [Postmodernism and Cultural Theories], inspired many Chinese scholars in their own critique of culture and tradition. Their crucial differences notwithstanding, all the Western theories contributed to what Liu Zaifu, one of China's leading critics and former director of the Institute of Literature in the Chinese Academy of Social Sciences, called a methodological breakthrough, the "expanding of mental space in literary studies."[8] Thus formalism and Western Marxism, like the other Western literary theories grabbed by Chinese scholars, all exerted a liberating influence in China against a completely threadbare and ossified theory of class and class struggle that reduced all literature and criticism to a number of rigid formulas.[9]

In reading Liu Zaifu's critical writings, we can have a sense of the strange but not surprising realignment of Western theories in China and the ambivalence with which Chinese critics face the sudden plethora of theoretical discourses. Liu is well-known in China for his work on Lu Xun and especially for championing "the subjectivity of literature," the necessity for literature "to return to itself." Like many other Chinese scholars, Liu heartily welcomed the arrival of contemporary Western theories, in which he saw the possibility of opening up new ways and constructing an entirely new critical apparatus that would help Chinese literature and criticism break away from the straitjacket of Maoist orthodoxy. The newly introduced Western theories, he thought, would also help reclaim an essentially human and humanistic subjectivity, which had been totally suppressed in the Maoist reification of abstract collectivity and in the name of class struggle and the "dictatorship of the proletariat." On the other hand, however, insufficient knowledge of any Western language impeded Liu's understanding of Western theory and confined his critical vision to a limited horizon. His plea for subjectivity, for the autonomy of literature and literary studies, his humanistic interpretation of Karl Marx's *Economic and Philosophic Manuscripts*, as well as his employment of a Hegelian terminology and some Western critical notions that have been long out of fashion, all seem to make him hopelessly outdated vis-à-vis the sophistication of contemporary Western theory. In fact, Liu himself is not unaware of the discrepancy between his own theory and that of the contemporary West. "The moving away from the object toward the subject," as he put it, "and the centripetal direction of this movement are running in just the opposite direction to that of the centrifugal movement some Western sociological schools in literary studies are trying to attain at the present."[10] It may well be that just about everybody who is somebody in contemporary Western theory is associated, in one way or another, with what Liu calls "sociological schools," but that hardly matters to him. To a Chinese reader sensitive to the same political and ideological overtones, for whom Liu Zaifu wrote his essays, "sociological school" as a critical term almost suggests a kind of "vulgar Marxist" approach to literature, that is, to interpret a literary text in terms of social and material conditions, and to render crude judgment on an author or a text on the basis of an alleged progressive role in aiding social progress or a reactionary role in blocking social progress. In any case, Liu does not apologize for the theoretical discrepancy between what he does and what the Western "sociological schools" try to achieve; he does not even think much about such a discrepancy, because he is writing for the Chinese in contemporary mainland China, which runs in a direction opposite to that of the West, where the various "sociological schools" may or may not be flourishing.

This should give us pause in judging Liu Zaifu and his theory according to contemporary Western criteria. If we care to take a closer look at his advocacy of "subjectivity," for example, we can see that he is not bent on contradicting Foucault or Derrida, whom he probably has never read either in the original or in translation, but that he is responding to a much more tangible local problem, namely, the Maoist subjugation of all individuals and individuality to the collective reification of class and class struggle. In this subjugation, Liu argues,

all subjectivity (the human being) is defined as a being of class, as a screw on the class machine, and is required to be completely suited for, and to serve in, class struggle. With all individuality dissolved in class and class struggle, there appears a strange phenomenon: that a human being totally loses initiative and personality, that is, loses that which makes a human being a human being.[11]

To define man as a screw on the class machine, Liu maintains, is to create a new absolute idea, a new determinism and even fatalism, because it conceives, of necessity, "all human behavior and psychology as derived from class struggle, and all that one says or does as already predetermined." When applied to characterization and description in literary works, this political determinism makes everything stereotyped and totally predictable as a sign of class attributes, reducing literature to a "semiotics of class."[12] From this dehumanizing mechanization and this entirely politicized "semiotics of class," Liu argues, it is imperative that the human being restore vital and independent subjectivity and that literature return to itself.

Incidentally, the dehumanizing concept of man as a screw on a machine, a metaphor so reminiscent of the nightmarish vision of the impersonal numbers in Evgeny Zamyatin's *We* (1924), or the faceless Gammas, Deltas, and Epsilons hatched in "conditioning centers" in Aldous Huxley's *Brave New World* (1932), is neither invented by Liu nor borrowed from Western literature or theory. It is, rather, borrowed directly from a homemade political slogan that is viewed *positively* and understood without irony in Mao's China, namely, the Party's call to every Chinese to learn from Chairman Mao's good soldier Lei Feng and to be content as a "revolutionary screw" (*geming de luosiding*).[13] First announced in the early 1960s, this call to mechanization was reissued after the Chinese army had fired on thousands of Chinese civilians and students in Beijing in the fateful June of 1989.

Quite ironically, Liu's condemnation of the dehumanization of man sounds very much like Georg Lukács's condemnation of the alienation of human life and labor so brilliantly recapitulated in Said's essay on traveling theory. The process of reification under capitalism, according to Lukács, radically transforms "everything human, flowing, processual, organic, and connected into disconnected and 'alienated' objects, items, lifeless atoms"; the "mechanically objectified 'performance' of the worker [is] wholly separated from his total human personality," as human existence itself is "reduced to an isolated particle and fed into an alien system," while the same ruthless alienation happens to intellect, or "the subject," as well.[14] I said "ironically" because socialism is supposed to end the alienation of man under capitalism; in reality, however, we find that man was born integral but is everywhere in alienation, including in socialist China and the erstwhile Soviet Union. Moreover, it is ironical because, for Lukács, class or class consciousness is precisely what enables the subject to break through the spiritual torpor, the numbing effect of reification and alienation, since "class consciousness," as Said puts it, "is thought thinking its way through fragmentation to unity; it is also thought aware of its own subjectivity as something active, energetic, and, in a profound sense, poetic."[15] For Lukács, then, it would perhaps be like a bad dream that class and class consciousness should become the very stuff that make up the repressive alienation of man and human subjectivity.

In China's politically charged atmosphere, the plea for subjectivity and the autonomy of literature is not outside the sphere of politics but very much at its center as a powerful articulation of the demand for intellectual freedom, and the humanist argument advanced by Liu Zaifu and other Chinese critics proves to be more deeply and directly involved in social and political transformation than much of Western theory, despite the latter's rhetoric and claim to political relevance. The involvement of literary theory with political events, of scholarly argumentation with direct engagement, can be seen nowhere more clearly than in Beijing's Tiananmen Square in June 1989, when a powerful crisis suddenly put everyone, everything, and every theory to the test. Liu was one of the many intellectuals who went to the students in Tiananmen and publicly voiced their support for the students' demand for freedom and democracy; after the Tiananmen massacre, he was forced into exile together with some of his younger, more radical colleagues. Liu Zaifu and many other Chinese literary scholars, to put it simply, are not ivory-tower dwellers who talk about the autonomy of literature and the freedom of artistic expression only from a safe distance, somewhere outside history. They are men and women of enormous courage and moral integrity fighting for social justice and intellectual freedom in political actions.

The political critique of Liu Zaifu and others by spokesmen of the Chinese ideological establishment shortly after the Tiananmen massacre may further help us understand the condition of literary theory in China. One such critique pits Liu Zaifu and Li Zehou, another influential Chinese theoretician, in direct opposition to Mao Zedong's *Talk at the Yan'an Forum*, accusing them of encouraging some avant-garde literary and art works to "challenge socialist morality, law, and public opinion," and of "trumpeting bourgeois liberalization."[16] In pleading for the autonomy of literature and literary studies, the critique continues, Liu and Li are advocating "independence from the politics of the proletariat, which not only means to lead literature and art into the formalist impasse but to throw themselves wittingly or unwittingly into the arms of bourgeois politics," which amounts to no

less a crime than treason, "the betrayal of the politics of the proletariat and the people, and the propagation of the politics of
bourgeois liberalization."[17] Such a political analysis is accurate in
the sense that it shows what is at stake in the theoretical debate
in China, but it is not accurate in pretending to speak on behalf
of the "proletariat" and the "people" when it is in fact speaking
for a totalitarian regime.

Is There Violence Outside a Television Set?

If the students' demonstration and the ensuing massacre in
Beijing constitute one of the most important political events in
recent Chinese history, they also present an enormous challenge
to all the different theories to provide account, analysis, interpretation, and engagement. It has indeed generated a great deal
of discussion in the whole world, and there is certainly no lack of
insightful analysis in terms of social and political history. Insofar
as literary theory is concerned, however, there is a peculiar silence about all this not just in China, where the whole thing is
still taboo, but also in the West. It is even more disturbing to see
that in what little analysis there is, the attempt often makes one
wonder how much real understanding critics in the West may
have of Chinese reality.

   A case in point is an essay by W. J. T. Mitchell in which we
find a photograph of Mao's statue and another of the "Goddess
of Liberty" that the Chinese students erected in Tiananmen
Square shortly before the bloody crackdown. Brought together to
confront one another in two consecutive pages, these two images
immediately set the stage for some incisive observations and
commentaries. It turns out that Mitchell just uses the destruction
of the statue made by the Chinese students as an example to introduce his argument that in America there is legal and political
control of public art just as in China. He quotes the Chinese government's warning to the students that " 'Even in the United
States statues need permission before they can be put up.' "[18] The
omnipresence of political control grants validity to this implicit
analogy: "We may not have tanks mowing down students and

their statues," says Mitchell, "but we are experiencing a moment when art and the public (insofar as it is embodied by state power and 'public opinion') seem on a collision course."[19] This is disappointing because the rather casual use of the Chinese example serves to trivialize the momentum of a great and tragic event, and a difference found within—the conflict between "art and the public," which exists in both China and America—is enlisted to play down an important difference between cultures and political situations. Moreover, the repetition of the phrase "even in the United States" not only verges on endorsing the Chinese government's view but also fails to understand the true meaning of that phrase coming out of government loudspeakers. By linking the Chinese students' "Goddess of Liberty" with the Statue of Liberty and the United States—in other words, with the "foreign" and "Western," with "bourgeois liberalization" and all its ominous political overtones—the government tried to depict the confrontation in Tiananmen not as an inevitable outcome of China's internal political problems, but as a "counterrevolutionary turmoil" incited and manipulated by external forces, by some secret foreign agents, and thus made up a pretext for the tanks to roll in. Speaking to a rebellious young generation at the height of a political confrontation, the Chinese government was not really interested, after all, in making a simple statement of truth about the United States.

Mitchell never claims to be a China specialist, and in his essay, which is not concerned with the "Goddess of Liberty" as such, the Chinese example is marginal, though he believes that the Beijing massacre, the statue, and its destruction are "full of instruction for anyone who wants to think about public art and, more generally, about the whole relation of images, violence, and the public sphere."[20] Mitchell does, however, provide a footnote that refers the reader to an essay by Rey Chow "for an excellent discussion of the way the events in China in June 1989 became a 'spectacle for the West.'"[21] The essay Mitchell recommends was published in *Radical America*, in a special issue entitled, quite appropriately, "China and Mexico: Rebellions at the Grassroots."

By weaving the political events in Beijing into a rich textuality of the issues of gender and race, Orientalism, an analysis of two American movies (*King Kong* and *Gorillas in the Mist*), the deconstruction of democracy, a comment on Third World women, and a questioning of sinology, Chow's essay may easily be one of the most sophisticated analyses of the Chinese political situation that have been attempted in the West, a rare specimen of the effort to respond to the "China crisis" from a perspective equipped with the most powerful discourses of literary and cultural theories the West has to offer. Chow's obvious familiarity with Western theory, her skillful deployment of analytical strategies, and her avowedly leftist political stance all make her essay exemplary of the sophistication of contemporary Western critical discourse, which appeals to critics like Mitchell. After reading it, however, I find myself in profound disagreement not only with her particular analysis of the events in Beijing but also, and more importantly, with the basic underlying assumptions that seem to me directly related to the whole issue of Western theory and Chinese reality, as well as to the nature of oppositional discourse within Western academia and in a broader context of global political confrontations.

Watching the massacre in Beijing is a traumatic experience that seems to defy theoretical analysis because, as Chow puts it, there is "nothing subtle, nothing reflexive, about a government gunning down its own, and for that matter, any people."[22] Reality, which so often seems intangible and hard to grasp, is suddenly thrust, so to speak, straight to our face by brute facts like people gunned down in the streets, and renders our theoretical discourse, which tends to doubt and reject the primacy of simple actuality, morally and emotionally inadequate. Theoretical analysis, however, is always able to go beyond the brute facts of violence and reach a high level of reflexive subtlety by putting in question the *representation* of violence. This is precisely what we find in Chow's essay, for very quickly the massacre in Beijing is exposed as imagery and representation on Western television, as Western media's denigration of a non-Western Other, comparable to the imperialist agenda as symbolically represented by the subjugation of a monstrous gorilla in *King Kong*. The invading imperialists in this case are cameramen of the television networks who, "like director Denim's film crew," went into China as "the unknown jungle with its dark, abominable secrets" and made it "the 'other' (anti-U.S.) country," an ugly sight and a monster like King Kong for the West to watch and enjoy.[23]

Any number of theoretical analyses of representation or mimesis will tell us that representation is an arbitrary play of signifiers that does not really refer or point to the signified, the referent, or whatever it is supposed to represent. Translating the massacre in Beijing into the language of television and film and seeing the brute events as a popular movie thus turn out to be yet another performance of such theoretical analysis, which predictably discredits representation. The problem with such an easy use of theory, however, is that the brutal reality of massacre gets lost in the analysis, and that it not only collapses a crucial difference between the reality in China and the fictionality in *King Kong*, but has Chinese reality and its serious, extratextual substance displaced by Hollywood fictionality. The cameramen of Western television are certainly not without their bias, and television coverage of Tiananmen was indeed a complicated matter in which different political and ideological forces had their stakes and influence, but to claim that whatever appears on the television is all made up by the Western media is not just to exaggerate the power of the media but simply to refuse to accept the reality that makes one feel ideologically uncomfortable. Indeed, in reading theoretical analyses of representation, just as in reading representation itself, one needs to keep an eye on the undeclared ideological motivations. The point is that the gunning down of Chinese civilians in Beijing is not only not subtle and not reflexive, but also not fictional. Unlike King Kong, those who were killed by machine guns and crushed by the metal bellies of tanks in Beijing did not die a metaphorical death.

Reality may be hard to grasp, but ideology seems more tangible. Without a single word analyzing the repressive measures that the Chinese authorities used to silence any dissenting voice and to eradicate any attempt at social and political change (which led to the mass protest in Tiananmen in the first place), to analyze "China watching" as Western media's invasion of China serves only to exculpate the Chinese government, to transmogrify a critical moment in the history of China into a "foreign" and "Western" conspiracy, and to turn the whole thing literally into a spectacle made in and for the West, a popular horror movie that might as well have been shot in Hollywood studios instead of the streets in Beijing. If the June 1989 Beijing massacre were indeed produced by "director Denim's film crew," one may wonder why the same crew failed to produce a spectacular dramatic denouement for the August 1991 Soviet coup. Why didn't they reproduce the successful Beijing scenario or simply issue a rerun of the Tiananmen footage, when they had a perfect chance to entice tanks to mow down those Muscovites? Shall we blame this anticlimactic ending on director Denim's bad taste in aesthetics, his vulgar interest in a cheap poetic justice? But thinking in such cinematic terms may only represent a fetishizing of film theory, a reification of textuality that forgets or neglects the real political forces that shape the course—and discourse—of history. Here we may well recall Roger Chartier's remark that "experience is not reducible to discourse," and that we "need to guard against unconstrained use of the category of the 'text'—a term too often inappropriately applied to practices (ordinary or ritualized) whose tactics and procedures bear no resemblance to discursive strategies."[24]

The television coverage of the events at Tiananmen, according to Chow, reenacts the Western colonialist and imperialist intervention in a Third World country, an intervention that evokes "the whole issue of extraterritoriality that has been present in Sino-Western relations since the mid-nineteenth century." China is invaded again, this time by "people like Ted Koppel or Tom Brokaw" with their "intrusive filming and reporting."[25] Notice that the issue is not that Western filming and reporting distort what really happened in China, since Chow gives no analysis of how, in their reports, comments, and discussions, Ted Koppel, Tom Brokaw, Dan Rather, or any other anchor, politician, or China expert deliberately misled the television audience. In fact, without in some way acknowledging reality as the ontological world outside representation and its analysis, it is impossible for theoretical analysis to judge anything as misleading and distorting. The critique of Western media here is thus not epistemological but ideological—that is, the very act of filming and reporting is already intrusive, already an act of cultural or technological imperialism.

This is, of course, the standard position the Chinese government takes in matters of Sino-Western relations. In the official statement issued on 5 June 1989 by the Central Committee of the Chinese Communist Party and the State Council, what happened in Beijing the day before was described as the suppression of a "counterrevolutionary rebellion" started and organized by "political conspirators who have long stubbornly held to the position of bourgeois liberalization, and those who have worked in collusion with foreign and overseas enemies."[26] In the week after the Tiananmen massacre, *Renmin ribao* [People's Daily] reported on the one hand that good foreigners—such as officials of North Korea and the German Democratic Republic—all supported the Chinese government and considered its action fully justifiable.[27] On the other hand, it published a commentator's column to warn bad foreigners to mind their own business, reiterating that "the incident that happens currently in China is entirely China's internal affair," and that no foreign intruding or interfering can be tolerated.[28] The simplistic antagonism between Chinese and foreign Lu Xun ridiculed in his caricature still serves to legitimize this official position. An old Chinese witticism has it that whatever happens, one should never expose family ugliness to outsiders (*jiachou buke waiyang*). In its modern form, as a principle the Party urges the Chinese people to follow particularly in dealing with foreigners, the injunction becomes that the inside and the outside must be different (*neiwai you bie*). From the point of view of the Chinese general public rather than that of the gov-

ernment, then, the question here is not whether the corruption of
the political system and all the other "dark, abominable secrets"
of China are real or fabricated, but whether the Chinese would
be better off if those secrets were to continue to be kept, and
whether we would feel happy and satisfied if things were quietly
rotten in China, while everything looked pretty cheerful from the
outside and nobody out here gave a damn. It was again Lu Xun
who told us that "China had always practiced 'closed-doorism'
so that we would never go out, nor would others be allowed
in."[29] Presumably that was the situation in the good old days before the mid-nineteenth century, but one wonders whether it is
desirable for China to relive that moment of cultural isolationism
and, even if it is, whether it is still at all possible.

    In putting up a statue in Tiananmen in defiance of the official
warning, the Chinese students deliberately created an abomina-
tion to the government, a potent and provocative symbol that
was destined to be interpreted by all. Although the students call
their statue *minzhu nüshen*, which can be translated into English
only as "Goddess of *Democracy*"—not *Liberty*—the statue was
identified as a replica of "Lady Liberty" by the American media
to credit its creation to the influence of the West, and by the Chinese government to tie this symbol to the foreign and the Western. In the same issue of *Radical America* that features Chow's essay, Kay Johnson points out that it is the American media that
have wrongly identified the Chinese statue as "a 'replica' of the
Statue of Liberty," and that the goddess is unmistakably Chinese: "Her posture, apparel and facial features indicated that this
was not an attempt to create a duplicate."[30] Joseph Esherick and
Jeffrey Wasserstrom, who viewed the events in Tiananmen as
"political theater" and emphasized the symbolic meaning of
such theatrical performance, also note that "though Western
journalists often treated this twenty-eight-foot icon as a simple
copy of the Statue of Liberty, and the Chinese government in-
sisted that this was so, the goddess was in reality a more complex symbol combining Western and Chinese motifs, some employed reverently, others ironically."[31] Citing a Chinese source,

Wu Hung reports that the student demonstrators in Beijing indeed wanted at first to make a replica of the Statue of Liberty, but in the end "a Chinese image—a healthy young woman—was preferred instead."[32] Given the Chinese-foreign antagonism and the particular importance attached to names and naming in Chinese political practice, to ascertain the identity of the statue in Tiananmen becomes a pivotal point on which the judgment of the nature of the students' movement depends. There is no denying that the Statue of Liberty does hold a great attraction for the Chinese students, but the creation of a statue of their own is significant precisely because it shows the deepening of the students' self-understanding visibly articulated by this new Chinese image.

It seems strange that Rey Chow would ignore the Chinese name of the statue and insist that the Chinese symbol is indeed a "replica of the Statue of Liberty."[33] But this seemingly wrong identification does something quite significant as a theoretical move, as a strategy in arguing specifically for a Third World feminist theory. This seeming misidentification relates the Chinese statue to the "symbolism of the white-woman-as-liberty," thereby revealing the scandalous fact that all Chinese, "from the astrophysicist Fang Lizhi, to workers, intellectuals, students, and the overseas communities," harbor an illusion about democracy symbolized by this white woman, that they all utter "a naive, idealistic clamor for democracy 'American style.'"[34] So far as I know, Chow is the only one who has identified the Chinese "Goddess of Democracy" as a "white woman," and in doing so, she clearly expresses her frustration that in the "degendered" Chinese clamor for freedom and democracy, the race- and gender-specific Chinese woman or Third World woman is missing, that the Chinese students know nothing whatever about "the issues of gender and sexuality *and* their enmeshment in politics," and that the student leader Chai Ling "does not appear as 'woman' but as 'Chinese.'"[35] When they "should" be fighting as women for women's causes—which might be the key to the solution to all of China's problems—Chai Ling and the other Chinese women, owing to their ignorance of Western theories, are thus "degendered" and are fighting not just as mere Chinese but for a cause very much flawed and doomed: the cause of democracy.

The point of debunking the Chinese "Goddess of Democracy" as a "fetish of the white woman," as Chow indicates, is to lead to a politically superior position of "deconstructing Democracy."[36] That position is superior because it is empowered by a critical consciousness and theoretical reflection that are, unfortunately, "inaccessible to the Chinese who grew up on the Mainland in the past twenty to thirty years." Chow continues:

> They have been, precisely because of the cultural isolationism implemented by the Chinese government at different levels, deprived of the intellectual space that would allow them the kind of critical understanding I am suggesting. An emotional idealism that arises from desperation and that is displaced onto a fetish like the goddess of liberty is the closest they could come to a taste of freedom. There is yet no room—no intellectual room, no reflexive mobility—to understand the history in which the ideal of "democracy" deconstructs itself in the West.[37]

Here we may see the theoretical reason why the Chinese prodemocracy movement would necessarily fail, because even before it could be established in China, democracy has already deconstructed itself *in the West*. Worse still, simply by being who they are, Chinese on the mainland are invariably barred from recognizing democracy as the fraud and anachronism it really is, because it takes someone who has lived under democracy and has experienced the worst of its abuses to begin to have the kind of critical understanding exemplified in Chow's essay. That is to say, only a Western critic can understand critically the problem of China. Having no lived experience of democracy and lacking a critical language and theoretical sophistication as defined in the West, the Chinese on the mainland can at best provide raw materials for the critic in the West to examine and analyze. It is impossible for them to reach the level of intellectual rigor and reflexive mobility that we find in Western theoretical discourse, just as it is impossible for the gorilla King Kong to match the technological prowess of his human captors. Here the twist of political and ideological alliance may seem rather bizarre, but it is not altogether incomprehensible, because, as Henry Louis Gates, Jr., puts it succinctly, "to attempt to appropriate our own discourses by using Western critical theory uncritically is to substitute one mode of neocolonialism for another."[38]

But what if the mainland Chinese were demanding democracy *not* American style, *not* the democracy that has deconstructed itself in the West? In other words, can we think of the Chinese desire for democracy as a desire born on the Chinese mainland rather than a "foreign" and "Western" desire imported from the outside? In another issue of *Radical America*, Paul Thompson reports that among the demonstrators in Beijing, "the number who then believed that Western-style democracy was either desirable or possible was very small," and that the "lessons of democracy were learned on the streets. As traditional authority collapsed and physically disappeared, Beijing became an exhilarating city as people celebrated their capacity to govern everyday life."[39] If so, then "the lessons of democracy" in Beijing streets have little to do with democracy in the West. In fact, some Western scholars doubt whether one should call the events of China's 1989 spring by the name *democracy movement*. According to Esherick and Wasserstrom, "it would be hasty to associate *minzhu* (literally: 'rule of the people') with any conventional Western notion of democracy."[40] Of course, *minzhu* is used in Chinese as the *equivalent* of "democracy," just as *shangdi* has been the Chinese equivalent of "God," and *tian* the equivalent of "Heaven." A terminological controversy can flare up at any point on how exactly equivalent these Chinese terms are for their Western originals or counterparts, but one may argue that even if democracy in China must somehow follow a Western model, it will still be, when it materializes, not an exact and precise copy of the West, but a democracy as Chinese as the Yellow River. But what's wrong with that? Why is there such fixation on purity of terms on the one hand, and on the other such fear of losing one's own self and becoming like the Other? As Lu Xun observes, the fact that we eat beef and mutton does not mean that we are turning ourselves into something "that resembles cows and sheep."[41] After all, isn't this the whole point of the traveling of theory? Isn't the dissemination of ideas in different cultures over and above antagonism and resistance one of the basic cultural experiences of our times? Unlike the whiteness of a white woman, democracy is not racially "overdetermined" in the genes; it can migrate to a different cultural environment and reach what Said describes as the fourth stage of its journey, when "the now full (or partly) accommodated (or incorporated) idea is to some extent transformed by its new uses, its new position in a new time and place."[42]

Nevertheless, given the undeniable cultural isolation and theoretical ignorance of the young Chinese on the mainland, perhaps I should admit that there is indeed "no intellectual room, no reflexive mobility" in the Chinese mind to understand democracy and its self-deconstruction. That does not mean, however, that the Chinese mind on the mainland is totally empty, because the mind, like nature, abhors a vacuum. If the intellectual room of the Chinese mind is not yet filled with knowledge of democracy and its failure, it is unfortunately filled with something quite as horrible, namely, the knowledge of the evil of totalitarianism. The young Chinese may not have enough Western education to know what democracy is and whether it is really what they want, but they certainly have enough Chinese experience to know what they do *not* want. In fact, their "naive, idealistic clamor for democracy" may be better described as a negative reaction to totalitarianism than as a positive response to democracy. In this sense, then, it is perhaps justifiable to view, as Chow does, the volcanic agitation in Tiananmen during the demonstrations as nothing but "emotional idealism." In defying a repressive totalitarian regime controlled by octogenarian communist leaders, the young Chinese may very likely have idealized the West as a projected image of their own dream of freedom and democracy. But is it fair to claim that only the Chinese should plead guilty of this "emotional idealism"? Has not the myth of the Other also found its way into the heart of the West and made many Westerners idealize China as the site of *their* dreams and utopias? The stern look of a truly critical consciousness will then have to demythologize the Other and desentimentalize the emotional idealism that obscures our vision of reality, the political reality that is so fundamentally different in one as opposed to the other. China and the West—need we be reminded once again?—are two different worlds, and the traveling of theory from the one to the other may prove to be a very risky odyssey indeed.

What's in a Name?

The difference between the two worlds and the mutual idealization bring me back to the discrepancy mentioned earlier between Liu Zaifu's theory and its Western counterpart, and above all to my own discontent with an essay that appears excellent to Mitchell. As someone who tried to introduce contemporary Western literary theory to Chinese readers in the early 1980s and has since been interested in Chinese-Western comparative studies of literature, I have no problem whatsoever with Chow's "using Western theory on Chinese literature," and I certainly would not charge her with being "too Westernized," a charge she found both "moralistic" and "devastating," coming from some backwater quarters of sinology beclouded by the influence of Orientalism.[43] What I find problematic in her essay, then, is not so much a misapplication of Western theory to the Chinese situation as the very context of her discussion, the ideological and political context from which she speaks in response to the so-called China crisis. Chow has herself clearly outlined this ideological context when she explains why she feels upset by the symbolism of the Chinese statue: "In the eyes of many U.S. leftist intellectuals, it is disturbing to see young Chinese students fighting for their cause with this symbolism. Don't they know what atrocities have been committed in the name of liberty and democracy? we ask implicitly or explicitly."[44]

A simple answer to that question might be, first of all, that the

Chinese statue was created in China and understood by the Chinese; that it was not meant to disturb American leftist intellectuals. And second, it is a bit strange and unfair, to say the least, to deny the Chinese their right to choose freedom and democracy simply because some American intellectuals find it disturbing, or because American imperialists and British colonialists have committed atrocities "in the name of liberty and democracy." The abuse of democracy does not invalidate the democratic ideal, and what the Chinese fight for is, of course, not the *name* but the *substance* of a democratic society.

A question one may put to the "U.S. leftist intellectuals"— whoever they are—is, Why should they feel disturbed by the prodemocracy movement in China? This is precisely one of the questions the editors of *Radical America* are also asking. In the introduction to the special issue on China and Mexico, the editors express their mistrust of the Western media as well as their anxiety over "the either/or's through which China's crisis is being interpreted: socialism versus capitalism, communism or democracy." Such emotional as well as political reactions lead to a number of questions: "And yet, as Leftists, we are deeply troubled. Can we continue to insist that the vision of socialism we claim, inspired by Marx, is still to be realized, that none of the societies of 'actually existing socialism' deserve their names, that Marxism continues to live, but only outside history?"[45]

These are indeed important questions we constantly face in the historical reality of our times, and, like all important questions, they admit no easy answer. If one considers Marx's vision of the future communist society and his prophecy that socialist revolution would arise in the most developed industrial countries in Western Europe and North America, one may well argue that none of the countries of "actually existing socialism" really resembles what Marx had in mind. I do not know whether this is turning Marxism into a mere futuristic theory outside history, but I do believe that it is not in the best interest of the American Left to turn a deaf ear to the cry for democracy and freedom in China as if they had a moral obligation to support the Chinese government simply because it calls itself Marxist. The name and the thing do not always go together, and the discrepancy between a Marxist rhetoric and a totalitarian realpolitik may account for the apparent logical absurdity that the leaders of a People's Republic could order the People's Liberation Army to kill its own people. In fact, in cases like this, Western literary theory, or simply a little logic and common sense, may prove helpful in revealing the difference between the name and the thing, the signifier and the signified, or the political rhetoric of a reified People and the average Chinese in reality. To ease the anxiety of some U.S. leftist intellectuals, it may be therapeutically necessary to show how the political symbolism of the reified People has deconstructed itself in China.

"Serve the People" is the title of one of Mao's short essays, written before the Party took over China, and it quickly became the core of a political rhetoric that has provided legitimation for the rule of the People's Republic since its founding in 1949. As the motto of the Party, the five characters of this phrase are written on a big red wall facing the street at the Gate of New China [Xinhuamen], the main entrance to the huge compound where the Party and government leaders take their residence in Beijing. The gilded Chinese characters cast in bas-relief literally transform the wall into a gigantic quotation from Chairman Mao in his own handwriting, and designate the nature of the place as the residence of a People's government, while obliterating the old meaning of this place as the former palace of the emperor and the royal family. The palaces of Beijing have housed China's emperors since Kublai Khan in the thirteenth century, but the gate leading to the compound has been renamed to highlight the idea that those who now rule from here are no longer emperors of feudal China but leaders of New China, leaders of a proletarian revolution, the jealous guardians of the collective interest of all the Chinese people. Chairman Mao's dictum inscribed on the wall presents the guiding principle of this political theory as a primary text for every passerby to read; thus the gate with its new name and the wall with the inscription turn into a sort of symbolic text, what Mikhail Bakhtin would call "material bearers of meaning" or "bodies of meaning," of which "even a simple brick . . . expresses something through its form."[46] What is expressed by the gate and wall is of course an emphatically denoted difference, or rather a desire for difference, between New China and her imperial past, a difference called for by the very location of the gate and wall that form the entrance to what was once an imperial palace.

Put in the Chinese context, the renaming of the gate is by no means trivial. The "rectification of names [*zheng ming*]," as Confucius maintains, ought to be the first step in administration, because the proper word or name will indicate the appropriate nature of government policies and invest them with justification and legitimacy.[47] Here the name and the thing named are understood as one, and this politics of naming is essential to the politics of ruling. The place names in Beijing and elsewhere in China are thus thoroughly politicized; they all bespeak the political stability and social harmony under a benign government: *Xinhuamen* means "Gate of New China," *Tiananmen* means "Gate of Heavenly Peace," and *Changanjie*, the wide street leading to Tiananmen from both the east and the west side of the city, means "Avenue of Permanent Peace." Bearing such names, Chinese gates, walls, streets, and buildings weave into a gigantic geo-graphical text that inscribes the cultural myth of a perfect political order on the physical features of the land, a myth that renders the violent nature of power and domination almost invisible, and thereby fulfills, as Roland Barthes puts it, "the task of giving an historical intention a natural justification, and making contingency appear eternal."[48]

In Beijing's urban iconography, the gate and wall of the government leaders' residence thus function as "material bearers of meaning," and what is changed by a new name and an added inscription is of course not their materiality but the meaning they bear. Instead of being part of an imperial palace serving the emperor, they are now assigned a totally different function, a new meaning in the political rhetoric that designates the nature of the communist government as that of a public servant, one that operates to "Serve the People." Indeed, the elevated word *People* features prominently in the language of New China, which is now the People's Republic governed with the force of a People's Liberation Army. The People, as every Chinese citizen learned in the numerous meetings and political study groups, are now masters of the country. In reality, however, the Gate of New China and the wall bearing Chairman Mao's handwriting serve yet another purpose: they are not just material *bearers* of a rhetorical meaning but also material *barriers* that mark out a boundary, that open and close, selectively include and exclude. Therefore, as barriers that hide the other side—the physicality of an imperial palace and the absolute power of a centralized government residing in it—they form a facade of hypocrisy that has an uneasy and precarious relationship with the meaning they bear, and consequently run the risk of subjecting that allegorical meaning, the political rhetoric and cultural myth of the People's New China, to the exposure of irony, the undoing of a devastating literalization.

The citizens of Beijing who pass the Gate of New China in their daily routine probably seldom reflect on the meaning of such architectural symbolism, but even if they do, in their quotidian sanity they would understand the gate and wall in a literal sense—that is, as barriers that mark out the boundary of a sacred enclosure, a modern Forbidden City from which the ordinary Chinese are strictly excluded. The rhetorical meaning of the wall and the gate, the message that emanates so glaringly from Mao's gilded calligraphy, is not so much ignored as received and understood—that is, understood properly as sheer political rhetoric, as elevated words not to be taken literally. When the country as a whole seems to lie in a spiritual torpor, the tension between the literal and the rhetorical remains largely dormant; the rhetoric of political indoctrination has the look of high seriousness. It seems to reign supreme, and its self-inconsistency is not subjected to the damaging effect of a repressed Rabelaisian laughter.[49] In a time of crisis, however, such tension and inconsistency are no longer left unexposed and unexplored. When students and ordinary citizens in Beijing rose up to challenge the authority of China's communist leadership, one of the powerful means by which they questioned the legitimacy of the regime was precisely a deliberate literal reading of political rhetoric, an ironic gesture that forced the meaning, or meaninglessness, of politically elevated words to unfold in public.

In late April 1989, when the students came to the Gate of New China to demand a dialogue with the government leaders, more soldiers were immediately sent to guard the gate and the wall that instructs them to "Serve the People." On 22 April, three student representatives attempted to make a petition, on their knees, on the steps in front of the Great Hall of the People, the building on one side of Tiananmen Square in which the People's Congress holds its meetings, and also the building from which, on 4 June, the riot police and soldiers dashed out to "clear" the square. The students' gesture, the usual ritual of prostration that ordinary people must perform before the emperor, stands out in sharp relief against the hollow name of the hall as well as the empty words cast on the wall at the Gate of New China. Such a gesture thus turns out to be not one of humiliation but a provocative gesture of irony that reveals the true relationship between the people of China and their leaders, a relationship not so different from the one in Old China despite all the political rhetoric to the contrary. These gestures, the literalization of political slogans and rhetoric, all have the symbolic force to disclose the true nature of the official culture of the People's Republic, a culture of a politically elevated People, in which real people are subjugated by their alienated and "perverse double."[50] The decisive exposure of the totalitarian nature of this People's Republic, however, came from the barrel of a gun, when the People's Liberation Army did shoot the people despite the logic of its name. If Marx were alive to see all this, he probably would be the first to disown such state powers of communism.

And yet, many American leftist intellectuals are disturbed, and their anxiety is genuine. "When Western political leaders and media are trumpeting a 'crisis of communism,'" as Thompson puts it clearly and astutely, "the Left is understandably reluctant to appear to be endorsing their judgements."[51] Here we may have a sense of *déjà vu*, of seeing yet another rehearsal of the same kind of antagonistic mentality Lu Xun caricatured more than half a century ago. The antagonism here is of course not between the Chinese and the foreign, but between the Left and the Right, the radical and the conservative; nevertheless, the absurdity and stupidity of such a mentality remain the same. It is unlikely that many American leftist intellectuals would know that satirical passage from Lu Xun, but they probably have read this widely popular quotation from Chairman Mao, which was included in *Quotations from Chairman Mao Tse-tung*, the "little red bible," back in the 1960s: "We should support whatever the enemy opposes and oppose whatever the enemy supports."[52] This categorical statement of a political stance is logically dubious and practically inapplicable. The American Left would fall precisely into the pit of the "either/or's" if it appeared to endorse Chinese political leaders in order to oppose Western political leaders, to believe in the Chinese official media in order to mistrust Western media, and to deconstruct democracy in order to embrace "socialism."

But who is the real enemy? Where does that leave the Chinese students and the Chinese people? Should the American Left dismiss the whole mass movement in China, the former Soviet Union, and Eastern Europe as merely "a naive, idealistic clamor for democracy 'American style'"? And why should anyone hate democracy simply because it is "American" and "Western"? Or, to paraphrase Lu Xun, why should *we* eat flies simply because *they* emphasize hygiene? In much the same vein Liu Zaifu also asks: "Why should we send as gifts 'freedom,' 'democracy,' 'humanism,' 'love,' and all such beautiful words and concepts to the bourgeoisie?"[53] In facing the political situation in China and the other socialist countries, as Paul Thompson argues,

the Left not only needs to firmly back the reform process, but to finally dispense with talk of "bourgeois" democracy. There was nothing bourgeois about the freedoms to think, organize, demonstrate and choose a government being fought for by the people of Beijing and other cities. I believe that the people of China want a democratic socialism rather than a return to capitalism. But I also believe that they should have the right to choose.[54]

Never mind whether "the people of China," or actually the government, are now choosing, in the 1990s, capitalism or "a democratic socialism"; the relevant question is: Are the leftist intellectuals in the United States ready to grant the Chinese the right to choose? Is the American Left willing to look into the unpleasant reality in China rather than preserve its ideological purity intact "outside history"? This is, of course, by no means to forgo the critical responsibility of the intellectuals to criticize. The right to criticize political corruption and social evil without peril and retaliation is precisely what the Chinese intellectuals fight for in their hope for democracy. And in that cause, they definitely need support from intellectuals and people all over the world. American leftist intellectuals can begin to dissolve their anxiety by refusing to be cornered in the mentality of the "either/or's," the antagonistic mentality that Lu Xun urged us to discard. They will not find the behavior of the Chinese students disturbing once they stop misreading the symbolism the students use and stop judging according to Western critical standards what the Chinese do on the Chinese mainland.

This is not to say that Western literary and cultural theories are useless in China. On the contrary, Western theory, when grabbed and assimilated by Chinese intellectuals, plays an important role in the cultural, ideological, and political transformations of China. The tremendous official Chinese resistance to Western theory already testifies to its power and relevance. But when theory travels to a different culture and plays a role in the transformation of that culture, theory itself is also transformed. The role of Western theory in China must therefore be understood and evaluated from a perspective grounded in Chinese reality. Otherwise it will only be misunderstood and misevaluated.

But what is Chinese reality, and for that matter, any reality? Given the skeptic and sometimes even agnostic attitude characteristic of much of contemporary Western theory, this seems a question to which any confident answer is likely to be contested by all sorts of theoretical inquisitions. Indeed, if the ability to analyze television *representation* of reality *as fictionality* and to translate Chinese political events into the film language of *King Kong* is considered theoretical sophistication, any argument for the existence of reality outside fictional discourse and the textuality of representation will surely appear "naive" and "superficial." After all, I was watching the events at Tiananmen Square on a color television in the United States, far from the danger of the immediate political confrontation in China. How can I be sure that what I was watching was really not Tiananmen but *King Kong*? How can I be sure that there *was* a massacre in Beijing? I did not die in Beijing in June 1989, and those who did cannot come to America to bear witness to their own deaths. How can I be sure that here we are not facing again a theoretically interesting aporia where, as Shoshana Felman puts it so elegantly with regard to the Holocaust, there is a "radical impossibility of witnessing"?[55] But being a Chinese who grew up on the mainland, I am afraid that to indulge in such profound theoretical meditations is an intellectual luxury I neither can afford nor care to procure.

Vis-à-vis the sophisticated argument for the impossibility of reality, then, I shall suggest not that we simply call a spade a spade but that we extend our skepticism to the very skeptic theory that relinquishes any hope of knowing and therefore acting upon and making changes in reality. To be sure, no one can claim to know the totality of what is real in one's individual understanding, but that ought not to paralyze and trap us in a vertiginous reflection on the endless deferring of the real in our necessarily finite knowledge. The stakes are simply too high. Instead I would suggest that Chinese reality, not unlike the Chinese philosophical notion of *tao*, exists nowhere and everywhere: nothing contains it in totality but everything bears it in part. Reality exists, as the philosopher Zhuangzi says in a deliberate decrescendo of the mysterious *tao*, in even the smallest and the meanest part of our world: in ants, in weeds, in earthen ware, in urine, and in excrement.[56] It exists, quite simply, in our daily experience of the world and constitutes the circumstances, the physical, social, and cultural environment of our lives, the very condition and substance of our being.

What I am calling "reality" here is similar to what Edward Said calls "the world," and I believe that it is important to reiterate the point he makes about the "worldliness" or "circumstantiality" of texts, that "texts are worldly, to some degree they are events, and, even when they appear to deny it, they are nevertheless a part of the social world, human life, and of course the historical moments in which they are located and interpreted."[57] As critics and scholars we may have different interpretations of the world and the events that happen in it, but the existence of the world and events is beyond question and, ultimately, it is reality or the world that places constraints on our interpretations. Chinese reality and what happened in June 1989 in Beijing, then, are not just a series of flickering pictures on the television screen but are rooted in the social and political history of China, and the analysis of television representation of the events in Beijing, no matter how profound and sophisticated it may appear, will only be truly superficial if it takes television texts as mere fictional representation without a trace of their worldliness and circumstantiality, and if it says nothing about the social and political history of China that gradually but inevitably led to the confrontation in Tiananmen.

If we do not negate the reality of political confrontation, how then should a truly oppositional discourse operate to engage itself in such a confrontation? If the Chinese students are opposed to the brute force of a state machine, it should follow that the oppositional discourse that speaks for the Chinese should also be courageously opposed to the same state machine and reenact the same opposition on the level of discursive theoretical analysis. This is what Western oppositional discourse does in the West, notably feminism, African American criticism, gay and lesbian studies, Marxist literary criticism and other politically leftist theories. Reading Chow's essay and Mitchell's endorsement, however, I find it hard to understand why they should stop at opposition when they confront the political reality in China. Could it be, as Bruce Robbins argues, that oppositional discourse is requisite for the literary profession, that "the words 'opposi- tional' and 'professional' are not antithetical"?[58] In other words, within the academic institution of the Western university and its professional literary critics, oppositional discourse is precisely conformist as professional performance; it is doing what the pro- fession requires, which has nothing to do with Chinese reality. "The thrust of the argument is to take any merit away from op- position; in being oppositional, [Stanley] Fish says, you are just following the profession's orders."[59] There is a certain danger in this argument that forecloses any possibility of genuine opposi- tion in critical discourse, which cannot be totally compromised by being cast as professional performance. And yet the question remains: How does one relate the oppositional discourse as pro- fessional performance in American academia to the political op- position in the real world? We now seem to return to the initial question of traveling theory: What can and does Western theory do in the cultural and political environment of China?

Said's idea, as I see it, of texts as worldly events and as placing themselves in the world emphasizes the actual force of texts to make a difference in the transformation of reality. The force of texts as texts, however, is not physical but mental, not material but spiritual. This is significant because the immateriality of texts as ideas and theories makes it very difficult and indeed impossi- ble for any state power to block completely the traveling of the- ory and effectively to stop the dissemination of ideas that may have potentially subversive implications. In China, historical evidence goes a long way back to the very first centralized state power under Qin Shi Huangdi, China's first emperor (third century B.C.E.), who not only initiated the project of building the Great Wall to ward off the physical force of the nomadic tribes coming from the northern steppes but also burned books in or- der to eliminate the spiritual force of ideas in China. The Great

Wall was never really the effective deterrent it was designed to be, and the burning of books was a complete failure. The spiritual edifice of ideas and theories cannot be destroyed by material fires, and that is bad news for all thought police and controllers of ideas, whether they are the first emperor of China, the Roman Catholic Index compilers, Adolf Hitler, or Mao and his Red Guards. The problem that the Chinese government has with metaphorical "spiritual pollution" lies precisely in its metaphoricity, in the fact that the "pollution" is spiritual. In fact, the spiritual force of ideas and theories manifests itself most powerfully when it is engaged in opposition to cultural and political orthodoxy, when it appeals to our critical consciousness, which, as Said observes, is nothing but "an unstoppable predilection for alternatives."[60] Reading contemporary Chinese literature and criticism, the search for alternatives is everywhere apparent and unstoppable in all their stylistic, methodological, and ideological experiments. Ultimately, it is in the light of such opposition and antagonism, such pursuit of alternatives, that we must understand the meaning of Western theory and the role it plays *within* the cultural and political environment of China.

CHAPTER 6

Postmodernism and the Return
of the Native

The year 1989 has particular significance in recent Chinese
history, for it will not only be long remembered as the year of
student demonstration and its subsequent bloody suppression
by the government, but it also marks the end of a period of cultural critique and the attempt at liberation of the mind during
the 1980s, in which Chinese intellectuals played an important
role, after decades of self-enclosure and isolation, in opening up
windows toward the outside world and introducing new ideas
and values into the cultural arena of post-Mao China. In many
respects, the cultural critique of the 1980s continued the critique
of China's past, especially Confucianism as the cultural and political mainstream, that an earlier generation of Chinese intellectuals had started in the May Fourth movement in 1919. The critique of traditional culture in the 1980s, however, took on a special contemporary relevance, implicitly and even explicitly criticizing the more recent past of Mao's China, and ultimately tend-
ing toward the transformation of China into a modern democratic society in which all the citizens should enjoy basic rights
and freedom. In the political context of China of the 1980s, such a
tendency clearly ran counter to the interest and agenda of the
political establishment, and as a result officially sponsored ideological campaigns against "spiritual pollution" and "bourgeois
liberalization" were launched one after another throughout the
whole period till the confrontation reached its height in Tiananmen Square in June 1989, symbolized by the destruction of the
students' statue—the "Goddess of Democracy." Seen in this per-

spective, then, the events of 1989 did not come about suddenly, without prelude or forewarning.

The massacre in Beijing, however, came as a shock to all sides of the political confrontation and had profound consequences in the social and economic life of China. In the 1990s, the government has relaxed its grip on economic reform and commercial activity in the private sector while further tightening its ideological control in schools and its censorship of publications. In a way, neo-authoritarianism, which had been briefly but intensely debated among Chinese intellectuals in the late 1980s, became a social practice rather than an academic discussion. That is to say, relaxation in economic policies and the tightening of ideological control put in practice the core idea of neo-authoritarianism: that China, owing to its special social and economic conditions, cannot afford to have democracy but must strengthen the authority and centralized power of the state in order to move the country into an economically and technologically defined modernity or, in the official discourse of the government, the "four modernizations" of agriculture, industry, national defense, and science and technology. To some extent, Singapore may offer a model for this kind of modern and prosperous neo-authoritarian state without democracy, and the talk of a Confucian ethic as allegedly contributing to the so-called miracle of East Asian industrialization serves to reinforce the idea of an East Asian alternative to modernization. At the same time, open, large-scale defiance and public protest have all but disappeared, and the cry for democracy and political freedom subsided in the wake of the horrible events at Tiananmen. Very quickly, waves of commercialization and consumerism have engulfed the entire Chinese society; the craze for money and the rise of popular culture seem to have rendered the ideas, values, and concerns of the intellectuals rather irrelevant. Economic changes have thus brought about new and serious challenges to Chinese intellectuals in addition to great political pressure, and the social environment of the 1990s has become markedly different from that of the 1980s.

In the Hong Kong journal *Twenty-first Century*, Yu Ying-shih

published an influential article in 1991 on the "marginalization of
Chinese intellectuals," in which he argues that modern history
has witnessed the rapid decline of the social status of Chinese
intellectuals from their central role of *shi* or literati-officials in the
traditional political system to their increasing marginalization,
both politically and culturally, since the beginning of this century, when Western ideas, especially Marxism, gradually took
over mainland China and made traditional, native cultural values insignificant or irrelevant. In the last hundred years, says Yu,
"Chinese intellectuals have withdrawn themselves toward the
very margin of Chinese culture on the one hand, and have constantly paced up and down the margin of Western culture on the
other, like a lonely boat lost at sea and unable to reach the shore
in either direction."[1] Although he clearly stated that in writing
the article, he wanted "to unfold a historical problem as objec-
tively as possible and not to make any value judgment,"[2] Yu's
argument helped initiate a debate on the role of intellectuals in
premodern and modern times that necessarily mixed discussion
of historical issues with evaluation of the historical process itself.
In the specific context of the 1990s, the "marginalization of intellectuals" rings particularly true and quickly takes on a meaning
of its own, not intended by Yu Ying-shih in his initial discussion
but particularly relevant to the current situation in mainland
China. Many scholars have begun to talk about the "loss of the
humanistic spirit" or the "decline of elite culture in modern China." What they mean by this is not the forced retreat of Chinese
intellectuals that Yu envisioned, from their traditional role of
literati-officials and active participation in the political system to
their marginalized irrelevance in modern times, but a recent
phenomenon in mainland China where intellectuals, as Chen
Pingyuan puts it, are turned into "modern Don Quixotes," who
are "not only punished by political authorities for their deviation
from the orthodoxy, but are also abandoned by the market for
their 'morality,' 'ideals,' and 'passion.'"[3] For Chen Pingyuan, the
decline of high culture is definitely an urgent current issue,
though it can be traced to some historical roots, especially mis-

takes that intellectuals themselves have made in their "cultural choices," in cultivating a "'pan-political' consciousness, the worship of 'revolution,' and the myth of a 'plebeian literature.'"[4] That is to say, Chinese intellectuals themselves have, in the last hundred years, advocated a radical populism that has finally materialized with a vengeance and pushed intellectuals and their spiritual values to the margin of social and cultural life in China.

Most scholars lament this marginalization of intellectuals in a society swept by commercialization, the rise of consumerism, and a lowbrow, valueless popular culture, but some also see it as part of the inevitable concomitant of modernization and market economy. For example, Zhao Yiheng, who teaches Chinese at the University of London, presents a view almost directly opposite to that of Yu Ying-shih. He does not see the marginalization of intellectuals as a decline, nor does he think the close involvement of Confucian literati-officials in the traditional political system an enviable position, because that involvement made it almost impossible to have any critique of institutional rules and regulations, while such cultural critique, the subversion and transformation of the social and cultural mainstream, Zhao maintains, should be "the proper business of intellectuals."[5] In a modern society, according to Zhao, intellectuals should carry out a "pure critique" from the haven of the academy or university to counter the utilitarian and mammonist tendencies of the populace in society, and therefore the marginalization of intellectuals in China today, he declares, "is fortunate rather than disastrous, a success rather than failure," because it offers Chinese intellectuals, for the very first time in history, the opportunity to discard their traditional roles as literati-officials, as revolutionaries or spiritual leaders, or as obedient singers in praise of officially sanctioned social values. Instead, marginalization makes it possible for intellectuals to engage in "pure critique" of the orthodoxy according to their humanistic values and from an outside but independent position.[6] The call to embrace marginalization is evidently a deliberate overstatement, almost a stylistic indulgence on Zhao's part. Moreover, the independence of intellectuals in the safe haven of the academy as Zhao describes it is more an ideal situation to be devoutly hoped for than a political reality in China, where educational, research, and publishing institutions are under tight—though not always effective—control and surveillance, now compounded with the pressure of decreasing funds and the loss of respectability for intellectual work. The idea of cultural critique as the specific responsibility of intellectuals from outside the political system and cultural establishment, rather than from within, however, is an important point. The "pure critique" is thus ultimately a political critique, a resistance to and critique of the official discourse in culture and politics. Whatever one may think of the marginalization of intellectuals or the decline of high culture, it is clear that marginalization is a fact in the China of the 1990s, which provides a cultural and political environment significantly different from that of the 1980s, and it is in this new environment that a whole set of new problems, new theories, and new debates has emerged, and it is also in this new environment that we must consider their impact and significance.

Orientalism in the Chinese Context

Edward Said's pathbreaking book *Orientalism* was first published in 1978, when China had just come out of the nightmare of a ten-year-long self-inflicted torture known as the Great Proletarian Cultural Revolution, in which the official discourse of anti-imperialism, anticolonialism, antifeudalism, anticapitalism, and antirevisionism, produced and propagated through official news media and the Communist Party organs, served to justify widespread violence in the country and to legitimize China as the self-appointed center of world revolution, with Mao Zedong as its godlike supreme leader. That is to say, the radical anti-Western discourse of the Cultural Revolution was in fact a political rhetoric to justify the totalitarian rule at home and to disguise a modern version of sinocentrism abroad. In this context, Said's book and its anti-imperialist and anticolonialist argument, though radical and subversive in the context of the Western world, would strike many Chinese readers, if in an unlikely situation they were able to find the book and read it, as imparting a message that seemed in the end surprisingly familiar, reminiscent in subtle ways of what they had heard during the Cultural Revolution about the hegemony of the capitalist West and the heroic struggle of two-thirds of the world's population yet to be liberated from hegemonic domination by the superpowers. That would probably be a gross misreading of Said, but if the "text" of Said's book is to have any bearing on the Chinese "world," as Said himself would have argued in a manner suggested by his essay "Traveling Theory," the argument of Orientalism would have to assume "a new position in a new time and place."[7] Perhaps because of the difference in the political and cultural conditions in China and the West, it was difficult for Said's work to assume a position that would have had an inspiring and liberating effect in China at that time, and consequently Orientalism, despite its tremendous impact in American academic circles, was neither widely known to Chinese readers nor appreciated by them in the 1980s.

In the very different cultural environment of the 1990s, however, Said, like many other postmodern and postcolonial theorists and critics, has become quite well known on the Chinese mainland. Both Orientalism and the more recent Culture and Imperialism have been discussed in Chinese publications, initiating a serious debate not just about Western representations of the Orient but, more important, about the relationship between China and the West in the twentieth century and the function of Western theories and critical concepts when they are introduced to Chinese readers and adopted by Chinese critics. Quite in conformity with Said's own convictions, the theoretical debate in China inspired by Orientalism is not literary or purely textual, but directly involved with political issues, as indeed all debates in China tend to be. Those who introduce Said's works to China are often Chinese students educated in American universities; they are mostly young scholars well informed of the latest developments in Western literary theory and criticism, and they often speak with the sense of being a new generation of critics who differentiate themselves from all earlier generations in modern times at home, above all from critics of the 1980s who had inherited the critical legacy of the May Fourth new-culture movement in promoting freedom and democracy in post-Mao China. In other words, from 4 May 1919 to 4 June 1989, the entire modern period is seen by these critics as dominated by a misplaced trust in Western values of freedom and democracy and the efficacy of modernization, by the influence of the Western discourse of Orientalism. If the Cultural Revolution and its anti-imperialist rhetoric were discredited during the 1980s, in opening up discussions of Orientalism and postcolonialism, critics of the new generation tend to take a revisionist view of both that political rhetoric and its critique. When considering the significance of Said's works in post-Mao China, as we read in an article that introduced Said to the Chinese reading public in 1993, written by a Chinese student studying in the United States, Chinese readers are likely to ask, given their experience of the Cultural Revolution and its rhetoric: Have we not heard enough of the talk about imperialism, about hegemony? The question is meant to be rhetorical, and the answer given in that article is firm and clear: No, not enough, indeed. For China is still, we are told, under "the shadow of imperialist hegemony," and "the 'culture fever' of the 1980s testified yet once more to the persistence of imperialist hegemonism."[8] Thus the appropriation of Said's works in the 1990s serves to revamp the old discourse in China on imperialism, colonialism, and Western hegemony, and to react against the cultural critique of the 1980s, which is seen as reiterating the modernist discourse predicated on such Western concepts and values as freedom, democracy, and modernization itself. Transplanted into the Chinese context, then, Said's theory of Orientalism is employed to resituate a domestic cultural critique onto a map of global confrontation, in which sentiments of nationalism tend to be easily rekindled, and vaguely conceived native values easily embraced as desirable alternatives, while discussion of modern Chinese history and culture is increasingly cast in the binary op-

position between the East and the West, Third World victimization and Western hegemonic imperialism.

It is interesting to note, however, that the East-West dichotomy
works rather differently in Said's theory and its transformation
in China. If Said in his critique aimed at Western imperialism
and colonialism, especially the discourse of Western scholars in
Oriental studies that misrepresent peoples and cultures of the
East, discussions of Said's works in China often target domestic
cultural productions as a sort of self-colonization or shameful
surrender to Western hegemony. The rather surprising connection of the cultural critique of the 1980s with "the persistence of
imperialist hegemonism," as we just saw above, is an indication
of how the critical discourse of Said's *Orientalism* is assimilated
to participate in discussions of Chinese culture and history that
have real political implications in this domestic orientation. For
example, having introduced the basic ideas of *Orientalism* and
Culture and Imperialism, a critic writing in the widely read Beijing
journal *Dushu* [Reading Monthly] quickly turns his critique to
works by Chinese writers and artists and maintains that many
artistic works, including films made by Zhang Yimou that have
won a number of foreign awards, all try to "offer some unthinkable and improbable objects to make Westerners feel stimulated,
intoxicated, or sickened, to produce in Western audiences what
in aesthetics is called the 'sense of the sublime,' the feeling of
pity and racial superiority in culture." Autobiographical works
that reflect on their authors' sufferings in China during the Cultural Revolution, such as Nien Cheng's *Life and Death in Shanghai*,
Chang Jung's *Wild Swans*, and Wu Ningkun's *A Single Tear*, draw
especially sharp criticism from him. "It would perhaps be too
cruel," the critic intones with a vehement sarcasm, "to blame
them for deliberately catering to the taste of Western readers and
soliciting pity and money with their wounds and pus-oozing ul-
cers. The point I want to make is that the appreciation of these
works by the Western reading public has something to do with
the mode of Orientalism."[9] Likewise Chinese scholarly works, he
continues, do nothing but mimicking of Western Orientalist dis-

course: "In the 'cultural reflections' of the mid- to late 1980s, some people cursed their own ancestors and knocked them down. They scolded the Chinese for their conservatism, xenophobia, and selfishness, their muddleheadedness, their being unscientific, illogical, unhygienic, and immoral."[10] From the critical perspective informed by Said's works, this critic feels empowered enough to lump together the various cultural theories and discussions in China from the late nineteenth century up to the 1980s and dismiss them all as inadequate reactions to the impact of the West, as one form or another of "Occidentalism," which he defines as "an impetuous, blind, and irrational attitude toward Western culture produced by Chinese scholars under the impact of a strong and dominant Western civilization."[11]

Such a sweeping dismissal of all the ideas and theories that have been proposed in the last hundred years of Chinese history may strike one as incredibly arrogant and astonishingly self-righteous, and indeed it serves to empower those critics who claim to have escaped from Western influence and been able to counter the hegemony of Western imperialism on behalf of the native Chinese tradition. Polemically characterizing the cultural critique of the 1980s as "cursing ancestors" and "scolding" the Chinese for their alleged failings, this critic seems to make an emotional plea for preserving the native tradition, the honor of "ancestors," and the Chinese national pride against a Westernized modernist discourse, the discourse of Orientalism. And yet, such a burst of patriotic sentiment and defense of Chinese culture do not well up from any deep conviction of the intrinsic values of the native heritage, but as the result of contemporary Western education, the assimilation of the latest development in Western literary and cultural theories, especially the theories of Orientalism, postcolonialism, and postmodernism. The critic cited above, Zhang Kuan, identifies himself in the article as a graduate student from mainland China being educated in the United States, and thus speaks from the privileged position of someone privy to the inside of the West. From that position of intimate knowledge of Western theories, he is able to admonish

Chinese scholars at home, in a way that reminds one of a schoolmaster lecturing his naive pupils, "not to hasten to join in the chorus of Orientalism like a swarm of bumblebees."[12] What appears in his article as vindication of the native Chinese tradition against a hegemonic West turns out to be the outcome of a Western education, and his quick dismissal of all the native cultural theories since the late nineteenth century serves to prove an implied point that the latest Western theory supersedes all earlier theories. Ironically, then, it is still the West that offers the framework for a critique of Western hegemony and provides correct answers to all the questions in China.

The response to Said's works in mainland China is of course quite diverse, and at the core of many discussions is again the relationship between China and the West, native tradition and foreign ideas. Because of the different problems they face in their own cultural and political environment, Chinese scholars have responded to the theory of Orientalism in ways that differ significantly from how Said's work was received in the West. One interesting example is a conversation among five scholars in Beijing, published in *Dushu* in January 1994 as a response to articles on Said in earlier issues. Although not speaking as one unified voice, the five interlocutors all consider the implications of Orientalism in the context of Chinese society in modern times, and they are obviously concerned more about what Said's theory means or does in China than about the specifics of that theory itself. Because of such a perspective, what they see as dangerous and directly relevant to the current Chinese situation is not so much the threat of Western imperialism as that of a narrow-minded nationalism and conservatism in the native tradition. Tao Dongfeng identifies the problematic relationship between national characteristics and modernization as the "paradoxical anxiety" of Chinese intellectuals since the May Fourth movement, and so he believes that "the condemnation of Orientalism has at least to some extent satisfied the sinocentric sentiments of some intellectuals and has an intrinsic connection with the cultural conservatism, the Eastern culture regenerationism, and the trend of anti-Westernization that have surfaced in the cultural debate in recent years."[13] Zhang Fa expresses some doubt about West-centeredness as a "conscious conspiracy" deliberately propagated by Westerners, and he argues that though moderniz-ation may be a global tendency, cultural traditions are varied and different, and that each culture will face the question of "cre-ative transformation" in the global tendency toward moderniza-tion.[14] Wang Yichuan acknowledges that Said's *Orientalism* has played the positive role of "deconstructing the fictionality of the image of the Orient" in Western colonialist discourse, but he also warns against the "blind self-enclosure in fighting Western-centrism," for otherwise the assimilation of Said's critique of Orientalism would become more "reactionary" than "progres-sive."[15] Sun Jin goes even further and states that putting forward the theory of Orientalism at the present in China "will have a much greater reactionary effect than that of progressivism," and by "reactionary" he means the tendency "to move against a modernized civilization."[16] Zhang Rongyi, on the other hand, tries to go beyond the East-West opposition and argues that "cul-tures located in marginal areas should also have the right to speak."[17] That is to say, not everything in a non-Western culture or history is to be understood as a reaction to the threat of the West or an imitation of the Orientalist discourse, without consid-ering the internal dynamics in the indigenous cultural and politi-cal conditions. What becomes immediately clear in reading this conversation is that modernization, understood not just in terms of modern science and technology but above all in terms of cul-ture and political system, modernization as political change in terms of freedom and democracy, is for many Chinese scholars a positive goal not to be forsaken, a goal no less than the self-strengthening of China as a country and a nation. "Moderniza-tion is the main theme that takes precedence over everything else in China today," Tao Dongfeng puts it emphatically. "Any de-viation from this main theme will lead to conservatism."[18] It may be surprising that a radical and politically leftist theory in the West, such as Said's work on Orientalism and imperialism, may seem "conservative" and even "reactionary" in the eyes of these Chinese scholars, but whether a theory from the West plays a radical or conservative role in a non-Western environment depends on the cultural and political context within which that theory interacts with the reality of the non-Western society, and, just as crucially, on the way scholars writing for a non-Western audience understand that theory and use it in their own social and cultural criticism.

The limitations of the theory of Orientalism have of course been recognized by many scholars. Lisa Lowe, for example, rejects any "totalizing orientalism as a monolithic, developmental discourse that uniformly constructs the Orient as the Other of the Occident."[19] Arran Gare also sees Said's work as somewhat inflexible and argues, with special reference to sinological studies, that the problem with Said's work is "not that he has identified a close relation between the discourse of Orientalism and imperialism," but "that in following Foucault he has not allowed for any other possibility."[20] In a non-Western cultural and political environment, like that of China, however, the problem with the theories of Orientalism and postcolonialism is not that they do not sufficiently acknowledge the plurality of the Orientalist discourse in the West, but that they can be easily misappropriated to serve the purposes of cultural conservatism, narrow-minded nationalism, and sinocentrism, and thus have the radical significance of their challenge to hegemony and domination seriously compromised. Of course, as a sophisticated and nuanced argument, Said's *Orientalism* can hardly be reduced to simplistic and monolithic anti-Western propaganda that it is often said to be. The criticism those Chinese scholars put forth in their conversation, however, is directed not so much toward Said as to those who misappropriate his ideas. How to retain the nuance and theoretical sophistication of Said's theory in a world that is often fiercely confrontational and impatient with careful analysis and scholastic distinctions, and, more important, how to avoid turning the theory of Orientalism and postcolonialism into some kind of endorsement of cultural conservatism, political orthodoxy, and religious fundamentalism in the East, remains a serious challenge to all scholars and critics, including Said himself, who has always emphasized the political relevance of theory and tried to make theory work and have a real impact on the realities of our times.

Occidentalism Official and Unofficial

A controversial television series called *He shang* (River Elegy), which was broadcast in the summer of 1988 and viewed by millions of Chinese with fascination and agitation, may be taken as a salient example of the cultural critique of the 1980s, and its tendentious depiction of both China and the West can help situate the theoretical discussion of Orientalism in the specific context of contemporary Chinese culture and politics. *River Elegy* takes the form of a documentary, but it is more of an essay on Chinese culture and history, brilliantly conceived, passionately argued, and clearly articulated through the effective use of music, visual imagery, archive materials, and an emotionally engaging and forceful narration. With its six parts thematically organized around the Yellow River, the dragon, the Great Wall, and some other such potent images long considered to be symbols of Chinese culture and the Chinese nation, *River Elegy* mounts a strong critique of the entire Chinese tradition, especially Confucianism, and it unabashedly calls for a "great flood" to wash out "the dregs of the old civilization." Moreover, it further identifies that great flood as "none other than the industrial civilization," the open, "blue-water, maritime civilization," best represented by the culture, science, and democratic system of the West.[21] By declaring that Chinese civilization has declined and become decrepit, and by selectively presenting and commenting on certain historical moments and images of the Chinese, screenwriters Su Xiaokang, Wang Luxiang, and their collaborators set up a dramatic contrast between China and the West, between the old, declining culture of the Yellow River and the new, thriving civilization across the blue ocean. In looking back at the millennia of Chinese history, they set up another contrast between the past glories of ancient China, especially that of the great empires of Han and Tang, and the weaknesses and humiliation China repeatedly suffered from the hands of Japan and the Western powers in the last hundred years. In both cases, then, the contrast makes it clear that what they try to emphasize is the crisis of Chinese culture in the modern and contemporary period, and that the critique of China's past or the idealization of the West aims at a cultural critique as well as a political commentary on the present. In that commentary, the authors of *River Elegy* adopted a number of typical nineteenth-century Western notions—from Hegel's Eurocentric philosophy of history to Marx's problematic notion of the Asiatic mode of production—and constructed a grand narrative that tells of the decline and fall of the earthbound civilizations of the East—the Egyptian, the Babylonian, the Indian, and now the Chinese—while at the same time speaking of the rise and rapid progress of the West. From Alexander the Great to Columbus and to the expansion of European powers after the Industrial Revolution, even the colonialist history of the West is presented in a somewhat positive light as an indication of the force and vitality of an externally oriented civilization. In many aspects, therefore, *River Elegy* seems to reiterate the discourse of Orientalism, creating the mythological image of an idealized West above the mythological image of a stagnant and decrepit Orient, and it easily lends itself to the charge of "fulsomely worshipping things foreign," a charge often thrown at Chinese intellectuals or anyone with any indication of an interest in the outside world, especially the West.

That was of course one of the charges or major criticisms aimed at *River Elegy* as soon as the controversial program was shown on Chinese television. Its reception among the majority of Chinese viewers, however, was mostly positive and enthusiastic. The fact that a television documentary could touch a nerve with so many people and stimulate millions of viewers into serious discussion and heated debate, not just on the mainland but also in Taiwan, Hong Kong, and overseas Chinese communities, testifies not so much to the power of television as to the depth of anxiety that most Chinese feel about the present condition and the future destiny of their culture, their sense of urgency for a fundamental change so that the Chinese mainland will rid itself of poverty and weakness and emerge as one of the great nations in the world, which every Chinese has always wanted it to be. In dealing with such intellectual and also highly emotional issues and in presenting such a strong critique of culture and history, *River Elegy* is, as Su Xiaokang himself admits, a "television political commentary film that would take hold of the Yellow River as a subject from the viewpoint of cultural and philosophical consciousness," and in making connections between the past and the most pressing contemporary issues, it is trying to find answers to current problems "in the deepest and most mysterious 'cultural roots' of our nation."[22] That is to say, *River Elegy*, like so many other works engaged in the cultural critique of the 1980s, speaks the language of social allegory and addresses the present by commenting on the past; its concerns are entirely internal and domestic, its critique of traditional China is meant to implicate contemporary political reality, and its attack on the symbols of stagnation and self-enclosure has immediate relevance as an attack on the conservative forces in the present regime that have always resisted change and reform in whatever aspect of the Chinese society.

The politically radical and subversive meaning of *River Elegy* was well understood in mainland China by both the average people and the conservative ideologues in the establishment, and that may explain why there was such an overwhelmingly enthusiastic response from the general audiences on the one hand, and on the other such vehement condemnation by the hard-liners among the higher-ups in the government. A typical example of the latter is the reaction from Wang Zhen, China's vice-president, an army general, and one of the most conservative old-timers in the top leadership, who angrily denounced *River Elegy* as "counterrevolutionary," an always deadly incriminating charge in communist China. The debate about *River Elegy* was soon involved in the internal strife between different factions of the Party and was used by the moderates and the hard-liners alike in the leadership as a means of testing their opponents' strength. The banning of the program in November 1988 thus became an indication that the hard-liners had got the upper hand in the top leadership; and after the June massacre in Beijing in 1989, the printed texts of *River Elegy* were rooted out and destroyed, and critique of the program intensified. An article representing the official point of view attacked the screenwriters for sweeping away "five thousand years of the history of the culture and civilization of the Chinese people," but clearly it was really the implicit condemnation of recent history under the leadership of the Communist Party that made *River Elegy* culpable.[23] The talk of a "blue-water, maritime civilization" was not only refuted as an idealization of the West, but was condemned, more seriously in the specific political context, as advocating capitalism, as spreading the dangerous idea that "only capitalism can save China, and the path of development of Western capitalism is the only hopeful option."[24] The article further accused the screenwriters of "promotion of bourgeois liberalism," and singled out Su Xiaokang for his involvement in the student demonstration in Tiananmen and his "political action that planned for, and fanned up, seditious turmoil."[25] The television series was then officially condemned, and Su Xiaokang had to flee the country. The whole affair proved once again that the debate on *River Elegy*, like so many other incidents in what appeared to be literary, artistic, or cultural matters, was closely and dangerously intertwined with political strife and power struggles in China. Therefore, any analysis and criticism of the television program would miss the crucial point if it failed to take into consideration the complexity of China's internal politics and the way it is played out.

It is only as a foil to the image of China in need of change and reform that the image of a superior, idealized West is invoked in *River Elegy*. A thorough grasp of the political implications of such a contrastive framework, its subversive ramifications in the Chinese mainland, is thus prerequisite for an adequate understanding of the images of China and the West as represented in that television program. Of course, not all criticisms of *River Elegy* come from communist hard-liners in the government, but many who criticize it, especially those outside mainland China, often overlook or fail to understand its real political meaning and the possible manner of its expression. "*River Elegy* is not something that just dropped from the sky," as Su Xiaokang puts it; "it simply could not discuss things in a totally uncontrolled manner, heedless of the practical possibilities provided in today's Chinese mainland."[26] As for those who left China for the West when the communists took over and now feel angry that *River Elegy* has idealized the West while putting down China, Su comments that "it is easier for them to see the 'superiority' of Oriental culture, when they are looking at the problems of Western civilization as their frame of reference. . . . they have had nothing at all to do with the sufferings that have happened to the people on the Chinese mainland after they themselves had left. Thus, it is easy for them to express their love and pity for their 'homeland' gracefully, and with a sense of transcendence."[27] What Su Xiaokang stresses is the important point that *River Elegy*, its imagery, argument, and even its overstatements, should be understood within the specific context of contemporary Chinese culture and politics on the mainland, otherwise it will only be misunderstood and misinterpreted. As Xiaomei Chen argues convincingly, whatever else *River Elegy* may be, it is "without a doubt an expression of an anti-official discourse prevalent in China at the end of the 1980s, which painted the Occident as an oppositional and supplementary Other," and the depiction of China as "inferior" in this controversial work is "part of a strategy for exposing the inferiority of a monolithic, one-Party system."[28] The creation of an image of the West for domestic purposes, what Chen calls the "discourse of Occidentalism," can be used by the ideological establishment to suppress the marginal and heterodox forces in a non-Western society, but it can also be used by those forces to launch an attack on the state orthodoxy and its ruling ideology. In China, an official discourse of Occidentalism has always depicted the West as evil and inimical in the melodramatic government propaganda, and this anti-Western discourse has often been used to justify the suppression of any political opponents or any perceived deviation from the Party line. Given the presence of such an official Occidentalism, *River Elegy* with its favorable representation of a free and democratic West can certainly be understood, again as Chen argues, "as a powerful anti-official discourse using the Western Other as a metaphor for a political liberation against ideological oppression within a totalitarian society."[29] Because of the tremendous difference in political conditions, then, what appears to be a mindless repetition in China of the discourse of Orientalism and thus ideologically suspect, when measured by the yardstick popular in Western academia these days, is likely to turn out to be something quite different when situated in the cultural and political life of China, serving a totally different purpose and carrying a totally different meaning. To read such antiofficial Occidentalism as mimicry of Orientalism is only to misread it. Not only that, but such a misreading will de facto endorse the official anti-Western rhetoric of a repressive regime. To judge Chinese works in purely Western theoretical terms, then, would ironically repeat the same colonialist attitude so sharply criticized by Said and many other theorists and critics.

The image of the Other can be used to play the role of an effective contrast to the self in many different ways. Montaigne, as we have seen, used the Brazilian cannibals to facilitate his critique of European culture in his time, and in so doing he idealized the native Brazilians in order to comment on what he perceived to be European weaknesses. In a similar way, European or Western values have often been represented by Chinese writers since the late Qing period to promote their ideas of social change and the self-strengthening of China. Perhaps the most prominent example can be found in the works of Lu Xun, who was the most radical as well as the most influential among all antitraditional modern thinkers. In one of his essays, he contrasted Prometheus with the Chinese fire god: while the Greeks worshipped a hero who defied the gods to help human beings, the Chinese deified "a strange being that set things on fire at random," a nameless demon that bullied human beings and threatened them with destruction.[30] The comparison is hardly fair, but Lu Xun meant to expose what he saw as the weakness of the Chinese—their cowardice and blind submission to power. When the conservative critics of his time accused the new-culture movement of "worshipping foreign idols," Lu Xun replied bluntly that one would be better off with new foreign idols than stuck with old native ones: "It would be better to worship Darwin or Ibsen than Confucius or Guan Yu," he declares; "it would be better to make sacrifice to Apollo than to the God of Plague or the Deity of Five Ways."[31] Even more shockingly, in his answer to a questionnaire about required readings for young Chinese, Lu Xun advised, "read few—or even no—Chinese books, but read lots of foreign books."[32] Such statements are by no means rare in Lu Xun's works, in which the native cultural tradition, especially Confucian teaching, is often unfavorably compared with superior, more reasonable or more humane, foreign concepts and values. All these seem indeed embarrassing signs of self-colonization when viewed from Said's perspective or what has been presented to Chinese readers as Said's theory of Orientalism, and yet Lu Xun, of all modern writers, has been considered by most Chinese as a radical thinker, a great revolutionary, a leftist intellectual who was always opposed to the status quo, the cultural orthodoxy and political establishment. The superior image of the foreign in Lu Xun, like the Brazilian cannibals in Montaigne, serves the purpose of a thorough and comprehensive cultural critique, and it makes sense only in the internal dynamics of its indigenous condition. It would then seem incredibly arrogant to judge what Lu Xun said and did from the standpoint of contemporary Western theory, or to reject Lu Xun's legacy because we now have the privilege of reading Said's books. In such an arrogant negation, as Xiaomei Chen puts it, there is always "the danger of theoretically recolonizing the Third World with Western-invented and theoretically motivated languages of 'anti-colonialism.'"[33] And that, as we shall see, is not at all an imaginary danger these days as the various theories of Orientalism, postcolonialism, and postmodernism travel to China and become hot topics in Chinese criticism.

Postmodernism, Conservatism, and the Role of the Intellectual

The presence of that danger in Chinese literary and cultural criticism of the 1990s was brought to the fore in a recent debate on postmodernist theories. *Twenty-first Century*, a scholarly journal published by the Institute of Chinese Studies at the Chinese University of Hong Kong, carried two articles in February 1995 that commented on the cultural and political implications of the postmodernist trend in recent Chinese criticism, and the publication of these articles touched off a heated debate in the subsequent issues of that journal. The debate is just one of many that we can find in Chinese criticism, and there are many articles on postmodernism in other publications in Chinese, but this particular debate is more focused than most others and has involved a number of participants with quite different voices and views. A brief examination of the debate unfolded in the pages of *Twenty-first Century* may thus give us a clear sense of what is at stake in talking about postmodernism and Western theory in the Chinese context.

In an article entitled "'Postist Learning' and the Neo-Conservatism in China," Zhao Yiheng points out the current ludicrous overuse of the prefix *post-* not just in Western criticism, but also in its Chinese following, and he puts all the recently introduced Western theories of poststructuralism, postmodernism, and postcolonialism under the rubric of what he calls "postism" and relates them to the conservative tendency in Chinese criticism of the 1990s. Zhao maintains that cultural critique should be the task of Chinese intellectuals, and that the concern of such a critique is not to set up an opposition between China and the West in order to stir up the nationalist spirit, but to target and criticize "the institutionalized culture of one's own country (official culture, popular culture, essentialist culture)."[34] Insofar as cultural critique is a theoretical discourse, he argues, it is a critique of "institution, the theorizing and rationalizing of the cultural status quo."[35] In the 1990s, however, the spirit of such a cultural critique is lost in the facile and tendentious talk about postmodernism and postcolonialism on the Chinese mainland, which substitutes a China-West opposition for the critique directed at institutionalized culture or the status quo at home. From the standpoint of cultural critique, then, such a tendency is conservative culturally and politically because it compromises with the cultural orthodoxy and political authorities in China and discusses issues of culture and history with a simple "blame it on the West" approach. It is characteristic of this neo-conservatism that its relationship with the West is a preposterous and contradictory one, for on the one hand it claims to represent the interest of China as a Third World country against the hegemony of the West, while on the other it relies heavily on theories au courant in the West, those of postmodernism and postcolonialism in particular, and imitates the latest fashions in Western theoretical discourse for conceptualization and methodology, even for sentence structure and vocabulary or jargon. It is debatable whether the postmodern critique of modernity and the Enlightenment is making changes for the better in the West, but it is quite certain that, in a non-Western context, the self-critique of the Western tradition by Western scholars can easily be used by conservatives in the East as an excuse to maintain the status quo against any change, which they can readily dismiss as "Westernization," as copying something even Western scholars themselves have deconstructed and rejected. This tendentious use of Western theory by cultural conservatives in the East makes the role of theory across cultural and national boundaries much more complicated than it might be in its original context, and it poses the important question whether Western postmodernism that mounts a radical critique of the Western tradition may offer a convenient theoretical excuse for conservative Chinese intellectuals to shirk their responsibility of internal cultural critique and turn to embrace a narrow-minded nationalism. No wonder Zhao Yiheng would ask whether the foundations of Western "postist learning" may "have certain characteristics in themselves that make them lean to the conservative side in the concrete situation in China?"[36]

In a way Xu Ben's article "Third World Criticism," published together with Zhao Yiheng's in the same issue of *Twenty-first Century*, provides an apt answer to that question. Xu Ben first calls our attention to the fact that at a time when the various discussions of culture were suddenly put to an end after the suppression of the prodemocracy movement in 1989, "'Third World criticism' became almost the only thriving new trend in culture and ideology, and that is something worthy of our reflection."[37] According to Xu, the problem with so-called Third World criticism, as in what Zhao says about "postism," lies in avoiding confrontation with the cultural establishment and political authority in one's own country by shifting the aim of critique to the West, claiming that the primary task for Chinese critics today is to fight the cultural hegemony of the First World, that is, Western imperialism. Such a critical discourse is directly opposed to the cultural critique of the 1980s and thus also opposed to the ideals of democracy and freedom that inspired the student movement in Tiananmen; at the same time it bears some striking similarities with the official propaganda in its anti-imperialist and anticolonialist rhetoric, and its emphasis on collective interest and nationalism. "The core of such Third World criticism in China," as Xu points out, "is an emphasis on nativeness rather than rebellion against oppression." Or rather, it speaks only of rebelling against the "discursive oppression" of the Third World by the First World, as if that were "the major form of oppression in China today, and thereby it conceals and avoids, wittingly or unwittingly, the violence and oppression that do exist in real life in the indigenous society."[38] Those Third World critics talk about recovering "the memory of the people" from beneath its suppression by the Western First World, but in China, Xu asks, is "'the memory of the people' suppressed, ignored, and erased mainly by some Western discourse?" More important, does the official narrative of Chinese history "necessarily agree with the memory of the people?"[39] Speaking of memory, those Third World critics seem to have no remembrance of the domestic violence, political persecution, and total economic collapse in Mao's China during the Cultural Revolution, not to mention the other ideological campaigns and political movements that had a disastrous effect on the life of millions of Chinese. To speak in collective terms in the name of the People, to elevate that abstract notion, to idolize and deify it, while reducing every living person to naught, has always been the strategy of totalitarian rule. Why would some critics in the 1990s latch on to such a talk of the elevated People and sound so much like the official language of government propaganda? Questions like these necessarily put Chinese "postism" or "Third World criticism" in serious doubt, and ultimately the question comes down to this: How can "postist learning" and "Third World criticism," which have abandoned the intellectual responsibility of cultural critique and even denied the significance of the very existence of intellectuals, in any way contribute to the project of modernization, especially to the realization of democracy in China? How can they help advance the rights and interest of each individual Chinese in real life rather than those of the abstract, collective, reified People?

In an article that explores the seldom-discussed and little-understood relationship between Western postmodernist theory and the radical 1960s, especially the influence of Maoism and the Chinese Cultural Revolution among leftist students and intellectuals in Europe and America, Guo Jian offers another perspective for evaluating the significance of Western postmodernist theory in China. As one example of the Chinese influence on Western postmodernist theory, Guo points out that Fredric Jameson's exposition of "cultural revolution" as a theoretical concept in *The Political Unconscious* bears some obvious resemblance to Mao's views on class struggle in the realm of ideology and on the long-term coexistence of different classes and modes of production in China. Foucault's discussion with some French Maoists on "popular justice" provides another example of how this major Western thinker, whose ideas underlie much of postmodernist and post-colonialist theory, formulated his own theory in an environment in which the Chinese Cultural Revolution and Mao Zedong's thought certainly had a significant influence. The line of thought in many postmodernist thinkers and theoreticians can be traced back to the Chinese experience of the 1960s and the way it was imaginatively understood in the West. Thus Guo Jian argues that the Chinese Cultural Revolution and Mao's theory can be called "pre-postmodern," because they have influenced and anticipated some of the central ideas and important concepts in contemporary postmodernist theory. We may recall that Liu Kang has also called our attention to the connection of Foucault and Mao, but for him that connection is supposed to validate Maoism by the enormous authority Foucault enjoys in Western theoretical discourse. For Guo Jian, however, history and reality in China are more important than paying homage to the authority of Western theoreticians. To be able to see the connection between Foucault and Mao, or Western leftist theories and Maoism, says Guo, "will help us recognize the value and significance of Western 'postist learning' in the cultural criticism in contemporary China."[40] This is not to reject Western postmodernism and its value in China; in fact, in rethinking our own culture, he continues to argue, "Foucault's method of critique is not without its usefulness." But, says Guo emphatically, we cannot blindly import back something that came out of the influence of the Chinese Cultural Revolution some thirty years ago and show it off as the "eminent mark of 'the vitality and richness of . . . our culture in the 'post-new era.'"[41] He reminds us that for the Chinese on the mainland, "the painful historical lesson known as the Cultural Revolution offers a perspective far more reliable than any theory," and that we have no choice but to make an "'absolute' value judgment," and give precedence to this historical lesson over postmodernist theory if the latter "contradicts such a historical perspective or line of reference."[42] The influence of Maoism and Cultural Revolution on radical postmodernist theory still needs to be carefully studied,[43] but given the experience of calamities during the Cultural Revolution, the reception of such theory in China cannot be a simple transference and assimilation, and debate on Western theory will always be part of a larger debate on Chinese culture, history, tradition, and modernity.

Although there have been a number of responses to the initial articles by Zhao and Xu—of which some are rather critical and others have made useful corrections of what they may have overlooked—none has really challenged their main argument concerning the conservative tendency in discussions of Chinese culture and history in the 1990s. Indeed, some other scholars have also pointed out the conservative nature of the Chinese appropriation of Western theory. In an article published in 1994, for example, Wang Hui already noticed the problematic role postcolonialist theory played in mainland China when it was connected with the native tendency of nationalism. "In different cultural contexts," says Wang, "the same proposition may have completely different meanings."[44] Postmodernism and postcolonialism are radical theories of cultural critique in the West, while in China in its modern history, especially in the legacy of the May Fourth new culture, radicalism has always been associated with an antimainstream and antitraditionalist orientation. "In the early 1990s, however," Wang observes, "when they are introduced to China, those Western radical theories give rise to precisely a force that strengthens the mainstream. In other words, the introduction of some Western radical theories has reinforced some Chinese intellectuals' cultural nationalism."[45] Wang continues to argue that cultural conservatism in China manifests itself today in two forms, "of which one is a reexamination of radicalism in modern time, and the other mixes up the preservation of traditional culture with the upholding of the interest of the nation and state. This is not radical in either cultural or political terms, but works to reinforce the mainstream, and thus it is completely opposite to the significance of the same type of theories in the United States."[46] Perhaps to claim that neo-conservatism has become the main trend in current Chinese criticism, as Zhao Yiheng argued in his article, may have

overstated the case, but the abandonment of a critical and oppositional stance toward cultural orthodoxy and the political establishment in much of what has been written in the name of postmodernist, postcolonialist, or Third World criticism in mainland
China indeed presents a serious problem for the continuation of
cultural critique and the role of intellectuals.

Chinese "postism" has in effect relinquished the critical role of
intellectuals and contributed to their marginalization, and that
can be seen clearly in some of the responses to Zhao and Xu from
those "postist" scholars. In his reply to Zhao and Xu, Zhang
Yiwu, who is one of the most active and articulate "postist" or
"Third World" critics in mainland China, does not so much re-
fute their argument as confirm it by reiterating precisely the line
of talk that they have found problematic and inherently conservative. Quite predictably, Zhang Yiwu dismissed any critique of
Chinese "postism" or "Third World criticism" as yet another exercise of "Western" victimization of China, as if "postist" critics
were alone invested with some kind of Chinese authenticity and
thus capable of truly representing the interest of China and the
Chinese People. The talk of victimization and hegemonic suppression, of course, turns out to be an old strategy of empower-
ment, for once a Third World critic identifies himself with China,
anyone criticizing him must be accused of being anti-Chinese, of
evoking "Western cultural hegemony" to suppress the voice of
an innocent Third World country, even though the voice of that
so-called Third World critic sounds like an echo of contemporary
Western theories of Orientalism, postcolonialism, and postmodernism. Zhang Yiwu declares that those Chinese critics who do
their theorizing from the perspectives of postcolonialism and
Third World criticism "have completely changed the unconditionally 'subordinate' position to Western discourse and the
senseless infatuation with 'modernity,' which one finds in Chinese intellectuals of the 1980s who indulged in the discourse of
'Enlightenment.'"[47] The irony is, however, that at the precise
moment when these Chinese postmodern and postcolonial critics
claim to have escaped the shadow of Western discourse, they are

sinking deeper than anyone else into "the unconditionally 'subordinate' position to Western discourse" and "the senseless infatuation with '*post*modernity.'" As Guo Jian observes, "what Zhang Yiwu calls the viewpoint of the 'Third World' is nothing but the viewpoint defined by 'First World' 'postist' theoreticians who claim to speak for the 'Third World.'"[48] In a sense, Chinese "postism" is a discourse that does not find its own voice in the reality of Chinese social and political life but echoes other discourses: the Western theoretical discourse of postmodernism and postcolonialism and, even worse, the official discourse of the cultural and political establishment at home.

An example of the striking similarity between the language of such Third World criticism and that of official government speech can be seen in a brief passage in which Zhang Yiwu comments on Western notions of human rights, freedom, and democracy:

"Human rights" has long become a bargaining chip in managing the Chinese market and controlling Chinese trade, and the last illusory shadow to situate the Otherness of "China." Democracy represented by Lady Liberty, as Rey Chow has pointed out, is nothing but "a naive, idealistic clamor for democracy 'American style,' symbolized by a white woman."[49]

Whether the average Chinese would rather have basic human rights, freedom, and democracy than totalitarianism in their social and political lives, however, is a question never raised in the critical discourse that supposedly speaks for China. To reject human rights, freedom, and democracy because they are "Western" values hardly makes a convincing argument, and to judge them on the basis of race or nation is simply dangerous. During the Second World War, as Lei Yi's contribution to this debate reminds us, the problematic notion that the Japanese and the Chinese belonged to the same Asian race was used by Japanese militarists and imperialists to legitimize their invasion of China and other Asian countries, and the theoretical justification they proposed for their "Great East Asian War" was precisely the idea of yellow Asians fighting against white Europeans and Americans.[50] It seems that Chinese Third World critics tend to forget historical reality, or perhaps more accurately, they never have the memory of history in the first place. That may be the reason why they do not seem to detect the dangerous implications of theoretical arguments based on race or color. In the specific political situation of mainland China today, a radically anti-Western rhetoric is never really radical, as it is likely to coincide with, if it does not actually originate in, the official discourse of the political establishment. It is this political situation that one must take into consideration in examining the significance of Western theories of Orientalism, postcolonialism, and postmodernism in the Chinese context.

Anti-Westernism, however, is not what Said's theory is all about or intended to promote. According to Said himself, the "alleged anti-Westernism" is a big misunderstanding in the reception of *Orientalism* that he "most regret[s]" and finds himself "trying hardest now to overcome." The misinterpretation of his theory, says Said, usually argues that Orientalism is "a synecdoche, or miniature symbol, of the entire West," and therefore "the entire West is an enemy of the Arab or Islamic or for that matter the Iranian, Chinese, Indian and many other non-European peoples who suffered Western colonialism and prejudice."[51] Said is evidently aware of and feels uncomfortable with the fact that his work on Orientalism has been made use of in the Middle East and some other non-Western countries to legitimize the cause of fundamentalism or nationalism, but he refuses to be so co-opted by any such group. From a theoretical position that rejects essentialist claims about either the East or the West, he categorically dissociates himself from any "defense" of Islamic fundamentalism or its "secular equivalent"—nationalism. Nor does he want to dismiss all Oriental studies in the West as cultural imperialism or colonialism. "It is benighted to say that Orientalism is a conspiracy," Said remarks, "or to suggest that 'the West' is evil."[52] Therefore, whatever else Said's theory may be, it is not the kind of simplistic anti-Westernism that the "Third World" critics in China depict it to be. Even more significant, Said does not argue for abandoning the critical position of intellectuals with regard to the cultural establishment and political authorities anywhere, in the East as well as the West. In fact, in *Representations of the Intellectual*, he defines the intellectual as "someone whose place it is publicly to raise embarrassing questions, to confront orthodoxy and dogma (rather than to produce them), to be someone who cannot easily be co-opted by governments or corporations, and whose *raison d'être* is to represent all those people and issues that are routinely forgotten or swept under the rug."[53] With that put in the Chinese context, then, it is clearly not those "Third World critics" but cultural critics in the May Fourth movement and in the 1980s that can best lay claim to the name of intellectual as Said understands it, because what Said calls for are the critical spirit and social responsibility that make the intellectual enterprise worthwhile. That critical spirit and social responsibility are also what Chinese intellectuals in their cultural critique try to hold on to even under the constraint of political control and the increasing pressure of commercialization. China is changing more rapidly than ever, but intellectuals are charged with the task of cultural critique no matter what the status quo is, and in that sense, they transcend the immediate concerns of the day; or as Said also says, drawing on the ideas of Julien Benda, they are fiercely independent and courageous, willing "to risk being burned at the stake, ostracized, or crucified. They are symbolic personages marked by their unyielding distance from practical concerns . . . and, above all, they have to be in a state of almost permanent opposition to the status quo."[54] The discussion of the marginalization of intellectuals and the recent debate on Orientalism and postmodernism in the Chinese context testify to the fact that the critical spirit is still very much alive in China, and paradoxically it is this spirit that will sustain the vitality of the very culture and tradition that it subjects to constant critique and rethinking. It is in the dialectic relationship between tradition and its critique that Chinese culture will find its power to endure and regenerate, and that is our hope for the future.

Notes

Notes

Introduction

1. According to Friedrich Schleiermacher, it is a weak version of hermeneutics to assume that understanding comes naturally because the speaker and hearer share a common language and a common way of thinking. A "more rigorous practice of the art of interpretation," he argues, "is based on the assumption that misunderstanding occurs as a matter of course, and so understanding must be willed and sought at every point." Schleiermacher, *Hermeneutics: The Handwritten Manuscripts*, trans. James Duke and Jack Forstman (Missoula, Mont.: Scholars Press, 1977), p. 110.

2. Roger Chartier, *On the Edge of the Cliff: History, Language, and Practices*, trans. Lydia G. Cochrane (Baltimore: Johns Hopkins University Press, 1997), p. 8.

3. Ibid., pp. 19–20.

4. The former of these two views is typical of the kind of linguistic determinism or what some historians call a "linguistic turn," that sees language, as Roger Chartier notes, as "a closed system of signs whose relations autonomously produce signification. Thus the construction of meaning is detached from all subjective intention or control and assigned to an automatic and impersonal linguistic function. In this view reality is no longer to be thought of as an objective referent, exterior to discourse, because it is constituted by and within language" (ibid., p. 18). In his philosophical reading of Hölderlin, ". . . Poetically Man Dwells . . . ," Martin Heidegger proposes the famous thesis that "language speaks," arguing that "man acts as though he were the shaper and master of language, while in fact language remains the master of man" (*Poetry, Language, Thought*, trans. Albert Hofstadter [New York: Harper & Row, 1975], p. 215). In literary theory, Roland Barthes follows the Heideggerian thought and argues, in his well-known essay "The Death of the Author," that "it is language which speaks, not the author; to write is, through a prerequisite impersonality . . . to reach that point where only language acts, 'performs,' and not

'me'" (*Image-Music-Text*, trans. Stephen Heath [New York: Hill and Wang, 1977], p. 143). The latter view of an interpretive subjectivism can be found in much of reader-oriented critical theory, which, as Tzvetan Todorov remarks, "transforms all reading into that sort of 'picnic' Lichtenberg described with reference to Jakob Böhme's works: the author brings the words and the reader supplies the meaning" (Tzvetan Todorov, *Literature and Its Theorists: A Personal View of Twentieth-Century Criticism*, trans. Catherine Porter [Ithaca: Cornell University Press, 1987], p. 187).

5. Emmanuel Levinas, *Time and the Other [and Additional Essays]*, trans. Richard A. Cohen (Pittsburgh: Duquesne University Press, 1987), p. 79.

6. For "hermeneutic nihilism," see the section "Critique of the Abstraction Inherent in Aesthetic Consciousness" in Hans-Georg Gadamer, *Truth and Method*, where Gadamer offers a critique of Paul Valéry's claim that a text means whatever the reader reads into it. "From this it follows," says Gadamer, "that it must be left to the recipient to make something of the work. One way of understanding a work, then, is no less legitimate than another. There is no criterion of appropriate reaction. Not only does the artist himself possess none—the aesthetics of genius would agree here; every encounter with the work has the rank and rights of a new production. This seems to me an untenable hermeneutic nihilism" (2d rev. ed., trans. rev. Joel Weinsheimer and Donald G. Marshall [New York: Crossroad, 1989], pp. 94–95).

7. Ibid., pp. 268, 269.

8. Emmanuel Levinas, *Outside the Subject*, trans. Michael B. Smith (Stanford: Stanford University Press, 1994), p. 158.

9. Levinas, *Time and the Other*, p. 83.

10. Zhang Xuecheng, *Wen shi tongyi* [Comprehensive Study in the Arts and History] (Beijing: Zhonghua shuju, 1961), p. 1.

11. See Huang Junjie (Huang Chün-chieh), *Mengxue sixiangshi lun* [Studies in the History of the Thoughts of Mencius], vol. 1 (Taipei: Dongda tushu gongsi, 1991), pp. 4–27. For a brief discussion in English, see D. C. Lau, trans., *Mencius* (Harmondsworth: Penguin Books, 1970), appendix 5, "On Mencius' Use of the Method of Analogy in Argument," pp. 235–63.

12. Mikhail Bakhtin, *Problems of Dostoevsky's Poetics*, ed. and trans. Caryl Emerson (Minneapolis: University of Minnesota Press, 1984), p. 252. Katerina Clark and Michael Holquist first made the connection between Bakhtin and Levinas. They emphasize Bakhtin's skeptic attitude toward systematizing and put him in a tradition of thinkers "from Heraclitus to Emmanuel Levinas, who have preferred the powers that

inhere in the centrifugal forces" (*Mikhail Bakhtin* [Cambridge, Mass.: Harvard University Press, 1984], p. 8). David Patterson devoted a whole chapter to that connection in his book *Literature and Spirit: Essays on Bakhtin and His Contemporaries* (Lexington: University Press of Kentucky, 1988).

13. Levinas, *Time and the Other*, p. 39.

14. David D. Buck, "Editor's Introduction to Forum on Universalism and Relativism in Asian Studies," *The Journal of Asian Studies* 50 (Feb. 1991): 30. As Buck points out, relativist interpretations of cultures are "advanced with much more frequency among Asianists" than "universalist ideas" that believe in the commonality of human thinking and human behavior across cultures.

15. Patrick Colm Hogan, "Beauty, Politics, and Cultural Otherness: The Bias of Literary Difference," in Hogan and Lalita Pandit, eds., *Literary India: Comparative Studies in Aesthetics, Colonialism, and Culture* (Albany: State University of New York Press, 1995), p. 6.

16. Ibid., p. 8.

17. Buck, "Editor's Introduction to Forum on Universalism and Relativism in Asian Studies," p. 32.

18. *Chuang Tzu: Basic Writings*, trans. Burton Watson (New York: Columbia University Press, 1964), p. 138.

19. Xu Yi (fl. ca. 1111), *Yanzhou shihua* [Yanzhou's Remarks on Poetry], in *Lidai shihua* [Remarks on Poetry from Various Dynasties], ed. He Wenhuan (1732–1809), 2 vols. (Beijing: Zhonghua shuju, 1981), 1: 382.

20. Technically speaking, Su Shi's use of the metaphor is not an allusion to the *Zhuangzi*, for the word he used to describe the woman's red face is *ping*, not *nu*. The commentator, however, explains that the word *ping* means "the color of anger [*nu se*]," thus establishing an allusive relationship with the phrase in the *Zhuangzi* as we discussed above. Allusion is an important rhetorical device often used in classical Chinese poetry, but unlike the critical concept of *intertextuality* in Julia Kristeva or Roland Barthes ("a text is . . . a tissue of quotations drawn from the innumerable centres of culture" ["The Death of the Author," *Image-Music-Text*, p. 146]), allusion in Chinese writing establishes the author of the alluded text as a historical presursor with authority and prestige, carrying the weight of tradition, the source of depth and richness of meaning.

21. Eric Partridge, *The World of Words: An Introduction to Language in General and to English and American in Particular*, 3d ed. (London: Hamish Hamilton, 1948), p. 154. Partridge goes on to give this example: "The names of flowers show that the same likeness has been observed by

various races. The spice called *clove* and the *clove*-pink both belong to Latin *clavus*, a nail. The German for pink is *Nelke*, a . . . diminutive . . . of *Nagel*, nail" (pp. 154–55). I may add that the Chinese name for this flower is *dingxiang*, literally "nail fragrance" or "a fragrant nail."

22. Hoyt Alverson, *Semantics and Experience: Universal Metaphors of Time in English, Mandarin, Hindi, and Sesotho* (Baltimore: Johns Hopkins University Press, 1994), pp. xi, 6–7.

23. Ibid., p. 130.

24. Helen Vendler, *The Poetry of George Herbert* (Cambridge, Mass.: Harvard University Press, 1975), pp. 10, 19.

25. Jiao Xun (1764–1820), *Mengzi zhengyi* [The Correct Meaning of the Works of Mencius], vi.9, in vol. 1 of *Zhuzi jicheng* [Collection of Distinguished Philosophical Works], 8 vols. (Beijing: Zhonghua, 1954), p. 263.

Chapter 1. The Myth of the Other

1. Michel Foucault, *The Order of Things: An Archaeology of the Human Sciences* (New York: Vintage, 1973), p. xv.

2. Ibid.

3. Ibid., p. xix.

4. Jorge Luis Borges, "The Analytical Language of John Wilkins," *Other Inquisitions, 1937–1952*, trans. Ruth L. Simms (Austin: University of Texas Press, 1964), p. 101.

5. Ibid., p. 103.

6. Ibid., p. 104.

7. Borges, "The Congress," *The Book of Sand*, trans. Norman Thomas di Giovanni (New York: E. P. Dutton, 1977), p. 37.

8. Borges, "Tlön, Uqbar, Orbis Tertius," trans. James E. Irby, *Labyrinths: Selected Stories and Other Writings*, ed. Donald A. Yates and Irby (New York: Modern Library, 1983), pp. 3, 4.

9. Borges, "The Garden of Forking Paths," trans. Yates, *Labyrinths*, p. 24.

10. Borges, *Borges on Writing*, ed. Norman Thomas di Giovanni, Daniel Halpern, and Frank MacShane (New York: E. P. Dutton, 1973), p. 86.

11. Borges, "Facing the Year 1983," *Twenty-Four Conversations with Borges, Including a Selection of Poems*, trans. Nicomedes Suárez Araúz et al. (Housatonic: Lascaux Publishers, 1984), p. 12.

12. See, for example, "The Other" in *The Book of Sand*, pp. 11–20, and "Borges and I" in *Labyrinths*, pp. 246–47.

13. Benedict de Spinoza, *The Ethics*, in *The Chief Works of Benedict de Spinoza*, trans. R. H. M. Elwes, 2 vols. (New York: Dover Publications, 1951), 2: 67.

14. Spinoza, *Correspondence*, in *The Chief Works of Benedict de Spinoza*, 2: 370.

15. Plato, *Parmenides* 164c, trans. F. M. Cornford, *The Collected Dialogues of Plato, Including the Letters*, ed. Edith Hamilton and Huntington Cairns (Princeton: Princeton University Press, 1961), p. 954.

16. Rudyard Kipling, "The Ballad of East and West," *Collected Verse of Rudyard Kipling* (New York: Doubleday, Page & Co., 1907), p. 136.

17. Levinas, "Ideology and Idealism," *The Levinas Reader*, ed. Seán Hand (Oxford: Basil Blackwell, 1989), p. 246.

18. Edward Said, *Orientalism* (London: Routledge & Kegan Paul, 1978), pp. 4–5.

19. Giambattista Vico, *The New Science*, ed. and trans. Thomas Goddard Bergin and Max Harold Fisch (Ithaca: Cornell University Press, 1968), p. 96.

20. Ibid., p. 112.

21. Erich Auerbach, "Vico's Contribution to Literary Criticism," in *Studia Philologica et Litteraria in Honorem L. Spitzer*, ed. A. G. Hatcher and K. L. Selig (Bern: Franke, 1958), p. 33.

22. Robert Lloyd, *Poems by Robert Lloyd* (London, Printed for the author by Dryden Leach, 1762), pp. 43 ff.; quoted in Qian Zhongshu [Ch'ien Chung-shu], "China in the English Literature of the Eighteenth Century (I)," *Quarterly Bulletin of Chinese Bibliography* 2 (June 1941): 31.

23. Vico, *The New Science*, pp. 32, 45.

24. Ibid., p. 33.

25. Ibid., p. 51.

26. Foucault, *The Order of Things*, p. xix.

27. Adolf Reichwein, *China and Europe: Intellectual and Artistic Contacts in the Eighteenth Century*, trans. J. C. Powell (New York: A. A. Knopf, 1925), pp. 25–26.

28. See Alexander Pope, *The Rape of the Lock, Selected Poetry and Prose*, 2d ed., ed. William K. Wimsatt (New York: Holt, Rinehart and Winston, 1972), pp. 99, 105, 110.

29. Hugh Honour, *Chinoiserie: The Vision of Cathay* (New York: E. P. Dutton, 1961), pp. 7–8.

30. Michel de Montaigne, "Of Experience," III: 13, *The Complete Essays of Montaigne*, trans. Donald M. Frame (Stanford: Stanford University Press, 1958), p. 820.

31. Donald F. Lach, *Asia in the Making of Europe*, 2 vols. (Chicago: University of Chicago Press, 1965–77), 2: 297.

32. Gottfried Wilhelm Leibniz, "Preface to the *Novissima Sinica*," in Leibniz, *Writings on China*, trans. Daniel J. Cook and Henry Rosemont, Jr. (Chicago: Open Court, 1994), p. 51.

33. Ibid., p. 45.

34. Alastair Laing, "Catalogue of Paintings," *François Boucher, 1703–1770* (New York: The Metropolitan Museum of Art, 1986), p. 202.

35. Ibid., p. 207.

36. Honour, *Chinoiserie*, p. 101.

37. François Marie Arouet de Voltaire, *Essai sur les moeurs et l'esprit des nations et sur les principaux faits de l'histoire depuis Charlemagne jusqu'à Louis XIII*, ed. René Pomeau, 2 vols. (Paris: Editions Garnier Frères, 1963), 1: 224.

38. Ibid., 1: 68.

39. Ibid., 1: 70.

40. Reichwein, *China and Europe*, p. 77.

41. See Qian Zhongshu [Ch'ien Chung-shu], "China in the English Literature of the Seventeenth Century," *Quarterly Bulletin of Chinese Bibliography* 1 (Dec. 1940): 351–84. See also Qian, "China in the English Literature of the Eighteenth Century (I)," pp. 7–48, and "China in the English Literature of the Eighteenth Century (II)," *Quarterly Bulletin of Chinese Bibliography* 2 (Dec. 1941): 113–52.

42. Francis Bacon, *Of the Proficience and Advancement of Learning, Human and Divine*, in *The Works of Francis Bacon*, 10 vols. (London: Baynes and Son, 1824), 1: 147.

43. Ibid., 1: 146.

44. Thomas Browne, "Of Languages, and Particularly of the Saxon Tongue," *The Prose of Sir Thomas Browne*, ed. Norman Endicott (Garden City: Anchor Books, 1967), p. 427. "Poncuus" is probably Peng zu, the legendary figure of remote antiquity who lived an exceptionally long life of eight hundred years.

45. John Webb, *An Historical Essay Endeavoring a Probability That the Language of the Empire of China Is the Primitive Language* (London: Printed for Nath. Brook, 1669) [p. ii].

46. Ibid. [p. iii].   47. Ibid. [pp. iii–iv].

48. Ibid. pp. 31–32, 44.   49. See ibid., pp. 191–212.

50. Ibid., pp. 32, 93.   51. Ibid., p. 98.

52. Ibid., pp. 98, 99.

53. Qian, "China in the English Literature of the Seventeenth Century," p. 371.

54. Honour, *Chinoiserie*, p. 83.

55. Daniel Defoe, *The Life and Strange Adventure of Robinson Crusoe*, in *The Works of Daniel Defoe*, 8 vols., 16 pts. (Boston: David Nickerson, 1903), 1: 2: 256–57.

56. Ibid., 1: 2: 257, 258.

57. Defoe, *Serious Reflections during the Life and Strange Adventures of*

Robinson Crusoe with His Vision of the Angelic World, The Works of Daniel Defoe, 2: 3: 123, 127.

58. James Boswell, *Life of Johnson*, ed. R. W. Chapman (Oxford: Oxford University Press, 1980), pp. 929, 984–85.

59. Ibid., p. 1211 n. 2.

60. Reichwein, *China and Europe*, pp. 94, 145.

61. Ibid., p. 150. For a full treatment of nineteenth-century Western concepts of China, see Mary Gertrude Mason, *Western Concepts of China and the Chinese, 1840–1876* (Westport: Hyperion, 1939).

62. Harold R. Isaacs, *Scratches on Our Minds: American Views of China and India* (New York: John Day Co., 1958), p. 40.

63. Ibid., p. 381.

64. Cao Xueqin, *The Story of the Stone*, trans. David Hawkes and John Minford, 5 vols. (Harmondsworth: Penguin, 1973–86), 2: 539, 540.

65. *Zhou li zhushu* [*Rites of Zhou* with Annotations], *juan* 2, in Ruan Yuan (1764–1849), *Shisan jing zhushu* [Thirteen Classics with Annotations], 2 vols. (Beijing: Zhonghua shuju, 1980), 1: 648.

66. *Li ji zhengyi* [The Correct Meaning of the *Records of Rites*], *juan* 52, ibid., 2: 1630.

67. Quoted in *China's Response to the West: A Documentary Survey, 1839–1923*, ed. Ssu-yü Teng and John K. Fairbank (Cambridge, Mass.: Harvard University Press, 1961), p. 19.

68. For a discussion of the absurd rigidity of ritualized protocols in dealing with foreign embassies in the late Qing, see the multivolume Qing documents and travelogue literature edited by Zhong Shuhe under the general title *Zouxiang shijie congshu* [Walking toward the World Series], particularly vol. 1 (Changsha: Yueli shushe, 1985), pp. 231–32.

69. Ge Jianxiong, "Shijie shang buzhiyou Zhongwen: *Ying shi Majia'erni lai pin an* yu *Ying shi yejian Qianlong jishi* zhi duikan" [Chinese is Not the Only Language in the World: Comparison of the *Qing Royal Archive Documents of the British Embassy of George Macartney* with Sir George Staunton's *An Authentic Account of an Embassy from the King of Great Britain to the Emperor of China*], *Dushu* [Reading Monthly] (Nov. 1994): 102. For a recent study in English of the Macartney embassy, see James L. Hevia, *Cherishing Men from Afar: Qing Guest Ritual and the Macartney Embassy of 1793* (Durham: Duke University Press, 1995). It is interesting to note that we may find in Hevia's book something of a reversal of what Ge Jianxiong argues in his article. The title of that book, *Cherishing Men from Afar*, is a translation of the Chinese phrase *huairou yuanren*, which means "to summon those from remote places and submit them under the kingly rule," a phrase that repeatedly occurs in Qianlong's decrees, which can be traced back to the phrase we men-

tioned earlier from the *Record of Rites,* and is central to the notion of a tributary framework. What Hevia does in his translation, then, can be said to turn a phrase that signifies a superior nation's control and sub-jugation of foreign barbarians into a discourse of equality and kindness. Perhaps the discrepancy between Ge Jianxiong's and James Hevia's readings of the Chinese imperial documents is yet another indication of the different cultural and political contexts in China and the West with-in which scholarship is produced as a response to social conditions and questions.

70. Ge Jianxiong, "Yaoshi shijie shang zhiyou Zhongwen" [If Chinese Is the Only Language in the World], *Dushu* [Reading Monthly] (July 1994): 130.

71. Raymond Dawson, "Introduction," *The Legacy of China,* ed. Dawson (Oxford: Oxford University Press, 1964), p. xiii.

72. Dawson, "Western Conceptions of Chinese Civilization," *The Legacy of China,* p. 4.

73. Foucault, "Language to Infinity," *Language, Counter-Memory, Practice: Selected Essays and Interviews,* ed. Donald F. Bouchard, trans. Bouchard and Sherry Simon (Ithaca: Cornell University Press, 1977), p. 56.

74. Foucault, *The Order of Things,* pp. 38, 39, 38.

75. Matthew Ricci, *China in the Sixteenth Century: The Journals of Matthew Ricci, 1583–1610,* trans. Louis J. Gallagher (New York: Random House, 1953), p. 28.

76. Henri Cordier, "Chinese Language and Literature," in Alexander Wylie, *Chinese Researches* (Shanghai, 1897), p. 195.

77. George Steiner, *After Babel: Aspects of Language and Translation* (Oxford: Oxford University Press, 1975), p. 357.

78. William Boltz, *The Origin and Early Development of the Chinese Writing System* (New Haven: American Oriental Society, 1994), p. 6.

79. Ibid., pp. 6, 9.

80. Jacques Derrida, *Of Grammatology,* trans. Gayatri Chakravorty Spivak (Baltimore: Johns Hopkins University Press, 1976), p. 90.

81. Dawson, "Western Conceptions of Chinese Civilization," p. 22.

82. Martin Heidegger, *Being and Time,* trans. John Macquarrie and Edward Robinson (New York: Harper & Row, 1962), p. 191.

83. Ibid., p. 195.

84. Gadamer, *Truth and Method,* p. 266.

85. Ibid., pp. 267, 269.

86. Oscar Wilde, "The Decaying of Lying: An Observation," *Intentions* (New York: Bretano's, 1905), pp. 46–47.

87. Eugenio Donato, "Historical Imagination and the Idioms of Criticism," *Boundary 2* 8 (fall 1979): 52.

88. Roland Barthes, *Empire of Signs*, trans. Richard Howard (New York: Hill and Wang, 1982), pp. 3, 6.

89. Ibid., p. 18.

90. Roland Barthes, "Well, and China?" trans. Lee Hildreth, *Discourse* 8 (fall–winter 1986–87): 116, 117.

91. Ibid., p. 118.

92. Ibid., p. 119.

93. Simon Leys, "Footnote to a Barthesian Opuscule," *Broken Images: Essays on Chinese Culture and Politics*, trans. Steve Cox (New York: St. Martin's Press, 1979), p. 89.

94. Lisa Lowe, *Critical Terrains: French and British Orientalism* (Ithaca: Cornell University Press, 1991), p. 163.

95. Ibid., p. 154.

96. Barthes, "Well, and China?" p. 117.

97. Barthes, *Empire of Signs*, p. 108.

98. Ibid., p. 110.

99. Victor Segalen, *Essai sur l'exotisme: Une esthétique du divers (notes)* (Montpellier: Editions Fata Morgana, 1978), p. 19.

100. Ibid., pp. 76, 77.

101. Gadamer, *Truth and Method*, p. 42.

102. Ibid., p. 35.   103. Ibid., p. 14.

104. Ibid., p. 17.   105. Ibid., pp. 306 ff.

Chapter 2. Montaigne, Postmodernism, and Cultural Critique

1. Ann Kaplan, to cite one such example, speaks of the postmodern as "representing a cultural 'break' in the sense of Foucault's 'episteme,' or Kuhn's paradigms: the postmodern moment is a break initiated by modernism, which is here viewed as a transitional period between nineteenth-century Romanticism and the current cultural scene." E. A. Kaplan, ed., *Postmodernism and Its Discontents: Theories, Practices* (London: Verso, 1988), p. 1. But see also Fredric Jameson, *Postmodernism; or, The Cultural Logic of Late Capitalism* (Durham: Duke University Press, 1991), pp. 26, 167 ff.

2. Jean-François Lyotard, *The Postmodern Condition: A Report on Knowledge*, trans. Geoff Bennington and Brian Massumi (Minneapolis: University of Minnesota Press, 1984), p. 46.

3. Ibid., p. 51.

4. Ibid., p. xxv.

5. See Steven Conner, *The Postmodern Culture: An Introduction to Theories of the Contemporary* (Oxford: Basil Blackwell, 1989), pp. 32–43.

6. Linda Hutcheon, *A Poetics of Postmodernism: History, Theory, Fiction* (London: Routledge, 1988), p. 4.

7. Fredric Jameson, "Foreword," in Lyotard, *The Postmodern Condition*, p. viii.

8. Jameson, *The Ideologies of Theory: Essays, 1971–1986*, 2 vols. (Minneapolis: University of Minnesota Press, 1988) 2: 103.

9. Jameson, "Foreword," in Lyotard, *The Postmodern Condition*, p. xvi. See Richard Shusterman, "Postmodernism and the Aesthetic Turn," *Poetics Today* 10: 3 (fall 1989): 605–22.

10. Jameson, *The Ideologies of Theory*, 2: 195–96.

11. Fredric Jameson, *Postmodernism; or, The Cultural Logic of Late Capitalism*, p. 2.

12. Jameson, "Foreword," in Lyotard, *The Postmodern Condition*, p. xiv.

13. Ibid., p. xvi.

14. Lyotard, "Answering the Question: What Is Postmodernism?" trans. Régis Durand, ibid., p. 79.

15. Ibid., p. 81.

16. Ibid.

17. Umberto Eco, *Postscript to the Name of the Rose*, trans. William Weaver (New York: Harcourt Brace Jovanovich, 1984), pp. 66, 68.

18. See Montaigne, "Of Presumption," II: 17, *The Complete Essays*, p. 481.

19. Lyotard, *The Postmodern Condition*, p. 75.

20. Arthur C. Danto, "Approaching the End of Art," *The State of the Art* (New York: Prentice Hall, 1987), p. 216.

21. Hans Robert Jauss, *Aesthetic Experience and Literary Hermeneutics*, trans. Michael Shaw (Minneapolis: University of Minnesota Press, 1982), p. 57.

22. Ihab Hassan, "Pluralism in Postmodern Perspective," *Critical Inquiry* 12 (spring 1986): 504.

23. Norman Holland, "Postmodern Psychoanalysis," in *Innovation/ Renovation: New Perspectives on the Humanities*, ed. Ihab Hassan and Sally Hassan (Madison: University of Wisconsin Press, 1983), pp. 300, 304–5.

24. Bakhtin, *Problems of Dostoevsky's Poetics*, p. 287.

25. Montaigne, "It Is Folly to Measure the True and False by Our Own Capacity," I: 27, *The Complete Essays*, p. 135.

26. Ibid., pp. 133, 134.

27. Montaigne, "Of Presumption," II: 17, ibid., p. 478.

28. Ibid., p. 480.

29. Montaigne, "Of Coaches," III: 6, ibid., pp. 692, 693.

30. Tzvetan Todorov, "L'être et l'autre: Montaigne," trans. Pierre Saint-Amand, *Yale French Studies* 64 (1983): 118.

31. Ibid., p. 125.

32. Ibid., pp. 127, 135.

33. Ibid., pp. 125, 126.

34. Montaigne, "Of Cannibals," I: 31, *The Complete Essays*, p. 150.

35. Ibid., p. 152.

36. Todorov, "L'être et l'autre: Montaigne," p. 123.

37. Montaigne, "Of Cannibals," *The Complete Essays*, p. 153.

38. Ibid., p. 155.

39. Ibid., p. 158.

40. Todorov, "L'être et l'autre: Montaigne," p. 118.

41. Segalen, *Essai sur l'exotisme*, p. 13.

42. See Edwin M. Duval, "Lessons of the New World: Design and Meaning in Montaigne's 'Des Cannibales' (I: 31) and 'Des coches' (III: 6)," *Yale French Studies* 64 (1983): 95–112.

43. Michel de Certeau, *Heterologies: Discourse on the Other*, trans. Brian Massumi (Minneapolis: University of Minnesota Press, 1986), p. 73.

44. M. Blanchard, "Of Cannibalism and Autobiography," *MLN* 93 (May 1978): 654.

45. Duval, "Lessons of the New World," p. 102.

46. Montaigne, "Of Cannibals," pp. 153, 155.

47. Ibid., p. 156.

48. Todorov, "L'être et l'autre: Montaigne," p. 122.

49. Ibid., p. 123.

50. Ibid., p. 125.

51. Ibid.

52. Tzvetan Todorov, *On Human Diversity: Nationalism, Racism, and Exoticism in French Thought*, trans. Catherine Porter (Cambridge, Mass.: Harvard University Press, 1993), p. 12.

53. Ibid., p. 42.

54. Todorov, *Literature and Its Theorists*, p. 157.

55. Ibid., p. 159.

56. Leo Ou-fan Lee, "On the Margins of the Chinese Discourse: Some Personal Thoughts on the Cultural Meaning of the Periphery," *Daedalus* 120 (spring 1991): 217.

57. Todorov, *Literature and Its Theorists*, pp. 159–60.

58. Ibid., p. 160.

59. Jiao Xun, *Mengzi zhengyi* [The Correct Meaning of the Mencius], iii.6, p. 138.

60. Ibid., xi.2, pp. 433–34.

61. Irene Bloom, "Human Nature and Biological Nature in Mencius," *Philosophy East and West* 47 (January 1997): 23.

62. Conner, *Postmodernist Culture*, p. 9.

63. Foucault, *The Order of Things*, p. xv.

64. See Lyotard, *The Postmodern Condition*, pp. 20–23.

65. Mario Vargas Llosa, *The Storyteller*, trans. Helen Lane (New York: Farrar, Straus and Giroux, 1989), p. 158.

66. Keith Booker, *Vargas Llosa among the Postmodernists* (Gainesville: University Press of Florida, 1994), p. 121.

67. Conner, *Postmodernist Culture*, p. 9.

68. Ibid., pp. 9–10.

69. Henry Louis Gates, Jr., "Editor's Introduction: Writing 'Race' and the Difference It Makes," *Critical Inquiry* 12 (fall 1985): 5.

70. Ibid., p. 13.

71. Ibid., p. 15.

72. Blanchard, "Of Cannibalism and Autobiography," p. 658.

73. Ernst Robert Curtius, *European Literature and the Latin Middle Ages*, trans. Willard R. Trask (Princeton: Princeton University Press, 1953), p. 291.

74. M. Bakhtin, *The Dialogic Imagination: Four Essays*, trans. Caryl Emerson and Michael Holquist (Austin: University of Texas Press, 1981), p. 272.

Chapter 3. Jewish and Chinese Literalism

1. Dionysius of Halicarnassus, *Critical Essays I*, trans. Stephen Usher, Loeb Classical Library vol. 465 (Cambridge, Mass.: Harvard University Press, 1974), p. 7.

2. John M. Steadman, *The Myth of Asia* (New York: Simon and Schuster, 1969), p. 15.

3. For a warning against the danger of facile invocation of collective identities and mistaking cultures for isolated, free-floating entities, see Henry Louis Gates, Jr., "Beyond the Culture Wars: Identities in Dialogue," *Profession 93*: 6–11. Gates reminds us with the French anthropologist Jean-Loup Amselle that cultures "aren't situated one by the other like Leibniz's windowless monads," but rather, "the very definition of a given culture is in fact the result of intercultural relations of forces" (p. 8).

4. Steadman, *The Myth of Asia*, p. 30.

5. Martin Hengel, *Jews, Greeks and Barbarians: Aspects of the Hellenization of Judaism in the pre-Christian Period*, trans. John Bowden (Philadelphia: Fortress Press, 1980), p. 78.

6. Jiao Xun, *Mengzi zhengyi* [The Correct Meaning of the Mencius], i.7, p. 54.

7. Philip Carrington, *The Early Christian Church*, 2 vols. (Cambridge: Cambridge University Press, 1957), 1: 14.

8. See Martin Hengel, *Judaism and Hellenism: Studies in Their Encoun-*

ter in Palestine during the Early Hellenistic Period, trans. John Bowden, 2 vols. (Philadelphia: Fortress Press, 1974).

9. See Saul Lieberman, "How Much Greek Is Jewish Palestine?" in *Essays in Greco-Roman and Related Talmudic Literature*, ed. Henry A. Fischel (New York: KTAV Publishing House, 1977), pp. 325–43.

10. Carrington, *The Early Christian Church*, 1: 10.

11. John Milton, *On the Morning of Christ's Nativity*, in *Complete Poems and Major Prose*, ed. Merritt Y. Hughes (Indianapolis: Bobbs-Merrill, 1957), p. 48.

12. Heinrich Heine, *Concerning the History of Religion and Philosophy in Germany*, trans. Helen Mustard, in *The Romantic School and Other Essays*, ed. Jost Hermand and Robert C. Holub (New York: Continuum, 1985), p. 136.

13. Ibid., p. 137.

14. See Hengel, *Judaism and Hellenism*, pp. 306, 309.

15. See Hans Dieter Betz, "The Birth of Christianity as a Hellenistic Religion: Three Theories of Origin," *Journal of Religion* 74 (Jan. 1994): 1–25.

16. Morna D. Hooker, *Continuity and Discontinuity: Early Christianity in Its Jewish Setting* (London: Epworth Press, 1986), p. 27.

17. P. Sanders, *The Historical Figure of Jesus* (London: Penguin, 1993), p. 96. For important works in New Testament scholarship that emphasize the Jewish background of Jesus, see Geza Vermes, *Jesus the Jew: A Historian's Reading of the Gospels* (London: Collins, 1973); and Vermes, *The Religion of Jesus the Jew* (Minneapolis: Fortress Press, 1993).

18. Hooker, *Continuity and Discontinuity*, p. 26.

19. Averil Cameron, *Christianity and the Rhetoric of Empire: The Development of Christian Discourse* (Berkeley: University of California Press, 1991), pp. 2, 38.

20. Karlfried Froehlich, ed. and trans., *Biblical Interpretation in the Early Church* (Philadelphia: Fortress Press, 1984), intro. p. 10.

21. Robert M. Grant with David Tracy, *A Short History of the Interpretation of the Bible*, 2d revised ed. (Philadelphia: Fortress Press, 1984), p. 63.

22. Wayne A. Meeks and Robert L. Wilken, *Jews and Christians in Antioch in the First Four Centuries of the Common Era* (Decatur: Scholars Press, 1978), p. 21.

23. Quoted in Harry Austryn Wolfson, *Philo: Foundations of Religious Philosophy in Judaism, Christianity, and Islam*, 2 vols. (Cambridge, Mass.: Harvard University Press, 1948), 1: 116, 123.

24. Quoted ibid., p. 160.

25. David Dawson, *Allegorical Readers and Cultural Revision in Ancient Alexandria* (Berkeley: University of California Press, 1992), pp. 74, 107.

26. Jean Daniélou, *From Shadows to Reality: Studies in the Biblical Typology of the Fathers*, trans. Wulstan Hubberd (Westminster: Newman Press, 1960), p. 202.

27. Froehlich, *Biblical Interpretation in the Early Church*, p. 20.

28. Origen, *On First Principles: Book Four* (II, 9, III, 5), in Froehlich, *Biblical Interpretation in the Early Church*, pp. 62, 67.

29. See Wolfson, *Philo*, 1: 158–59.

30. Jean Daniélou, *Origen*, trans. Walter Mitchell (New York: Sheed and Ward, 1955), p. 184.

31. See ibid., pp. 174–78.

32. Nicholas Robert Michael de Lange, *Origen and the Jews: Studies in Jewish-Christian Relations in Third-Century Palestine* (Cambridge: Cambridge University Press, 1976), p. 7.

33. Ibid., p. 30.

34. Origen, *On First Principles: Book Four* (III, 1), in Froehlich, *Biblical Interpretation in the Early Church*, p. 63.

35. Origen, *On First Principles: Book Four* (I, 6), in Froehlich, ibid., pp. 52–53.

36. Ibid., p. 53.

37. Gerard E. Caspary, *Politics and Exegesis: Origen and the Two Swords* (Berkeley: University of California Press, 1979), p. 53. See also Henry Chadwick, *The Early Church* (Harmondsworth: Penguin, 1967).

38. James Kugel, "Two Introductions to Midrash," *Prooftexts* 3 (May 1983): 146.

39. Harry Austryn Wolfson, *The Philosophy of Church Fathers: Faith, Trinity, Incarnation* (Cambridge, Mass.: Harvard University Press, 1956), pp. 24, 43.

40. *Mekilta de-Rabbi Ishmael*, ed. and trans. Jacob Z. Lauterbach, 2 vols. (Philadelphia: The Jewish Publication Society of America, 1933; rpt. 1961), 2: 135, 142.

41. Wolfson, *Philo*, 1: 138.

42. Kugel, "Two Introductions to Midrash," p. 143.

43. St. Augustine, *On Christian Doctrine*, trans. D. W. Robertson, Jr. (Indianapolis: Bobbs-Merrill, 1958), II.vi.8, p. 38.

44. Thomas Aquinas, *Basic Writings of St. Thomas Aquinas*, ed. Anton Pegis, 2 vols. (New York: Random House, 1945), 2: 17.

45. Martin Luther, *Works*, ed. Helmut T. Lehman, trans. Eric W. Gritsch and Ruth C. Gritsch, vol. 39 (Philadelphia: Fortress Press, 1970), p. 178.

46. Karlfried Froehlich, "Problems of Lutheran Hermeneutics," in *Studies in Lutheran Hermeneutics*, ed. John Reumann with Samuel H. Nafzger and Harold H. Ditmanson (Philadelphia: Fortress Press, 1979), p. 127.

47. De Lange, *Origen and the Jews*, p. 112.

48. George Minamiki, *The Chinese Rites Controversy from Its Beginning to Modern Times* (Chicago: Loyola University Press, 1985), p. ix.

49. David E. Mungello, *Curious Land: Jesuit Accommodation and the Origins of Sinology* (Honolulu: University of Hawaii Press, 1989), p. 355.

50. Arthur Lovejoy, "The Chinese Origin of a Romanticism," in *Essays in the History of Ideas* (Baltimore: Johns Hopkins University Press, 1948), p. 105.

51. Reichwein, *China and Europe*, p. 77.

52. Lionel M. Jensen, "The Invention of 'Confucius' and His Chinese Other, 'Kong Fuzi,'" *Positions* 1 (fall 1993): 415.

53. Quoted in Jacques Gernet, *China and the Christian Impact: A Conflict of Cultures*, trans. Janet Lloyd (Cambridge: Cambridge University Press, 1985), p. 27.

54. For detailed discussion of Bouvet and his relationship with Leibniz, see David E. Mungello, *Leibniz and Confucianism: The Search for Accord* (Honolulu: University of Hawaii Press, 1977), chapter 3; and the same author's *Curious Land: Jesuit Accommodation and the Origins of Sinology*, chapter 9. Though Bouvet was much later than Ricci and belonged to a group of the so-called Figurists who applied the Hermetic idea of Ancient Theology to the interpretation of Chinese classics, there was essential continuity between them in terms of Jesuit accommodationism. As Mungello argues, "Ricci's formula of accommodation had been evolving throughout the seventeenth century and the intellectual leap to Figurism was a rather small one" (*Curious Land*, pp. 17–18).

55. Joachim Bouvet, letter to Leibniz (Peking, 4 November 1701), in *Leibniz korrespondiert mit China: Der Briefwechsel mit den Jesuitenmissionaren (1689–1714)*, ed. Rita Widmaier (Frankfurt am Main: Vittorio Klostermann, 1990), p. 151.

56. Bouvet, letter to Leibniz (Peking, 8 November 1702), ibid., p. 174.

57. Claudia von Collani, ed., *Eine wissenschaftliche Akademie für China: Briefe des Chinamissionars Joachim Bouvet S.J. an Gottfried Wilhelm Leibniz und Jean-Paul Bignon über die Erforschung der chinesischen Kultur, Sprache und Geschichte* (Stuttgart: Franz Steiner, 1989), p. 111.

58. Bouvet, letter to Leibniz (8 November 1702), in *Leibniz korrespondiert mit China*, p. 174.

59. Bouvet, letter to Leibniz (4 November 1701), ibid., pp. 150, 154.

60. Mungello, *Curious Land*, p. 307.

61. Leibniz, *On the Civil Cult of Confucius*, in *Writings on China*, p. 64.

62. Zhu Jing, "16–18 shiji de xifang chuanjiaoshi yu Zhong Xi wenhua jiaoliu" [Western Missionaries and the Chinese-Western Cultural Exchange from the Sixteenth to the Eighteenth Century], in *Jidujiao yu*

jindai wenhua [Christianity and Modern Chinese Culture], ed. Zhu Wei-zheng (Shanghai: Shanghai renmin, 1994), p. 44.

63. Leibniz, *Discourse on the Natural Theology of the Chinese*, in *Writings on China*, p. 78.

64. Gernet, *China and the Christian Impact*, p. 29.

65. Mungello, *Curious Land*, p. 49. For an account in Chinese, see Luo Guang, *Jiaoting yu Zhongguo shijie shi* [History of Diplomatic Missions between the Vatican and China] (Taipei: Zhuanji wenxue, 1983).

66. Quoted in Gernet, *China and the Christian Impact*, p. 33.

67. Quoted in Gernet, ibid., p. 203.

68. Quoted in Arthur F. Wright, "The Chinese Language and Foreign Ideas," in *Studies in Chinese Thought*, ed. Wright (Chicago: University of Chicago Press, 1953), p. 291.

69. Ibid., p. 287.

70. Gernet, *China and the Christian Impact*, pp. 3, 239.

71. Ibid., p. 241.

72. Quoted in Gernet, ibid., pp. 206, 207.

73. Gernet, ibid., p. 239.

74. Ibid., p. 244.

75. See Chad Hansen, *Language and Logic in Ancient China* (Ann Arbor: University of Michigan Press, 1983).

76. See David L. Hall and Roger T. Ames, *Thinking though Confucius* (Albany: State University of New York Press, 1987).

77. See Stephen Owen, *Traditional Chinese Poetry and Poetics: Omen of the World* (Madison: University of Wisconsin Press, 1985); Pauline Yu, *The Reading of Imagery in the Chinese Poetic Tradition* (Princeton: Princeton University Press, 1987); François Jullien, *La valeur allusive: Des catégories originales de l'interprétation poétique dans la tradition chinoise (Contribution à une réflection sur l'altérité interculturelle)* (Paris: École Française d'Extrême-Orient, 1985); and Michael Fuller, "Pursuing the Complete Bamboo in the Breast: Reflections on a Classical Chinese Image for Immediacy," *Harvard Journal of Asiatic Studies* 53 (June 1993): 5–23. Opposed in principle to the classification of individual human beings into collective categories and group mentalities, I certainly do not believe that *all* sinologists hold views that present China as the opposite of the West. Scholars like James J. Y. Liu, Andrew Plaks, Kang-i Sun Chang, to mention just a few, have all used the concept of allegory in their discussions of Chinese literature. Even Stephen Owen and Pauline Yu are aware of some of the nuances. For example, while insisting on the literal reading of *shi* poetry, Owen allows certain subgenres of Chinese poetry to entertain fictionality, and more recently he has questioned the authenticity of the historical ground of Chinese poetry (see Owen, "Po-

etry and Its Historical Ground," *Chinese Literature: Essays, Articles, Reviews* 12 [Dec. 1990]: 107–18).

78. Haun Saussy, *The Problem of a Chinese Aesthetic* (Stanford: Stanford University Press, 1993), p. 36.

79. Louis H. Feldman, "Hebraism and Hellenism Reconsidered," *Judaism* 43 (spring 1994): 118.

80. Saussy, *The Problem of a Chinese Aesthetic*, p. 34.

81. Guo Qingfan (1844–1896), *Zhuangzi jishi* [Variorum Edition of the *Zhuangzi*], in *Zhuzi jicheng* [Collection of Distinguished Philosophical Works], 8 vols. (Beijing: Zhonghua shuju, 1954), 3: 31.

82. Wang Xianqian (1842–1917), *Xunzi jijie* [Collected Annotations of the *Xunzi*], in *Zhuzi jicheng* [Collection of Distinguished Philosophical Works], 2: 258.

83. See David Stern, *Midrash and Theory: Ancient Jewish Exegesis and Contemporary Literary Studies* (Evanston: Northwestern University Press, 1996), especially pp. 21 ff.

84. Daniel Bonevac, "What Multiculturalism Should Not Be," *College Literature* 21 (Oct. 1994): 158.

85. Antoine Berman, *The Experience of the Foreign: Culture and Translation in Romantic Germany*, trans. S. Heyvaert (Albany: State University of New York Press, 1992), p. 4.

Chapter 4. Out of the Cultural Ghetto

1. Gerald Graff, *Professing Literature: An Institutional History* (Chicago: University of Chicago Press, 1987), p. 3.

2. Fredric Jameson, "Literary Innovation and Modes of Production: A Commentary," *Modern Chinese Literature* 1 (Sept. 1984): 67.

3. Ibid., p. 71.

4. Ibid., p. 72.

5. Ibid., pp. 75–76.

6. Fredric Jameson, *Postmodernism; or, The Cultural Logic of Late Capitalism*, p. 36.

7. Fredric Jameson, "Third World Literature in the Era of Multinational Capitalism," *Social Text* 15 (fall 1986): 69; italics in the original.

8. Ibid., p. 71.   9. Ibid., p. 74.

10. Ibid., p. 80.   11. Ibid., p. 68.

12. Ibid., p. 69, emphasis added.

13. It would be tedious to rehearse here the many uses Lu Xun and his works have been put to in China for ideological control of the country and in power struggles within the Communist Party itself. A typical example is an article by Jiang Zemin, the Party chief, published in *Renmin ribao* or *People's Daily* (25 Sept. 1991) on the occasion of Lu Xun's 110th

birthday, in which Jiang claims that "Lu Xun's road leads from patriotism to communism," and makes Lu Xun a booster of "national pride" in the struggle against "international enemy forces" and their accomplice, the ubiquitous "bourgeois liberalization." For an account of the changing allegorical interpretations of Lu Xun's works that have been used to legitimize the various Party policies, see Merle Goldman, "The Political Use of Lu Xun in the Cultural Revolution and After," in *Lu Xun and His Legacy*, ed. Leo Ou-fan Lee (Bloomington, Indiana University Press, 1985), pp. 180–96.

14. Leo Ou-fan Lee, *Voices from the Iron House: A Study of Lu Xun* (Bloomington: Indiana University Press, 1987), p. 3.

15. Ibid., p. 68.

16. Even a casual reading of literary works published in the last decade and of Chinese-language journals with a wide intellectual appeal that regularly feature critical essays on literature, such as *Dushu* [Reading Monthly] in Beijing, *Ershiyi shiji* [Twenty-first Century] in Hong Kong, *Dangdai* [Con-Temporary] in Taiwan, and *Jintian* [Today] overseas, to mention just a few, will make it abundantly clear how much change has taken place in contemporary Chinese literature, how greatly it differs from that of an earlier generation of established modern writers like Mao Dun, Ba Jin, or Ding Ling, and how notions, terms, and critical approaches of an unmistakably Western origin have traveled across linguistic borders and have settled in Chinese critical discourse (which is nothing new in the whole history of modern Chinese literature, but has an especially strong political resonance in post-Mao China). Whether Chinese literature of the 1980s is legitimately "modern" or "postmodern" or whether it is just a poor imitation of some Western model or fashion is a vexed question still plaguing its critics, detractors and defenders alike. Part of what I am trying to do in this chapter is to look at this question from a different perspective so that we will not be so obsessed with the problem of influence and authenticity, but may understand this problem and its cultural context in terms of the recent changes in Chinese literature and literary studies.

17. Jonathan Chaves, "Forum: From the 1990 AAS Roundtable," *Chinese Literature: Essays, Articles, Reviews* 13 (Dec. 1991): 77.

18. Ibid., p. 80.

19. Paul de Man, *Allegories of Reading: Figural Language in Rousseau, Nietzsche, Rilke, and Proust* (New Haven: Yale University Press, 1979), pp. 16–17.

20. Jameson, "Third World Literature in the Era of Multinational Capitalism," p. 68.

21. Stephen Owen, "The Anxiety of Global Influence: What Is World Poetry?" *New Republic* (19 Nov. 1990): 29.

22. Ibid.

23. Jameson, "Third World Literature in the Era of Multinational Capitalism," p. 66.

24. Owen, "The Anxiety of Global Influence," p. 28.

25. Michelle Yeh, "Chayi de youlü: Yige huiying" [The Anxiety of Difference: A Rejoinder], *Jintian* [Today] 1 (1991): 94.

26. Owen, "The Anxiety of Global Influence," p. 32.

27. Ibid., p. 30.

28. Ibid.

29. Ibid., p. 31.

30. Bonnie McDougall, "Bei Dao's Poetry: Revelation and Communication," *Modern Chinese Literature* 1 (spring 1985): 247.

31. Owen, "The Anxiety of Global Influence," p. 28.

32. Ibid., p. 31.

33. Yeh, ""A Rejoinder," p. 95.

34. Leo Ou-fan Lee, "Huli dong shihua" [Ramblings on Poetry from the "Foxhole Studio"] *Jintian* [Today] 2 (1992): 204.

35. You Yi, "Ye tan bashi niandai wenxue de xihua" [Also on "Westernization" in Literature of the 1980s], *Jintian* [Today] 3–4 (1991): 31.

36. Yeh, "A Rejoinder," p. 95.

37. Ibid., p. 96.

38. Stephen Owen, *Traditional Chinese Poetry and Poetics*, p. 57.

39. Stephen Owen, *Remembrances: The Experience of the Past in Classical Chinese Literature* (Cambridge, Mass.: Harvard University Press, 1986), p. 67.

40. Owen, "The Anxiety of Global Influence," p. 30.

41. Pauline Yu, *The Reading of Imagery*, p. 5.

42. Ibid., p. 35; italics in the original.

43. Ibid., p. 76.

44. Jameson, "Third World Literature in the Era of Multinational Capitalism," pp. 80, 69.

45. Yu, *The Reading of Imagery*, p. 17.

46. Ibid., p. 82.

47. Chaves, "Forum: From the 1990 AAS Roundtable," p. 78; italics in the original.

48. Liu Kang, "Politics, Critical Paradigms: Reflections on Modern Chinese Literature Studies," *Modern China* 19 (Jan. 1993): 38.

49. Ibid., p. 14.

50. Ibid.

51. Stanley Rosen, *Hermeneutics as Politics* (New York: Oxford University Press, 1987), p. 6; see also pp. 190–93.

52. Liu Kang, "Politics, Critical Paradigms," p. 14.

53. Whether China ever had or has a civil society is a question to which historians, sociologists, and political scientists have devoted much attention in the last few years. A conference "Public Sphere and Civil Society in China" was held in May 1992 at UCLA, and it seems to me that the most convincing argument (made by Philip Huang, Frederic Wakeman, Jr., and others) is the one that not only questions the existence of a civil society in China but raises the methodological question of how theoretical concepts like "civil society" and "public sphere" may be appropriately used to discuss the Chinese situation. For discussion of this important issue from various perspectives, see the special issue of *Modern China* 19 (April 1993), subtitled *Symposium: 'Public Sphere'/ 'Civil Society' in China? Paradigmatic Issues in Chinese Studies, III.*

54. Chicago Cultural Studies Group, "Critical Multiculturalism," *Critical Inquiry* 18 (spring 1992): 532. The Chicago Cultural Studies Group (CCSG) is a group of scholars who began to gather in Chicago in 1990 from different disciplines and cultural backgrounds in India, China, Africa, and North America. The "multicultural" as well as interdisciplinary composition of this group makes it possible for these scholars to articulate, in their recent essay "Critical Multiculturalism," some extremely valuable ideas and opinions, because they are able to relate theoretical discussions in American academia to a larger and specifically "Third World" context. From a refreshingly new perspective, these scholars as a group are able to see things, to raise questions, and to suggest some answers that are often different from what we normally find in Western theoretical discourse. The voice of this group is thus in many ways unique; it has, as is so rare in Western theoretical discussions, incorporated the voice of the Other that speaks for certain non-Western cultural identities and positions.

55. Liu Kang, "Politics, Critical Paradigms," pp. 18, 19.

56. Ibid., p. 20.

57. CCSG, "Critical Multiculturalism," p. 534.

58. Ibid., pp. 534–35.

59. Gadamer, *Truth and Method*, p. 356.

60. For a recent survey of the 1980s and the excitement of "culture fever," see Jing Wang, *High Culture Fever: Politics, Aesthetics, and Ideology in Deng's China* (Berkeley: University of California Press, 1996).

61. Li Tuo, "Yijiu bawu" [Nineteen Eighty-Five] *Jintian* [Today] 3–4 (1991): 71.

62. Liu Zaifu, "Gaobie zhushen: Zhongguo dangdai wenxue lilun

shijimo de zhengzha" [Farewell to the Gods: The *fin de siècle* Strife of Contemporary Chinese Literary Theory] *Ershiyi shiji* [Twenty-first Century] 5 (June 1991): 127.

63. Ibid., p. 129.   64. Ibid., p. 131.
65. Ibid., p. 129.   66. Ibid., p. 133.
67. Ibid., p. 134.

68. Wu Xiaoming, "Du 'Gaobie zhushen'" [On "Farewell to the Gods"], *Ershiyi shiji* [Twenty-first Century] 8 (Dec. 1991): 152, 156.

69. Ibid., p. 153.

70. Ibid.

71. Henry Louis Gates, Jr., "The Master's Pieces: On Canon Formation and the African-American Tradition," in *The Politics of Liberal Education*, ed. Darryl J. Gless and Barbara Herrnstein Smith (Durham: Duke University Press, 1992), p. 111.

Chapter 5. Western Theory and Chinese Reality

1. Lu Xun, "Cong haizi de zhaoxiang shuo qi" [Reflections Starting from My Son's Photographs], in *Lu Xun quanji* [The Complete Works of Lu Xun], 16 vols. (Beijing: Renmin wenxue, 1981), 6: 82.

2. Edward Said, "Traveling Theory," in *The World, the Text, and the Critic* (Cambridge, Mass.: Harvard University Press, 1983), p. 227.

3. Lu Xun, "Nalai zhuyi" [Grabism], in *Quanji* [Complete Works], 6: 40.

4. Ibid., p. 39.

5. See Friedrich Schleiermacher, "On the Different Methods of Translation," trans. André Lefevere, in A. Leslie Willson, ed., *German Romantic Criticism* (New York: Continuum, 1982), p. 9.

6. See Lu Xun, "Nahan zixu" [Preface to *A Call to Arms*], *Quanji* [Complete Works], 1: 419.

7. For an illuminating analysis of Lu Xun's complicated relationship with left-wing writers, Marxist aesthetics, and Soviet literature, see Leo Lee, *Voices from the Iron House*, pp. 151–72. As Lee points out, in his time and mainly through secondhand Japanese sources of information, Lu Xun "could never have conceived of the 'new epoch' [of Soviet literature] as ushering in two decades of Stalinist bureaucracy and terror" (p. 154); moreover, the tight control of literary expression as we know it later, the "pervasive impact of the so-called *partinost* (party spirit), to the extent of dictating to writers what and how to write, simply did not exist in China in Lu Xun's time" (p. 165). It therefore becomes an intriguing hypothetical question many Chinese intellectuals often ask themselves: What and how would Lu Xun write had he lived to see the complete marginalization of intellectuals, the tightening of ideological

control, and the incessant political campaigns since the early 1950s in which many of his close friends and disciples—Hu Feng, Feng Xuefeng, and others—were purged and branded as counterrevolutionaries or rightists? Mao Zedong himself once answered this question by making the remark to the effect that Lu Xun would not dare to write the way he did, if he were alive in 1957 when the antirightist campaign was raging over China. But even in his Yan'an talks of 1942, as Merle Goldman argues, Mao already rejected Lu Xun's satirical style of writing as "inappropriate for life in a Communist society" (Goldman, "The Political Use of Lu Xun in the Cultural Revolution and After," in Leo Lee, ed., *Lu Xun and His Legacy*, p. 181).

8. See Liu Zaifu, "Wenxue yanjiu siwei kongjian de tuozhan" [The Expanding of Mental Space in Literary Studies], in *Wenxue de fansi* [Reflections on Literature] (Beijing: Renmin wenxue, 1986), pp. 1–39.

9. First produced as a film and then adapted for the stage and made into one of the eight "revolutionary model plays" during the Cultural Revolution, the celebrated *Hongdeng ji* [Story of a Red Lantern] can serve as an example of the use of such Chinese formulas in literary and artistic expressions. The characters in the story—the grandma, the father, and the daughter—are not related by blood but are members of three different families who have survived the persecution of their class enemy and have come together as one revolutionary unit. The point this story makes is that class relationship is more important than—and replaces—traditional family relations in the consciousness of communist revolutionaries. To make that obvious point explicit is the business of criticism that analyzes the characters in terms of their class origin and the whole story in terms of class and class struggle.

10. Liu Zaifu, "Wenxue yanjiu ying yi ren wei zhongxin" [Literary Study Should Put the Human Being at the Center], in *Wenxue de fansi* [Reflections on Literature], p. 46.

11. Ibid., p. 48.

12. Liu Zaifu, "Lun wenxue de zhutixing" [On the Subjectivity of Literature], in *Wenxue de fansi* [Reflections on Literature], pp. 64–65.

13. Like many other terms used in the Chinese Communist Party's political rhetoric, the "screw" metaphor may have a Soviet origin. Joseph Stalin, in a toast at the 1945 Kremlin reception in honor of World War II heroes, compared the Soviets to "'screws' that keep our large state mechanisms in a state of readiness in all areas of science, economics and the military" (quoted in Evgeny Dobrenko, "The Literature of the Zhdanov Era: Mentality, Mythology, Lexicon," in Thomas Lahusen with Gene Kuperman, eds., *Late Soviet Culture: From Perestroika to Novostroika*

[Durham: Duke University Press, 1993], p. 119). Neither Stalin nor Mao specified, however, who was or who held the screwdriver.

14. Said, "Traveling Theory," in *The World, the Text, and the Critic*, pp. 230–31.

15. Ibid., p. 233.

16. Yan Zhaozhu, "Lun wenyi de mei de qinggan: Chongdu *Zai Yan'an wenyi zuotanhui shangde jianghua*" [On the Feeling of Beauty in Literature and Art: Rereading *Talk at the Yan'an Forum on Literature and Art*], *Wenyi yanjiu* [Literature and Art Studies] 4 (July 1990): 9.

17. Ibid., p. 10.

18. J. T. Mitchell, "The Violence of Public Art: *Do the Right Thing*," *Critical Inquiry* 16 (summer 1990): 880.

19. Ibid., p. 883.

20. Ibid., pp. 880–81.

21. Ibid., p. 881, n. 2.

22. Rey Chow, "Violence in the Other Country: Preliminary Remarks on the 'China Crisis,' June 1989," *Radical America* 22 (July–Aug. 1988; pub. Sept. 1989): 24.

23. Ibid., p. 25.

24. Roger Chartier, *On the Edge of the Cliff*, p. 20.

25. Rey Chow, "Violence in the Other Country," p. 26.

26. "Statement to All Members of the Communist Party and All the People by the Central Committee of the Chinese Communist Party and the State Council," *Renmin ribao* [People's Daily], 5 June 1989, p. 1.

27. See *Renmin ribao* [People's Daily], 12 June 1989, p. 1.

28. "Zhongguo neizheng burong ganshe" [We Cannot Tolerate Interference in China's Internal Affairs], *Renmin ribao* [People's Daily], 14 June 1989, p. 1.

29. Lu Xun, "Nalai zhuyi" [Grabism], *Quanji* [Complete Works], 6: 38.

30. Kay Ann Johnson, "The Revolutionary Tradition of Pro-Democracy Students," *Radical America* 22 (July–Aug. 1988; pub. Sept. 1989): 7, 12 n. 2.

31. Joseph W. Esherick and Jeffrey N. Wasserstrom, "Acting Out Democracy: Political Theater in Modern China," *Journal of Asian Studies* 49 (Nov. 1990): 841.

32. Wu Hung, "Tiananmen Square: A Political History of Monuments," *Representations* 35 (summer 1991): 110.

33. Rey Chow, "Violence in the Other Country," p. 26.

34. Ibid., p. 27.   35. Ibid., p. 28.

36. Ibid., p. 27.   37. Ibid., p. 28.

38. Henry Louis Gates, Jr., "Editor's Introduction: Writing 'Race' and the Difference It Makes," *Critical Inquiry* 12 (fall 1985): 15.

39. Paul Thompson, "Democracy and Popular Power in Beijing," *Radical America* 22 (Sept.–Oct. 1988, pub. Dec. 1989): 22, 23.

40. Esherick and Wasserstrom, "Political Theater in Modern China," p. 837.

41. Lu Xun, "Lun 'jiu xingshi de caiyong'" [On "the Use of Old Forms"], *Quanji* [Complete Works], 6: 23.

42. Said, "Traveling Theory," in *The World, the Text, and the Critic*, p. 227.

43. Rey Chow, "Violence in the Other Country," p. 31.

44. Ibid., pp. 27–28.

45. "Introduction," *Radical America* 22 (July–Aug. 1988; pub. Sept. 1989): 3.

46. M. Bakhtin, "Response to a Question from the *Novy Mir* Editorial Staff," in *Speech Genres and Other Late Essays*, ed. Caryl Emerson and Michael Holquist, trans. Vern W. McGee (Austin: University of Texas Press, 1986), p. 6.

47. Tzu-lu said, "If the Lord of Wei left the administration of his state to you, what would you put first?"

The Master said, "If something has to be put first, it is, perhaps, the rectification of names."

Tzu-lu said, "Is that so? What a roundabout way you take! Why bring rectification in at all?"

The Master said, "Yu, how boorish you are. Where a gentleman is ignorant, one would expect him not to offer any opinion. When names are not correct, what is said will not sound reasonable; when what is said does not sound reasonable, affairs will not culminate in success. . . . The thing about the gentleman is that he is anything but casual where speech is concerned" (Confucius, *The Analects*, xiii.3, trans. D. C. Lau [Harmondsworth: Penguin, 1979], p. 118).

48. Roland Barthes, "Myth Today," in *Mythologies*, trans. Annette Lavers (New York: Hill and Wang, 1972), p. 142.

49. This is precisely what Paul Thompson noticed while teaching in Beijing: "Workers are officially described as 'masters of the enterprise.' But any mention of the term in workplace sessions I conducted for managers and employees while teaching and researching, produced nothing but contemptuous laughter" ("Democracy and Popular Power in Beijing," p. 17). For the famous analysis of the subversive Rabelaisian laughter, see Mikhail Bakhtin, *Rabelais and His World*, trans. Helene Iswolsky (Bloomington: Indiana University Press, 1984).

50. I borrow the term "perverse double" from Renate Lachmann's

helpful interpretation of Bakhtin's study of the Rabelaisian folk culture as politically set against the official Soviet "folk" culture. To a large extent the rhetoric of the People's New China consists of borrowings from the Soviet, or rather Stalinist, version of the culture of the People (*narod*), which may explain why Bakhtin is especially helpful in demythologizing the cultural myth in China as well as in the Soviet Union. "The 'prevailing order' of Bakhtin's day," Lachmann says, "was that of a folk culture from which the folk had been banished and replaced by its perverse double: 'folklore'" (Renate Lachmann, "Bakhtin and Carnival: Culture as Counter-Culture," trans. Raoul Eshelman and Marc Davis, *Cultural Critique* 11 [winter 1988–89]: 118).

51. Thompson, "Democracy and Popular Power in Beijing," p. 26.

52. Mao Zedong, "Interview with Three Correspondents from the Central News Agency, the *Sao Tang Pao* and the *Hsin Min Pao*," in *Selected Works*, 4 vols. (Beijing: Foreign Languages Press, 1965), 2: 272. The phrase became much more widely known during the Chinese Cultural Revolution, when it was included in the popular *Quotations from Chairman Mao*.

53. Liu Zaifu, "Peiyu jianshexing de wenhua xingge" [Cultivate a Constructive Character of Culture], in *Wenxue de fansi* [Reflections on Literature], p. 161.

54. Thompson, "Democracy and Popular Power in Beijing," p. 26.

55. Shoshana Felman, "Paul de Man's Silence," *Critical Inquiry* 15 (summer 1989): 744. For a response to Felman, see Susan Tarrow, "Editorial Note," *Critical Inquiry* 16 (spring 1990): 690. It is not without certain qualms that I have quoted Felman's felicitous phrase here, because I, along with Tarrow, may have given her notion a mere "misreading" and "a grave simplification," for "the radical impossibility of witnessing," according to Felman, is "a notion whose complexity can neither be reduced to the simplicity of a positivistic statement nor defined as my 'conclusion'" (*Critical Inquiry* 16 [spring 1990]: 690). By adding the epithet "radical" to the word impossibility, the whole notion is instantly transferred to a level of complexity that cannot be reached by its critics. Like the Holocaust that is impossible to witness, "the radical impossibility of witnessing" is itself impossible to be grasped; it is protected, as it were, by a radical impossibility of argument. It will therefore invariably appear simplistic and superficial to question such a complex notion and its claim to *radical* complexity.

56. See Guo Qingfan, *Zhuangzi jishi* [Variorum Edition of the *Zhuangzi*], xxii, in vol. 3 of *Zhuzi jicheng* [Collection of Distinguished Philosophical Works], p. 326.

57. Said, "Introduction: Secular Criticism," in *The World, the Text, and the Critic*, p. 4.

58. Bruce Robbins, "Oppositional Professionals: Theory and the Narratives of Professionalization," in Jonathan Arac and Barbara Johnson, eds., *Consequences of Theory* (Baltimore: Johns Hopkins University Press, 1991), p. 4.

59. Ibid., p. 12.

60. Said, "Traveling Theory," in *The World, the Text, and the Critic*, p. 247.

Chapter 6. *Postmodernism and the Return of the Native*

1. Yu Ying-shih, "Zhongguo zhishi fenzi de bianyuanhua" [The Marginalization of Chinese Intellectuals], *Ershi yi shiji* [Twenty-first Century] 6 (Aug. 1991): 25.

2. Ibid., p. 15.

3. Chen Pingyuan, "Jin bainian Zhongguo jingying wenhua de shiluo" [The Decline of Elite Culture in Modern China], *Ershi yi shiji* [Twenty-first Century] 17 (June 1993): 12.

4. Ibid., p. 18.

5. Zhao Yiheng, "Zouxiang bianyuan" [Toward the Margin], *Dushu* [Reading Monthly] (Jan. 1994): 37.

6. Ibid., pp. 40, 41.

7. Said, "Traveling Theory," in *The World, the Text, and the Critic*, p. 227.

8. Qian Jun, "Tan Sayide tan wenhua" [Said on Culture], *Dushu* [Reading Monthly] (Sept. 1993): 14.

9. Zhang Kuan, "Ou Mei ren yanzhong de 'feiwo zulei': Cong 'Dongfang zhuyi' dao 'Xifang zhuyi'" [The "Other" in the Eyes of the Europeans and the Americans: From Orientalism to Occidentalism], *Dushu* [Reading Monthly] (Sept. 1993): 7.

10. Ibid.

11. Ibid., p. 8.

12. Ibid., p. 9.

13. Wang Yichuan, Zhang Fa, Tao Dongfeng, Zhang Rongyi, and Sun Jin, "Bianyuan, zhongxin, Dongfang, Xifang" [Margin-Center-East-West], *Dushu* [Reading Monthly] (Jan. 1994): 146.

14. Ibid., p. 147.

15. Ibid., p. 149.

16. Ibid., p. 150.

17. Ibid., p. 151.

18. Ibid., pp. 150–51.

19. Lowe, *Critical Terrains*, p. 4.

20. Arran E. Gare, "Understanding Oriental Cultures," *Philosophy East and West* 45 (July 1995): 323.

21. See Su Xiaokang, Wang Luxiang et al., *He shang* [River Elegy], in Cui Wenhua, ed., *He shang lun* [On *River Elegy*] (Beijing: Wenhua yishu chubanshe, 1988), pp. 1–80. For a complete English translation of the

script and related essays, see the three-issue series of *Chinese Sociology and Anthropology* under the general title of *The Chinese Television Documentary "River Elegy"*, of which part I (winter 1991–92) contains an English translation of *River Elegy*, part II (summer 1992) and part III (fall 1992) contain essays, commentaries, and review articles that offer a variety of views in the subsequent discussion and debate on the television series. Here I quote from the English translation in part I, pp. 18, 79.

22. Su Xiaokang, "Preface: Calling for a Self-Examination by the Entire Nation—A Brief Discussion of the Conceptualization of the Television Series *River Elegy*," *Chinese Sociology and Anthropology* 24 (summer 1992): 7, 10.

23. Jin Ren, "Comrade Zhao Zhiyang's Intervention Theory and the 'New Epoch' of *River Elegy*," *Chinese Sociology and Anthropology* 24 (summer 1992): 73.

24. Ibid., p. 75.

25. Ibid., p. 78.

26. Su Xiaokang, "A Discussion on *River Elegy*," *Chinese Sociology and Anthropology* 24 (summer 1992): 86.

27. Ibid.

28. Xiaomei Chen, *Occidentalism: A Theory of Counter-Discourse in Post-Mao China* (New York: Oxford University Press, 1995), p. 41.

29. Ibid., p. 8.

30. Lu Xun, "Guanyu Zhongguo de liangsan jian shi" [Two or Three Things about China], in *Quanji* [Complete Works], 6: 7.

31. Lu Xun, "Suigan lu, sishi qi" [Random Notes: 47], ibid., 1: 333.

32. Lu Xun, "Qingnian bidu shu" [Required Readings for Youth], ibid., 3: 12.

33. Chen, *Occidentalism*, p. 17.

34. Zhao Yiheng, "'Houxue' yu Zhongguo xin baoshou zhuyi" ["Postist Learning" and Neo-Conservatism in China], *Ershi yi shiji* [Twenty-first Century] 27 (Feb. 1995): 14.

35. Zhao Yiheng, "Wenhua pipan yu houxiandai zhuyi lilun" [Cultural Critique and Postmodernist Theory], *Ershi yi shiji* [Twenty-first Century] 31 (Oct. 1995): 150.

36. Zhao Yiheng, "'Houxue' yu Zhongguo xin baoshou zhuyi" ["Postist Learning" and Neo-Conservatism in China], p. 5.

37. Xu Ben, "'Disan shijie piping' zai dangjin Zhongguo de chujing" [The Condition of "Third-World Criticism" in Contemporary China], *Ershi yi shiji* [Twenty-first Century] 27 (Feb. 1995): 16.

38. Ibid., p. 17.

39. Ibid., pp. 21–22.

40. Guo Jian, "Wenge sichao yu 'houxue'" [The Ideological Trend of

Cultural Revolution and "Postist Learning"], *Ershi yi shiji* [Twenty-first Century] 35 (June 1996): 116.

41. Ibid., p. 120.

42. Ibid., p. 122.

43. For a recent study that makes some comments on the relationship of French theory and Maoism, see Peter Starr, *Logics of Failed Revolt: French Theory after May '68* (Stanford: Stanford University Press, 1995).

44. Wang Hui and Zhang Tianwei, "Wenhua pipan lilun yu dangdai Zhongguo minzu zhuyi wenti" [Theories of Cultural Critique and the Problem of Nationalism in Contemporary China], *Zhanlue yu guanli* [Strategy and Management] 4 (1994): 17.

45. Ibid., pp. 17–18.

46. Ibid., p. 18.

47. Zhang Yiwu, "Chanshi 'Zhongguo' de jiaolü" [The Anxiety of Interpreting "China"], *Ershi yi shiji* [Twenty-first Century] 28 (Apr. 1995): 132.

48. Guo Jian, "Wenge sichao yu 'houxue'" [The Ideological Trend of Cultural Revolution and "Postist Learning"], p. 118.

49. Ibid., p. 131.

50. See Lei Yi, "'Yangjingbang xuefeng' jufan" [Instances of "Pidgin Scholarship"], *Ershi yi shiji* [Twenty-first Century] 32 (Dec. 1995): 14–18.

51. Edward Said, "East Isn't East: The Impending End of the Age of Orientalism," *Times Literary Supplement* (3 Feb. 1995): 3.

52. Ibid., p. 5.

53. Edward W. Said, *Representations of the Intellectual* (New York: Pantheon Books, 1994), p. 11.

54. Ibid., p. 7.

Index

In this index an "f" after a number indicates a separate reference on the next page, and an "ff" indicates separate references on the next two pages. A continuous discussion over two or more pages is indicated by a span of page numbers, e.g., "57–59." *Passim* is used for a cluster of references in close but not consecutive sequence.

Philo, 92–94
Picasso, Pablo, 60
Plaks, Andrew, 230n77
Plato, Platonism, 25, 35, 69, 88, 91f, 95,
    102, 111, 145
Plekhanov, Georgy, 145, 155
Politicization, 123, 140f, 149, 158,
    175
Pope, Alexander, 30
Populism, 59, 187
Postcolonialism, 17, 118, 189–95 *pas-
    sim*, 203f, 207–11
Postmodernism, 14, 17, 55–64, 72, 77–
    81, 119–25 *passim*, 137, 143ff, 189,
    192, 203, 207, 210, 232n16; in China,
    17, 120, 125, 203–12 *passim*
Postmodernity, 56, 58–61, 64, 119
Pound, Ezra, 45
Prince Gong, 151
Prometheus, 201
Proust, Marcel, 128
Pyrrhus, 67f

Qianlong, emperor of China, 41
Qian Zhongshu, 33, 36, 140
Qin Shi Huangdi, first emperor of
    China, 182f
Qu Yuan, 132

Rabelais, François, 61, 176, 239n50
Racism, 8f, 80
Ralegh, Walter, 34
Ranke, Leopold von, 39
Rather, Dan, 166
Reality, 2–7 *passim*, 26, 37, 48f, 56–65
    passim, 74, 79, 94, 98, 108, 113, 115f,
    127, 134, 137ff, 163, 166, 173, 180f,
    195f, 198, 211; in China, 14, 16, 161,
    164, 179f, 182, 188
Reichwein, Adolf, 29, 32f, 38, 100
Relativism, 3, 8f, 12–18 *passim*, 24, 27,
    65f, 72f, 75, 80f
Religion, 37, 98, 113; natural, 31, 34,
    99–104 *passim*, 109f, 115
Ricci, Matteo, 43, 99–105 *passim*, 109,
    229n54

Rites controversy, 15, 99, 104ff, 109,
    146
River Elegy, 17, 196–201
Robbins, Bruce, 182
Rosen, Stanley, 138
Rousseau, Jean Jacques, 38, 151

Said, Edward, 14, 17, 26, 152, 159, 171,
    180, 182f, 188–96, 201f, 211f
Sanders, E. P., 90
Saussure, Ferdinand de, 25
Saussy, Haun, 109, 112
Schleiermacher, Friedrich Daniel
    Ernst, 2, 154, 215n1
Segalen, Victor, 52, 70
Shammai, House of, 114
Shen Congwen, 140
Sinocentrism, 40, 86, 188, 193, 195
Skepticism, 8f, 42, 62f, 180
Smith, Adam, 151
Socrates, 64, 88, 111
Spencer, Herbert, 151
Spingarn, Joel Elias, 145
Spinoza, Benedict de, 25
"Spiritual pollution," 153, 156, 183f
Stalin, Joseph, 236fn13
Steadman, John, 84–86
Steiner, George, 44
Sterne, Laurence, 61
Subjectivity, 58, 63, 82, 144–49 *passim*,
    156–59
Sun Jin, 194
Sun Yat-sen, 124
Su Shi, 10, 217n20
Su Xiaokang, 196, 198ff
Symbol, Symbolism, 17, 21, 28, 30, 40,
    49, 118, 148, 167f, 172, 179, 196, 198,
    211; architectural, 174ff; of people,
    174, 176f, 206

Tao Dongfeng, 193f
Taoism, 13, 101, 103, 113
Tarrow, Susan, 239n55
Tay, William, 119
Textuality, 2, 163, 165, 180, 189
Thompson, Paul, 170, 178, 238n49

Library of Congress Cataloging-in-Publication Data

Zhang, Longxi.
    Mighty opposites : from dichotomies to differences in the
comparative study of China / Zhang Longxi.
        p.   cm.
    Includes index.
    ISBN 0-8047-3259-0 (alk. paper).
    1. China—Civilization—Western influences.
2. Comparative civilization.   3. East and West.   I. Title.

DS721.C4726433   1998
951—dc21   98-26223
                                                            CIP

This book is printed on acid-free, recycled paper.

Original printing 1998
Last figure below indicates year of this printing:
07   06   05   04   03   02   01   00   99   98